PCs MADE EASY, SECOND EDITION

James L. Turley

Osborne **McGraw-Hill**

Berkeley New York St. Louis San Francisco
Auckland Bogotá Hamburg London Madrid
Mexico City Milan Montreal New Delhi Panama City
Paris São Paulo Singapore Sydney
Tokyo Toronto

Osborne **McGraw-Hill**
2600 Tenth Street
Berkeley, California 94710
U.S.A.

For information on translations or book distributors outside of the
U.S.A., please write to Osborne **McGraw-Hill** at the above address.

PCs Made Easy, Second Edition

34567890 DOC 99876543

ISBN 0-07-881929-6

Acquisitions Editor Scott Rogers	**Indexer** Kathy L. Turley
Technical Editor Matthew Lafata	**Computer Designer** Peter F. Hancik
Project Editor Wendy Rinaldi	**Illustrator** Marla J. Shelasky
Copy Editor Judith Brown	**Cover Designer** Compass Marketing
Proofreader Mick Arellano	

CONTENTS

ACKNOWLEDGMENTS

The creation of a new book is an ensemble effort. The author, it turns out, plays only one small part. Many others are involved in preparing the manuscript and artwork. I would like to thank Jeffrey M. Pepper, Editor-in-Chief of Osborne/McGraw-Hill, and Scott Rogers, who toiled as my editor. Hannah Raiden made sure it was on time, Wendy Rinaldi made sure it was correct, and Matt Lafata made sure it was true. A tip of the hat to Brendan P. Kehoe and his *Zen and the Art of the Internet*, for his valuable information. Thanks also to Tom and Fred, for allowing me the time.

Special thanks are in order for my young and attractive wife, Kathy, who created the idea for the New Word icons that appear in each of the chapters. She also wrote most of the marginal notes that appear throughout the book. I suspect that her contributions may outweigh my own.

And, of course, to Caroline and David, who can now have their Daddy back. Until the next book!

To my parents, for a brain;
my wife, for courage;
and my children, for a heart.

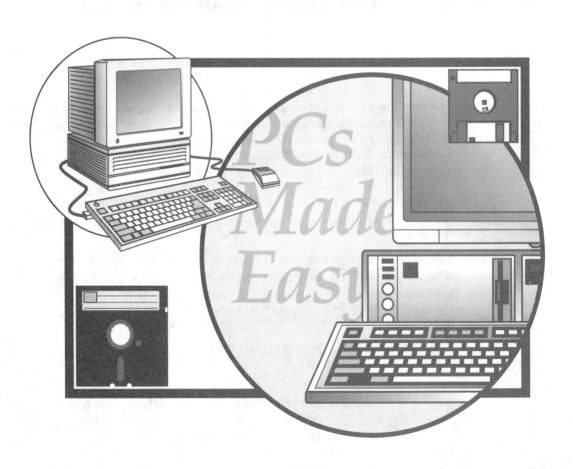

GETTING STARTED

Congratulations on your new personal computer! Or, if you don't have a computer yet, congratulations on your purchase of this new book!

This book is written for you, the absolute beginner with personal computers. You'll learn about all the different parts of your computer and what your computer can do for you. Before long, you'll be reading about how to use your PC or Macintosh computer to do the things you do, better—or maybe even to do things you could never do before! Best of all, you can get started without knowing a lot about computers.

Learning to use a computer is like learning to ride a bicycle or speak a new language. It seems like an awful lot of work, but once you've mastered the skill, you wonder how you ever got along without it. You'll see how using a computer, like so many other skills, is easy once you feel comfortable with it.

When it comes right down to it, computers are just electrical appliances; yet there's a definite difference between the way people feel about a computer and the way they feel about, say, a toaster. Computers aren't particularly "smarter" than toasters, they're just built to do a different job. One of the goals of this book is to show you how to use a computer as confidently as you'd use your toaster. You will have to learn some new words, though. The world of computers has a vocabulary all its own.

New Words

When you learn any new skill or start any new field of study, you encounter unfamiliar words. You've probably heard or read some computer terms before. Others you're likely to encounter—or already have—when you go shopping for computer equipment. Like a doctor's specialized vocabulary, computer terms serve their purpose, but there's no need for you to become an expert at "computerese." Your goal should be simply to understand the basics and to become "computer literate." Whenever a particularly important word appears in this book for the first time, it will be printed in *italics* and discussed in the text. Many of these words will also be defined in a special paragraph, set off from the regular text with a special picture, like this:

NEW WORD: Unfamiliar words like *megabyte* and *software* will be introduced in this book as you read along. You'll learn each one as you need to. What you read in one chapter will help you in other chapters. Just look for the "New Word" boxes like this one.

This book will inform you, but it won't make you a computer expert or "power user." Many people shy away from computers because they think they're too complicated. It's true that the newest computers are, by definition, "state of the art." But that doesn't mean you need an engineering degree to use a computer. There's a big difference between using a computer and programming one. Remember, you don't have to be a pilot to ride in an airplane or an auto mechanic to drive a car.

In science fiction, computers are sometimes portrayed as evil-minded contraptions, bent on causing as much grief as possible before finally overthrowing the world. The truth is somewhat tamer than late-night reruns would have you believe. Actually, computers are extraordinarily patient; willing to wait as long as it takes for the slowest typing and sit idle while you page through your book searching for some forgotten piece of information. As you will see in the next few chapters, your computer can't do a thing without you. No amount of mishandling or innocent mistakes is going to make your computer run amok like the fictionalized versions. Smoke and sparks are strictly for the movies.

Starting Your Computer for the First Time

If you already have your computer, now is the time to get it started for the first time. If you don't have your PC yet, you may want to read through this section now, with an eye toward preparing for when your computer arrives. If you're already familiar with setting up and *booting* your PC, you can skip ahead to the next section.

 NEW WORD: When you boot a computer, you're not kicking it out the door, you're starting it up. Boot comes from the word bootstrap, as in "pulling yourself up by your own bootstraps." It was once a technical term that described how a computer starts itself from nothing when it's turned on, but now it's in general use.

The most important thing to know for now is whether you have an IBM (or compatible) computer or a Macintosh computer. Each will be treated separately, because starting them up is different. What you do and what you see on the screen differs quite a bit depending upon your style of computer. You might find it interesting to browse through both sections, just to see how the "other half" lives and works.

Starting Your Macintosh

Let's say you have a Macintosh computer similar to the one in Figure GS-1. It doesn't matter if yours is a little bit different; all Macs work the same way. The first thing to check is that all of the parts are plugged together. You have three pieces that need to be plugged together: the main computer box, the keyboard, and the monitor. If you have an older Macintosh or one of Apple's laptop computers like the Portable or PowerBook, you get to skip this part entirely because they are already assembled.

Some Assembly Required

You should have a keyboard that connects to the main computer box with a curly cable. Make sure that the cable is plugged into the keyboard at one end and into the computer at the other end. There are usually two sockets on the keyboard, one at each end. It doesn't matter which one you use, they're both the same. The other end of the cable plugs into your main computer box. There are a lot of plugs on the Macintosh, so be sure you plug your keyboard cable into the right one. Look for the special picture on the back of the Mac that looks like this:

This is the mark that identifies the keyboard plug.

The three pieces of this Macintosh computer should be connected together **Figure GS-1.**

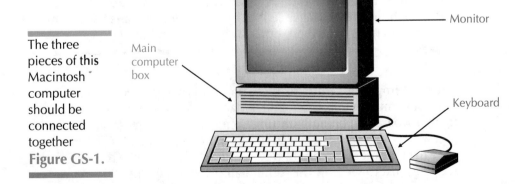

Monitor

Main computer box

Keyboard

A Little Bit of History

The first electronic computers were developed in the United States during the 1940s. They were built from components scavenged from other equipment. Originally just laboratory curiosities, they were used to demonstrate electrical concepts or to test theories. By the mid-1950s a few large corporations and universities had begun actually using computers. These were enormous machines, attended around the clock by flocks of white-coated engineers. By the 1960s, the demand for electronic computers stimulated office equipment companies like IBM, Burroughs, and NCR to start building and selling the new machines. New developments and discoveries appeared at an amazing rate. By the early 1970s, so much had been learned about digital electronics and computer design that companies routinely produced computers that were five times faster, half the size, and half the price of computers only a few years older.

As computer production increased, many companies that produced electronic components for televisions and radios turned their attention to new components especially designed for computers. This not only made it easier to build computer circuits, it also accelerated the trend toward making them smaller and less expensive.

By the early 1970s, so many of these "ready-made" computer components were available that any first-year engineering student could build a small computer. The finished product was small enough to sit on a desktop or be carried from room to room. To be sure, these small computers were not nearly as powerful as the "real" ones used by large corporations, but then, they didn't cost $100,000 either.

The novelty of being able to build and use your very own personal computer was such that a new national craze developed. Computer hobbyists traded stories, information, technical tips, and equipment the way schoolchildren trade baseball cards. Eventually, some of the more enterprising hobbyists started their own businesses to provide equipment or supplies to their fellow enthusiasts. Some of these companies still exist, such as Atari and Apple Computer.

(By the way, all of this information is in your Macintosh manual, too.) After you plug in the keyboard, check to see that you've plugged in your mouse, too. You won't be able to accomplish much on your Mac without a mouse!

Plug the mouse into the other end of the keyboard—the end that isn't plugged into the main computer box. That's why the keyboard has two sockets! If you're right-handed, you'll probably find it more convenient to plug your mouse into the right side of the keyboard (putting the cable to the main box on the left, of course). If you're fortunate enough to be left-handed, switch the two around, so that your mouse is plugged into the left side.

That takes care of the mouse and the keyboard. Now, make sure that your monitor, or screen, is plugged in, too. If you have an older Mac, or a IILC or Classic model, you can skip this step because your screen is already built right in. Attaching the screen takes two cords, one between the screen and the main computer box, and one to provide electricity. Your Mac's screen is a lot like a television, so it needs to be plugged into the electric socket. Instead of plugging it into the wall, though, your Mac provides a handy outlet for you.

Look around on the back of your Macintosh and you'll find both of the plugs you need. The one marked with this symbol,

is where you want to plug in the skinny cable from your monitor. You should have no trouble recognizing the electrical outlet provided on the back of your Mac. Plug in your monitor here, using the cord provided, and you're ready to go.

Now you've connected all the pieces. The last step is to plug in the computer. Before you do that, though, find a sturdy desk where you can set your new computer and sit comfortably. Don't place your Mac too close to the edge, in case it accidentally falls over. Now go ahead and plug it in.

After everything is plugged in and plugged together, press the power switch on your monitor. Look around the back of the monitor for the switch. There's only one, and it's marked with a circle with a line in it.

Ready to Start

Have you made it through all of the boring stuff? Good, now you're ready to start using your Macintosh. Get comfortable and place the keyboard where you can reach it. Look around on your keyboard for the key with the triangle on it:

It may be at the very top of your keyboard, or it may be near the upper-right corner. Once you've found it, press it once.

Did your computer turn on? It should have. If it didn't start, look in your Macintosh manuals to find out what might be wrong. Don't worry, your computer's probably not broken. There's just something that's been forgotten. Your Mac manuals will tell you what to do from this point.

When you press the "start" key described above, you should hear a beep, and your Macintosh will display the "happy Mac" picture. Right after that, you should see it change to the message that says "Welcome to Macintosh."

This tells you that your computer is working fine. That message will stay on for a few seconds while your computer gets things ready for you to work. Once that's done, you'll see the Mac's main working screen. Apple calls it your *desktop,* and it's a picture that you'll become very familiar with.

NEW WORD: The computer desktop is what the Macintosh shows on the screen when it's ready for you to start working. It's meant to look like a clean desk, with nothing on it. As you start working, other things will cover up much of the desktop.

Look at the picture of the Macintosh desktop in Figure GS-2. Your particular display may be a little bit different from this one, but the important stuff is the same. Across the top of the screen is the menu bar. It will have about a half dozen words on it. These are commands that

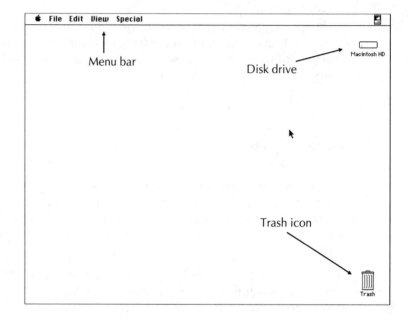

The Macintosh desktop is your main work screen
Figure GS-2.

you can point to with your mouse. Don't do that now, though. Let's look around some more first.

On the far left of the menu bar is a picture of an apple (note the similarity to the company's logo?). This works like an additional word in the menu bar. You'll see more about the "apple" menu later, in Chapter 5.

Near the upper-right corner of your screen, below the menu bar, you should see a picture similar to the one in Figure GS-2. This represents the Macintosh's disk, where your work is stored.

Near the lower-right corner of the screen you'll see the Macintosh Trash icon. Just like crumpling up a piece of paper and throwing it into a wastebasket, you can "throw away" something you're not happy with in the Trash can.

A Little More History

In 1975, Steve Wozniak and Stephen Jobs produced their first Apple computer from the fledgling Apple Computer Company. By today's standards, this was a pretty rudimentary machine, but the hobbyists and enthusiasts of the time welcomed it. In 1977 they began selling a better version, called simply the Apple II. The Apple II was a big hit with schools, which had already begun teaching a new field of study called "Computer Science." The Apple II has been followed by the II Plus, IIe, IIc, and IIGS. The members of the Apple II "family" still bear a strong resemblance to each other.

By 1981, the demand for small, affordable computers was so great that IBM, the office equipment giant, took notice. That was the year IBM introduced their own small computer for home or office, called simply the IBM Personal Computer Model 5150, or PC for short. They even advertised their new computer on television, featuring a friendly Charlie Chaplin look-alike and an ad slogan that went, "Imagine that. My own IBM computer." Heady stuff, indeed, for a generation that had grown up thinking of computers as million-dollar investments. Now a real IBM computer was within anyone's reach.

Although the new PC and Apple II were a great improvement over computers of the previous decade, they were still fairly difficult for a beginner to operate. To remedy this situation, Apple developed an entirely new line of computers called Macintosh, in 1984. This was a very different kind of personal computer, designed from the beginning to be easy to use and understand. The Macintosh introduced many people to the mouse and to icons. These represented a different way to make the computer work, instead of typing obscure commands. Its success is measured in the thousands of people who use Macintoshes (or "Macs") today; people who would never have considered buying a computer before. The original Macintosh spawned the Macintosh 512, Macintosh Plus, Macintosh SE, and Macintosh II. The Mac II now comes in many variations, like the Mac IIcx, IIci, and the powerful Quadra.

While Apple was busy with the Mac, IBM continued to upgrade and improve their original Personal Computer, producing the PC XT, PC AT, and PS/2.

Reach for your mouse and move it around. Note that the arrow on your screen moves around, too. You can move it around and around, up and down. If you move the arrow up to the very top of the screen, it stops moving. It doesn't "fall off" the screen if you move it too far.

Do you want to know how to turn your computer off now? Try to move the arrow over the word "Special" at the top of the screen. When you get there, hold the mouse still and press the big button on the mouse without moving the arrow away. That will make a menu appear on your screen. Just for fun, let go of the mouse button; the menu will disappear.

To turn your computer off, press the mouse button again to activate the menu. Without letting go of the button, slowly move the mouse towards you so that the arrow on the screen moves down. As the arrow moves down, it will highlight each of the words (menu choices) on the menu, one by one. When you get to the words "Shut Down," let go of the mouse button.

Voila! Your Macintosh has turned itself off. Now you know how to turn your computer on and off and you've seen what the Apple desktop looks like and what some of the pictures on the desktop are. You're already most of the way toward learning everything you need to use your Macintosh!

Starting Your PC

If you have a PC that looks more or less like the one in Figure GS-3, you must be sure that all of the pieces are assembled before you can start the computer. If yours is an all-in-one or laptop computer, you're excused from the assembly steps; skip ahead a few paragraphs.

The first step is to connect your keyboard to the main computer box. The keyboard should have a curly cable already attached to it, so your job is to find the matching plug on your PC. There should only be one round connector that matches, and it might be on the front of your computer, or (more likely) somewhere on the back.

The keyboard connector is tricky; it looks round but it only goes in one way. Look closely and you'll see an alignment pin or "dent" in the metal end of the keyboard cable. Carefully turn the connector so that it fits nicely into your PC's main box.

The next step is to connect your monitor (the computer's screen) to the main box. This takes two cables, one for the picture, and one for electricity. Plug one end of the monitor's cable into the monitor itself (if it isn't already attached) and the other end into your PC. For the second cable, your PC may or may not have a handy electrical outlet already located on the back. If so, plug your monitor into that one. It

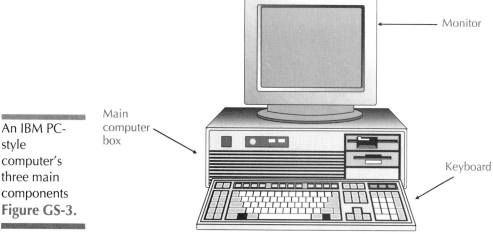

An IBM PC-style computer's three main components
Figure GS-3.

Monitor

Main computer box

Keyboard

will automatically turn your monitor on and off along with the rest of the computer. If your PC doesn't have a built-in power socket, you can plug your monitor directly into a nearby wall outlet. Finally, be sure your PC is plugged in, too!

Now you should be ready to go. First, make sure your monitor is switched on. Look for the power switch and press the button. If your monitor doesn't turn on right away, don't worry—your PC will turn it on automatically when it's time.

Now you can turn on the main switch to your PC. Many PCs have a big orange switch on the side marked with a vertical line (for "on") and a circle (for "off"). Others have more traditional on/off switches. Switch yours on and watch what happens.

You should begin to see something on your screen within five to ten seconds. It may take that long for your monitor to "warm up." You may also hear a ticking noise as your PC performs an automatic self-test to make sure everything is functioning normally. After the self-test completes, your PC makes a few beeps and chirps, and it's ready to go.

Getting Your PC Going

Take a look at your screen now and see if it looks like this:

```
Testing...
1024 KB Tested

BIOS (c) 1990 XYZ Software Inc.

C>
```

The stuff at the top isn't important. That will change depending on the particular brand of PC you have. Look at the very last line. Does it look like the example above? Or does it look like this:

```
System Error or non-system disk.
Insert system disk and strike any key to retry
```

If you get a message like this one, skip ahead to the section, "Loading Your DOS Disk." Otherwise, you're okay.

To start using your PC, you type commands at the keyboard. But don't type anything just yet. Let's take a longer look around first.

Still More History

Although Apple and IBM are two of the best-known companies producing personal computers, they are by no means the only ones. Atari Corporation (of video game fame) has produced some very inexpensive computers suitable for home use, like the 520 ST and 1040 ST. Commodore also makes some inexpensive home computers. The most popular of these is the Amiga, which has an excellent color screen and can make good, clear music as well. The Amiga is sometimes used as a computer-controlled video tape editor or for managing electronic musical instruments.

By far, the three most popular and widely used computers are, in order, the IBM PC family, the Apple Macintosh family, and the Apple II family. These three broad types of personal computers make up the great majority of computers that you will see, and that are covered in this book.

Not long after the original IBM PC became a big seller, an interesting thing happened. Other computer companies began producing PCs that were compatible with IBM's computers, but for less money. In this case, *compatible* meant that the new computers would operate the same way, work the same, act the same, and were often even painted the same color as the IBM PC. The copies were sometimes so exact they were called PC *clones*. By the mid-1980s, these IBM-compatible computers were selling better than IBM's own equipment. In fact, in 1989, IBM finally threw in the towel and discontinued their entire line of PCs. Not until late 1992 did they resume the PC business, but this time under the name ValuPoint. Today, most retail computer stores carry at least one brand of IBM-compatible computers. Some of the most successful clone makers are AST Research, Compaq, Dell Computer, and Toshiba.

Unlike IBM computers, there are almost no Apple-compatible computers. Because of the way Apple's engineers have designed the Apple II and Macintosh, their computers are protected under U.S. copyright law and, therefore, cannot be copied legally. (Yes, computers can be copyrighted just like books.) So, if you're looking for an Apple-compatible machine, you'll probably have to get it from Apple. If you're looking for an IBM-compatible computer, on the other hand, you can choose from several dozen companies' products.

The last line on your computer screen is called the *prompt.* The prompt is one letter—usually A or C—followed by a greater-than sign, like a small arrow pointing right. Whenever your PC displays this prompt, it means that you can type something. If the prompt isn't the last thing on the screen, it means your computer is working and you need to wait. Because there's a letter in front of the little arrow, people usually call this the "A prompt" or the "C prompt."

NEW WORD: A prompt is your PC's way of saying, "I'm ready." You could say that your PC is "prompting" you, as a drama teacher might prompt a student.

If you have a mouse, try moving it around now. Did anything happen? No? Good. That's because your PC doesn't use the mouse for everything, only sometimes. This is one of the times when it isn't paying attention to the mouse.

Press a couple of keys on the keyboard. Try typing your name. If you press a wrong key by accident and misspell your name, you can erase it by pressing the (Backspace) key. When you get to the end of your name, press the big gray key near the right side labeled (Enter). Your PC should say something like

```
C>David James
Bad command or file name

C>
```

That is your PC's (admittedly cryptic) way of telling you that it doesn't understand what you mean, and it doesn't know what to do. So it says your name is a "Bad command or file name." Instead of fooling it, let's try something that your PC *does* know how to do.

Type the word **DIR** and press (Enter). It doesn't matter if you type it in uppercase letters or not, by the way. Your PC is fairly forgiving as far as that goes. After you press the (Enter) key, you should see something similar to this:

```
C>DIR

Volume in drive C has no label
Directory of C:\

COMMAND  COM     36803  09-17-92
CONFIG   SYS        16  03-16-90
AUTOEXEC BAT        34  06-21-92

     3 File(s)          36853 bytes
                     10456928 bytes free

C>
```

So what is it, you may be asking? This is what a disk directory looks like. The command, DIR, tells your PC that you want to look at a directory listing of the information stored inside your PC. It doesn't matter if your PC exactly matches the example above (it would be pretty amazing if it did), but the overall design should look the same.

There are some other commands you can experiment with, if you want. Try typing **VER, DATE, TIME,** or **CLS**. Can you guess what the last one does?

REMEMBER: You must press the (Enter) key after the end of every command. Otherwise, your PC doesn't know for sure if you're finished typing.

When you are ready to turn your computer off again, just flip its on/off switch. That's it. Now that you know how to turn your computer on and off and how to type in some commands, you're well on your way to using your PC for more useful tasks!

Loading Your DOS Disk

If you get a nasty "Non-system disk..." kind of message when you try to start your PC, it is telling you that it can't find its instructions on how to run. It got part of the way and then got lost. That's no problem, and it's easy to fix.

Look around for your PC's floppy disks, which should have come with the PC itself, or in a box containing the DOS program. There's one disk in particular that you need to start your computer. It will be labeled "DOS System Disk," or something similar. Once you've found it, carefully insert the disk into your PC's disk drive. (If you're uncertain about this procedure, see Chapter 4 for help.) When the DOS disk is securely inside the floppy disk drive, press a key (it doesn't matter which key) on your keyboard. Now your PC should start up normally.

What Is Hardware?

Now it's time to start looking a little deeper into the personal computer world. Two of the most common words you'll hear used around computers are *hardware* and *software*. It's important to understand what these two words mean because they're going to appear again and again. You'll see them not only throughout this book, but in most computer advertising and catalogs, too.

Computer hardware is computer equipment. It's the stuff you can lay your hands on. It doesn't necessarily mean moving parts, or gears, or heavy machinery. Computer hardware may be just a handful of electronics in a plastic box (and often is). Hardware can also mean a big, noisy, mechanical printer. Basically, hardware is anything you can weigh on a scale or measure with a ruler.

What Is Software?

Computer software, on the other hand, is a little harder to define. Like a lot of computer words, "software" started out as an inside joke among computer engineers. They needed a word to describe the opposite of hardware. It's a part of the computer that you can't touch, see, or feel. But it's just as necessary for computer operation as its nuts and bolts. So, the word software was invented to describe "the part that isn't hardware."

Software is what actually makes your computer go, like fuel in a car. Without software a computer is just an expensive paperweight. Software is also another word for a computer program. *Software* and *program* are used interchangeably. Software is to a computer what a CD is to a CD player. The CD player is no use to you unless you have some CDs to play on it. The more CDs you have, the more you can enjoy your CD player. It's the same with computer hardware and software: the hardware is the part that shows, but the software is the part that goes.

You could just as easily use the computer words hardware and software to describe more familiar items. Table GS-1 compares the hardware and software of various everyday things. Even though these devices are very different, they all share the same concept: the hardware is just an appliance that lets you use the software. There's another similarity, too. Normally, you buy the hardware once and then build a collection of software to suit your tastes.

It's difficult not to confuse the software with the physical medium that it's stored on. Let's take the example of a CD recording. The *sounds* stored on the shiny disk are the software, but the disk itself is not. That's because the very same music could be stored on a cassette tape or on a vinyl record. The music doesn't sound any different, and you could copy the music from one medium (record, tape, or CD) to another if you wanted to. The recording medium is simply a holder for the music.

That's why it's difficult to visualize software. You can store the same recording of a symphony performance on a 33 1/3-RPM record, an audio tape, a video tape, or a compact disk. The software is the same in all four cases. The medium used to store it may differ, and you'd use different hardware to play it back, but the music itself—the software—remains constant.

Mixing Hardware with Software

The analogy between a computer and a record or tape player is a useful one. Suppose that you want to buy a new musical recording for your home stereo. At the music store you find that classical recordings are all

You Can Compare Hardware and Software for Everyday Items **Table GS-1.**

Hardware	Software
Computer	Program
Cassette recorder	Cassette tape
Record player	Records
Video cassette recorder (VCR)	Video tape
Compact disk player	Compact disk (CD)
Movie projector	Movie film

on compact disk, jazz is available only on cassette tape, rock and roll on video tape, and swing only on 33 1/3-RPM records. What can you do? Do you buy the type of recording that's compatible with your stereo equipment, or the kind of music that you want to listen to? If you want to buy a classical recording and you own only a cassette player, you're out of luck.

To a certain extent, this is what the current situation with computers is like. Not all kinds of software are available for all kinds of hardware, and what works on one computer won't necessarily work on another. It's not quite as bad as the hypothetical situation above, but this points out one very important rule: think about what you will use the computer for *before* you buy it. In Chapters 2, 6, and 15 you'll learn more about software and hardware.

PCs and Prices

The term *personal computer* is at least as vague as the term *compact car*. There are no hard and fast rules about what makes a computer "personal." Any machine you are likely to find in a store is certain to fall into this category. Large business computers aren't readily available at local computer dealers or through mail-order catalogs.

Because the category is so broad, prices vary widely. In the early 1980s you could buy a computer from Sinclair, Ltd., for $99 that was barely larger than a pocket calculator. On the other hand, manufacturers of high-powered engineering computers costing as much as $20,000 have been known to tout them as "personal" computers, too.

Generally speaking, an average computer for office or home will cost somewhere between $500 and $3000. This may sound like a pretty wide spread, and it is. But, like compact cars, there's a lot to choose from, and options vary. You might see ads for computers for around $99, but a price like that usually includes only the basic computer itself, without many of the pieces that you'll need to start working. You'll find more information about buying computers in Chapter 15.

The Future

It is a truism in the computer industry (as in so many other things) that the only thing that remains constant is change. After IBM and Apple virtually invented the personal computer, they now hold precious little of the market. Most PCs are made by companies less than ten years old. The growth of the personal computer industry—some would say explosion—has been so fast that it is difficult for PC professionals to keep up with developments, much less the average person.

The good news is, we all benefit from this growth as personal computer users. PC prices are constantly falling as today's hot machine is suddenly yesterday's dinosaur. Fierce competition means that prices are down while service and value are up. New and interesting products are introduced every day. You can have your pick of computers, computer stores, and computer programs to run.

Certainly, PCs are becoming faster and faster, even as they get cheaper and cheaper. But they are also becoming more and more alike. The IBM-type computers are starting to work more like the Macintosh computers, and vice versa. Those IBM clones that weren't quite 100 percent compatible are long gone, and many of the smaller computer companies have folded their tents.

As computers get smaller, faster, and cheaper, you will see more and more of the once-exotic features become commonplace. Things like color screens, stereo sound, lightning fast speed, and lots of memory become more and more affordable. Smaller and lighter portable computers make it easier to take your computer along when you're traveling, or just away from a desk—or an electrical outlet. Perhaps in time, all personal computers will fit into a coat pocket.

Ten Questions

When learning something new, you sometimes have all kinds of questions in mind that you want answered. Other times, you can't **even** think of what questions to ask until you know a little more. This book helps in both instances. Listed here are ten of the most important questions that will be answered in this book. Some of them may be questions that you have right now; some you may already know the answers to; others you may not have thought of yet. The chapters where you can find the answers are listed right after the questions.

✦ What are hardware and software? (Getting Started, Chapter 2, Chapter 6)

✦ What can I use a computer for? (Chapter 1, Chapter 11)

✦ Are all computers the same? (Chapter 2, Chapter 7)

✦ What is a chip; a byte; a floppy disk; a compiler? (Chapter 2, Chapter 3, Chapter 4, Chapter 12, Chapter 15)

✦ What's the difference between an operating system and an application program? (Chapter 7, Chapter 8)

✦ How do I make my printouts look professional? (Chapter 9)

✦ How can I make two (or more) computers work together? (Chapter 10, Chapter 15)

✦ How much information can my computer store? (Chapter 5)

✦ What happens if I do something wrong? (Chapter 14)

✦ Do I have to learn to be a programmer? (Chapter 8)

In this chapter we have looked at some basic computer terminology. Each chapter that follows will cover a different aspect of personal computer use. You can skip around if you like and read the chapters that interest you. The next chapter discusses some of the things computers are—and aren't—good at. You'll see how computers can be used in your business or home, and also learn about some chores that are best left to people.

C H A P T E R

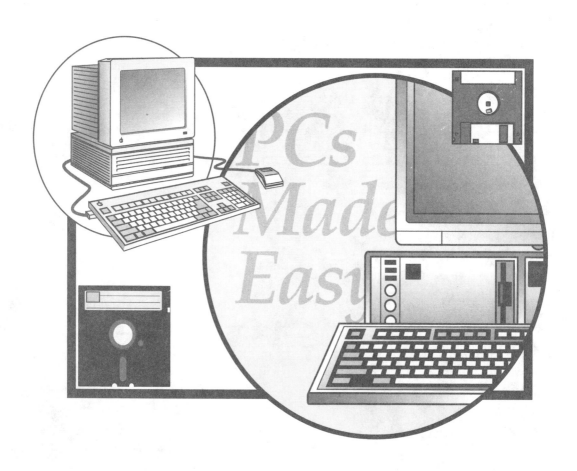

1

WHAT CAN A COMPUTER DO FOR ME?

Perhaps the biggest question facing you as a new or prospective computer user is, what can a computer do for me? The short answer is, a whole lot of different things. For a more complete answer, read on. This entire chapter is devoted to showing you just what you can do with a computer.

A personal computer can become one of those things that you wonder how you ever got along without. If you use a photocopier or those peel-off notepads, you know how indispensable they are. People who have a microwave oven or a VCR at home swear by them (or is it at them?). It's the same with PCs. They help so many different people with different needs that PCs have become a natural part of the modern home and office.

What Your Computer Can Do?

Some myths about computers and what they can do still exist. Most people who don't already have a PC have a very vague notion about what PCs do and how they do it.

If you throw an arbitrary question at an average adult, he or she can usually either give you an answer or tell you where to find the answer. People can draw upon their experience and education, filling in the gaps in their own knowledge. Computers aren't like that at all.

You can't just toss a question or a problem at a computer and expect it to be solved. PCs aren't nearly as advanced as they might appear to be on television or in the movies. A PC can't draw upon its past experience of anything, and it can't guess at the answers to things it doesn't already know. Your PC has to have very specific and precise "training" in whatever problems you want it to solve for you. And, you have to work with the computer on its own terms. PCs are not smart enough (yet) to speak your language, so you'll have to learn a bit of their computer language.

A computer plays computer programs the way a radio plays radio programs.

A good comparison might be a radio: Imagine living around the turn of the century (the nineteenth, that is) and describing the wonders of the "wireless" to someone for the first time. "It plays music," you say, "all by itself. You just switch it on, and music comes out!"

"Fine," says your skeptical friend, "make it play Mozart for me. Or a Sousa march. On second thought, I like that song the neighbor's kid was playing last night. Make it play that."

"It doesn't work that way," you explain. "It only plays what they're broadcasting. You have to choose the program you want to listen to by turning this dial." And so it goes. The original idea sounds great, almost too good to be true, but there are limits, and your friend has to learn what's possible. Turning the dial chooses from a selection of what "they" are broadcasting.

Similarly, your PC won't perform arbitrary miracles after pressing a few keys. It only does what "they" have programmed it to do. Like selecting radio programs, you can pick from thousands of different computer programs, each one different from the others. After you learn how to use each one (how to "turn the dial"), you've added a new capability to your PC.

You can decide how many programs to add to your PC. Some people have only one program, some have hundreds. You could say a program "trains" your PC for a specific task. Some programs are used for work and some for fun. You can create your own programs; a task comparable to composing your own musical radio program. This chapter describes some of the capabilities that programs add to computers, giving you an idea of what kinds of "programming" you have to choose from.

Writing and Editing

In the "old days," you could write a letter with a pencil, pen, or typewriter. If you made a mistake, you could (maybe) erase the error and correct it. Otherwise, you crossed it out or covered it over. When typing a long formal letter, the tension would rise as you neared the end of the letter, for making a mistake here meant retyping the whole thing over again. Correction fluid relieved some of that stress, but nobody likes to send a letter covered with white patches. And that just covered typing mistakes—what about adding a paragraph or two? When it was all done, making duplicates of the letter entailed either carbon paper, photocopying, or typing the entire thing over again. Finally, you probably would want to keep at least one copy of the letter on file.

Word processing is more than just using your computer as a typewriter.

Now enter the computer age. Imagine being able to write and rewrite your letter as much as you like; add a few words here, erase a paragraph there; make as many corrections as you want without splotching or tearing the paper; and never misspell a word again. Should the margins be indented, or flush left? Doesn't matter, you can try it both ways. When it's absolutely perfect, you can make as many identical copies as you like with just a press of the button. Sound good? It is.

Word processing software provides all of these features and many more. Word processing is the most popular use for personal computers today, both in businesses and at home. Most PCs get used for at least occasional word processing, even if they were originally bought for some other purpose. But what exactly does it mean to process words?

NEW WORD: Word processing means using a computer to write and edit words. You can use it for personal letters, business correspondence, newsletters, or even books (like this one).

Admittedly, "word processing" is not a phrase that rolls off the tongue. Nearly anything would be better. But the idea is simple, and the results can be dramatic. Word processing is like typing except that, unlike a typewriter, your words don't appear on paper right away. Instead, your words appear on the computer's screen, like the one shown in Figure 1-1. As you type, you can correct errors on the screen without having to "white out" your mistakes.

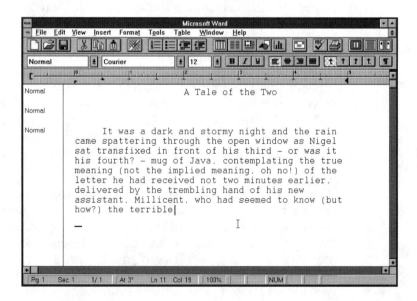

With word processing you can write nearly anything
Figure 1-1.

NOTE: You don't have to be good at typing to use your PC for word processing. The PC lets you fix your mistakes much more easily than you can on a typewriter. And, you can type as slowly as you want. Nobody but you has to know that it took 15 minutes to type one paragraph.

While you type, you can read what you've written so far and make any changes you like—again, before setting a single word on paper. You can reword a sentence, correct spelling mistakes or grammatical errors, and even move whole paragraphs around. If you want to insert a new sentence (or additional paragraphs), the computer makes room for them on the screen by automatically moving everything else down. You can erase words, sentences, or paragraphs in a similar fashion. You can have the computer check your spelling for you by automatically looking up every word in its electronic dictionary, and it can guide you in correcting misspelled words. When it looks exactly the way you want it, you can print your work on paper.

You can do a lot of things with your computer that you can't do with a typewriter.

You see one of the most common uses for word processing programs in your mailbox every day. These programs have made it easy to do bulk mailings of advertising and other promotional material. After typing a standard form letter, it is a simple matter for the computer to replace the name and address at the top of the letter with another name and address from a mailing list. After printing a copy of the letter, the computer can replace the name and address with the next name on the list, and so on.

Desktop Publishing

A more advanced form of word processing is called *desktop publishing*. Desktop publishing, or DTP for short, gives you even more creative freedom in your writing and page design and allows you to achieve results that look professional. Your final printed material can be in many colors, with photographs, multiple columns, and high-quality printing that looks as if it were typeset at a print shop.

NEW WORD: Desktop publishing is one step beyond word processing. It lets you design an entire document, like a brochure or a newsletter. It also lets you add fancy features like graphics, photos, and headlines to your document.

Desktop publishing is great for producing company newsletters, advertisements, brochures, flyers, and even small booklets. With a computer equipped for desktop publishing you can print pages in multiple columns like a newspaper or print in several different sizes and styles of type, for example, italics, boldface, and superscript. You can print around corners, you can print headlines across the top of the page, and you can reproduce photographs or original artwork right in the middle of the page. Figure 1-2 gives but a glimpse of what is possible with today's desktop publishing programs and a PC. For more about desktop publishing, see Chapter 8.

As in word processing, you can compose, edit, and modify each page as much as you wish. Your computer's screen shows you just what the finished product will look like before you actually print it. This kind of what-you-see-is-what-you-get (also known as WYSIWYG) display allows you to adjust each page any way you want and experiment with different layouts. Then, when your editing is finished, you can print as many perfect copies as you wish.

NOTE: If you really want to impress your computer friends, try pronouncing WYSIWYG as a word, like this: "*whiz*-ee-wig."

Record Keeping and Accounting

Maintaining business records is a complex and demanding job. Whether it's for yourself, for a small company with a dozen co-workers, or for a corporation employing thousands, you might have payroll records to keep, accounts receivable to track, accounts payable to write checks for, and inventory to total. Furthermore, these factors and more must be calculated precisely before you can see the "bottom line." A

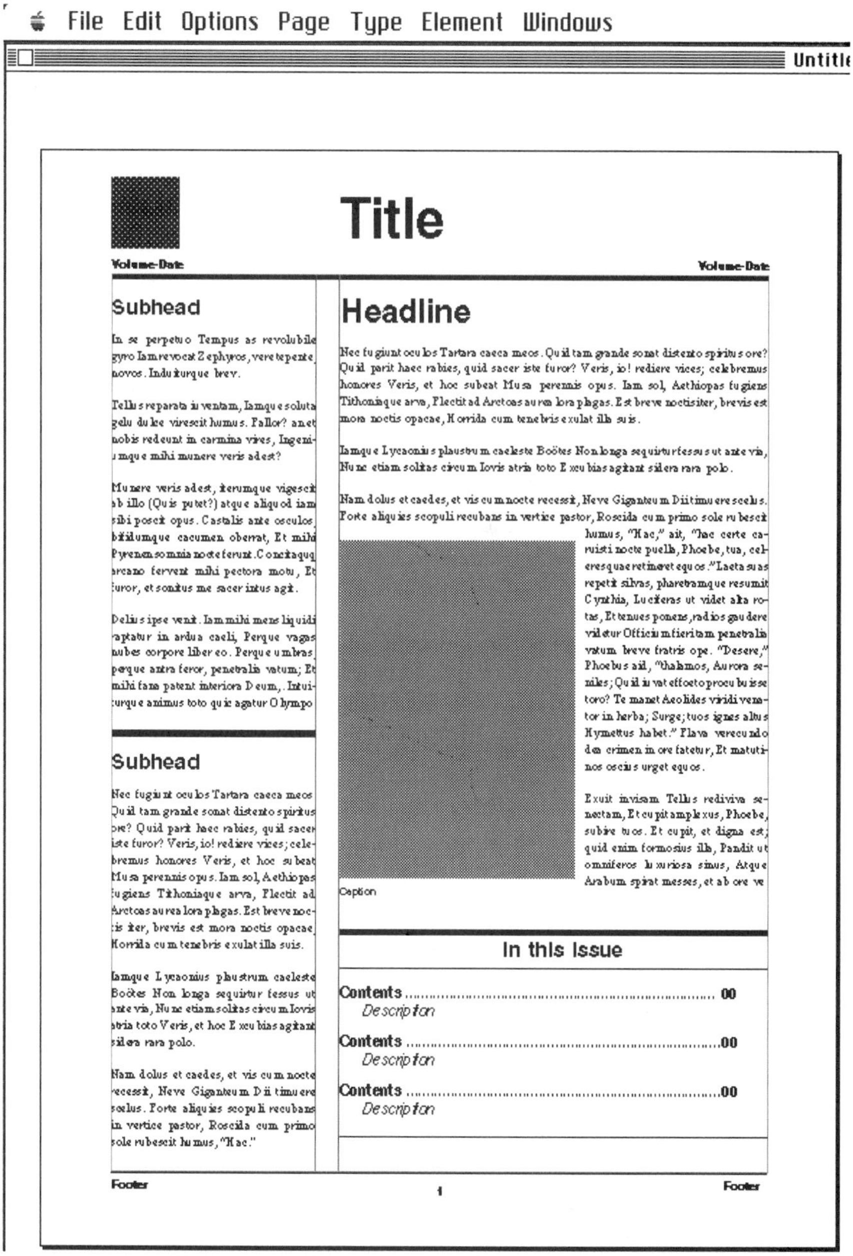

1

 🍎 File   Edit   Options   Page   Type   Element   Windows

□ ▤▤▤▤▤▤▤▤▤▤▤▤▤▤▤▤▤▤▤▤▤▤▤▤▤▤▤▤▤▤▤▤▤▤▤▤ Untitle

Title

Volume-Date   **Volume-Date**

Subhead

In se perpetuo Tempus as revolubile gyro Iamrevocat Zephyros, vere tepente novos. Induiturque brev.

Tellus reparata iu ventam, Iamque soluta gelu dulce virescit humus. Fallor? an et nobis redeunt in carmina vires, Ingeniumque mihi munere veris adest?

Munere veris adest, iterumque vigescit ab illo (Quis putet?) atque aliquod iam sibi poscit opus. Castalis ante oculos bifidumque cacumen oberrat, Et mihi Pyrenen somnia nocte ferunt. Concitaquq arcano fervent mihi pectora motu, Et furor, et sonitus me sacer intus agit.

Delius ipse venit. Iam mihi mens liquidi raptatur in ardua caeli, Perque vagas nubes corpore liber eo. Perque umbras, perque antra feror, penetralia vatum; Et mihi fana patent interiora Deum, Intuiturque animus toto quic agatur Olympo

Subhead

Nec fugiunt oculos Tartara caeca meos Quil tam grande sonat distento spiritu ore? Quid parit haec rabies, quid sacer iste furor? Veris, io! rediere vices; cele-bremus honores Veris, et hoc subeat Musa perennis opus. Iam sol, Aethiopas fugiens Tithoniaque arva, Flectit ad Arctoas aurea lora phagas. Est breve noc-tis iter, brevis est mora noctis opacae, Horrida cum tenebris exulat illa suis.

Iamque Lycaonius plustrum caeleste Boötes Non longa sequitur fessus ut ante via, Nunc etiam solitas circum Iovis atria toto Veris, et hoc E xeu bias agitant silera rara polo.

Nam dolus et caedes, et vis cum nocte recessit, Neve Giganteum Dii timuere soelus. Forte aliquies scopuli recubans in vertice pastor, Roscida cum primo sole rubescit humus, "Hac."

Headline

Nec fugiunt oculos Tartara caeca meos. Quil tam grande sonat distento spiritus ore? Quid parit haec rabies, quid sacer iste furor? Veris, io! rediere vices; celebremus honores Veris, et hoc subeat Musa perennis opus. Iam sol, Aethiopas fugiens Tithoniaque arva, Flectit ad Arctoas aurea lora phagas. Est breve noctisiter, brevis est mora noctis opacae, Horrida cum tenebris exulat illa suis.

Iamque Lycaonius plaustrum caeleste Boötes Non longa sequiturfessus ut ante via, Nunc etiam solitas circum Iovis atria toto E xeu bias agitant silera rara polo.

Nam dolus et caedes, et vis cum nocte recessit, Neve Giganteum Dii timuere scelus. Forte aliquies scopuli recubans in vertice pastor, Roscida cum primo sole rubescit humus, "Hac," ait, "hac certe ca-ruisti nocte puella, Phoebe, tua, celeresquae retinere equos."Laeta suas repetit silvas, pharetramque resumit Cynthia, Luciferas ut videt alta ro-tas, Et tenues ponens, radios gaudere videtur Officiu mfieritam penetralia vatum breve fratris ope. "Desere," Phoebus ait, "thalamos, Aurora se-niles; Quilit vat effoetoprocu buisse toro? Te manet Aeolides viridi vena-tor in herba; Surge; tuos ignes altus Hymettus habet." Flava verecundo dea crimen in ore fatetur, Et matutinos ocius urget equos.

Exuit invisam Tellus rediviva se-nectam, Et cupit amplexus, Phoebe, subire tuos. Et cupit, et digna est; quid enim formosius illa, Pandit ut omniferos luxuriosa sinus, Atque Arabum spirat messes, et ab ore ve

Caption

In this Issue

**Mixing words
and pictures
with desktop
publishing
Figure 1-2.**

Spreadsheets
can replace
the ledger,
the
calculator,
and the
eraser.

good accountant can analyze the results and find ways to move the figures around, or point out where adjustments should be made.

A computer is an ideal tool for managing these accounts. Your PC can easily, rapidly, and accurately calculate financial information once it has all of the relevant figures. Tedious chores like calculating interest or totaling columns can be done in a flash. What's more, it's simple to experiment with different financial strategies by asking "what would happen if..." kinds of questions. Testing different strategies by hand requires a lot of erasing and recalculating—perhaps even rewriting an entire ledger sheet—whereas your computer can perform hypothetical calculations and prepare the results for your analysis almost instantly.

NOTE: Your PC can even help you with your taxes. You can buy programs that will correctly fill out your federal Form 1040 and your state tax forms. New updates are available every year to take advantage of any changes in the tax laws. Plus, the computer itself may be tax deductible.

The computer can also process your records and display your figures in many different ways. One common format is to display the numbers in columns like an accountant's ledger or balance sheet. This kind of program is very popular with businesses large and small, and is known as a *spreadsheet*. A sample of a spreadsheet display is shown in Figure 1-3. A spreadsheet program for your PC can perform many different calculations on the financial data you enter. Spreadsheets will be covered in more detail in Chapter 8.

NEW WORD: A spreadsheet is a kind of program that lets you enter lots of numbers into rows and columns, as in a ledger. Then the computer can figure all sorts of information from the numbers.

People use spreadsheets for two main reasons. Some like to have the program calculate, check, and display financial data in an easy-to-read form that can be stored for future use. Others use a spreadsheet to

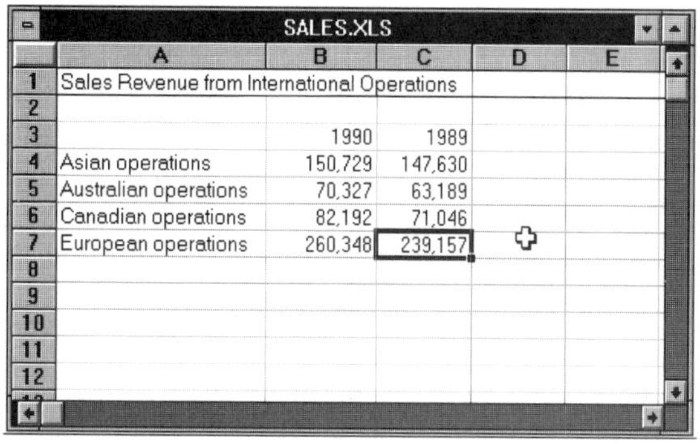

SALES.XLS

	A	B	C	D	E
1	Sales Revenue from International Operations				
2					
3		1990	1989		
4	Asian operations	150,729	147,630		
5	Australian operations	70,327	63,189		
6	Canadian operations	82,192	71,046		
7	European operations	260,348	239,157		
8					
9					
10					
11					
12					

A tiny sample from a spreadsheet, a kind of super calculator
Figure 1-3.

experiment with alternative business strategies. For example, the computer can show you right away what effect changing wholesale margins would have on your profits, making it very simple to evaluate the financial impact of such a change.

Record and File Storage

Almost everyone has a need to store and retrieve information at some time. Students write notes on 3 x 5 cards, scientists and engineers look up formulae in textbooks, salespeople keep names and numbers in card files, and cooks fill shoe boxes with recipes. A PC makes all these tasks easier by providing a reliable way to find that information when it's needed.

Storing It...

Your PC can be your file cabinet, card file, and paperweight all in one.

A trait that all computers share is a good memory. They can retain words, numbers, and pictures in enormous quantities. For instance, a typical PC can easily store all of the information in a small encyclopedia—but so can a small bookshelf. The difference is that the PC can find anything, anywhere in the encyclopedia in a moment. Even better, the PC can cross-reference the information for you, pointing out other references to your subject. Imagine the value this has as a study tool, or for corporate research.

Almost any kind of information can be converted to electronic form and saved in your computer's memory. After you've amassed a collection of information, or data, and put it in the computer, you've got a *database*. Your database can hold any kind of information that's important to you, from a store's inventory to the contents of the latest shipment; from a mailing list to a collection of baseball cards. There are even companies that sell already-compiled databases to PC users. For example, you can get a list of people living within a certain postal code or area code, weather information over the last 25 years, translations of religious texts, or astronomical data taken from orbiting satellites.

NEW WORD: A database is any collection of information that's stored in a computer for later retrieval. A database management program is what tells the computer how to find the information for you.

Storing the information is the first step. Now, what do you do with it once you've got it? What you really need is a manageable way of getting it back out again.

... and Finding It Again

Imagine a large library with thousands and thousands of volumes, arranged in no particular order, and having no card catalog. You could spend days searching for a particular book, and even then you might not find the right one unless you knew exactly what it looked like. Without a card catalog, you couldn't search for books on related topics at all.

A DBMS will do all the tedious searching and sorting for you.

Having a database by itself is like having such a library. The information it holds is of little or no use to you unless you also have an organized way to get it back out again. This is what *database management system,* or DBMS, software can do.

DBMS software allows you to use the PC as your own personal file clerk. It is the ultimate sorter, cataloger, and indexer. If you've previously stored the names and addresses of all of your company's clients in the computer, then you can use it to find all those clients who live in a particular city, or all those who have a middle initial "L." Customer records can be rapidly alphabetized, or sorted by ZIP code, or both. You can use the computer to sort the information into whatever form is most convenient for you.

If you store information about the customer each time you make a sale, along with information about the items they purchased and any other details that you think might be pertinent, then you can do some more interesting database management. For example, your computer could show you how many people purchased a particular product between any two dates, perhaps during a special sale period. Or it can show you how many customers who bought product A also bought product B. What is the average amount of a purchase? When are the busiest hours? How far away do your customers live? How often was an item out of stock? All of these questions, and more, can be answered almost instantly by the computer. Try to think how you would have answered these questions otherwise.

Drawing and Drafting

Many professions, such as architecture, mechanical engineering, and construction require precise drawings. An architect typically produces several drawings of a proposed structure seen from different angles, and highlights different details. For many architecture firms, their drawings are their primary product, and skilled drafters are valued employees.

A mechanical engineer or designer must also draw several views of a new machine part or tool, showing how the pieces fit together, with all dimensions carefully noted, like that shown in Figure 1-4. What all of these jobs have in common is the need for neat, clean, and accurate drawings, often to a particular scale (for example, 1 inch equals 10 feet), and with carefully drawn dimensions and measurements. These chores are usually categorized under the heading of mechanical drawing, or drafting.

Though normally for professional use, CAD programs can help you remodel a kitchen or bathroom.

Even if you're not an engineer, you might want to use a computerized drafting program. Lots of people use one when they plan some remodeling. Imagine being able to plan a new kitchen on your screen, moving cabinets and appliances around with just a few keystrokes. You don't have to be a full-time drafter to benefit from drafting programs.

In the past several years, personal computers have made real inroads in the engineering and design professions as unbeatable drafting tools, and they have made it possible for individuals to dabble in mechanical design. Now, instead of sitting at a large drawing table surrounded by T-squares, sharpened pencils, straight-edges, and erasers, you can use a

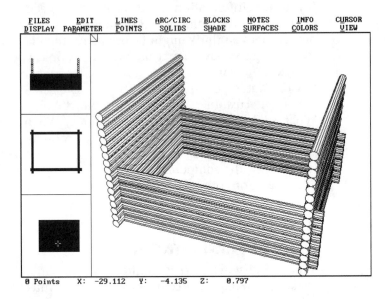

FILES	EDIT	LINES	ARC/CIRC	BLOCKS	NOTES	INFO	CURSOR
DISPLAY	PARAMETER	POINTS	SOLIDS	SHADE	SURFACES	COLORS	VIEW

0 Points   X: -29.112   Y: -4.135   Z: 0.797

Design your
dream house
with the help of
a CAD program
Figure 1-4.

personal computer with a *computer-aided design,* or CAD, program to
plan your project.

NEW WORD: A computer-aided design, or CAD, program lets you do
electronic drafting on your computer screen. There are special CAD
programs for use in architecture, electronics, engineering, aerospace,
and many other fields.

Drafting precise mechanical drawings using CAD software has many of
the same advantages as writing and editing letters using word
processing software. In both cases, you can create your rough draft on
the computer's screen quickly and easily. The major difference is that
with word processing software the computer screen displays words, and
with CAD software it displays your drawing.

After you've finished your basic drawing, you can move items around,
lengthen or shorten lines, adjust circles, or make any other changes
that you'd like before committing the drawing to paper. Of course, the
finished drawing will be free from erasure marks and, if properly

1

executed, will have no missing lines or errors. Outfitted with the proper equipment, a personal computer can draw on any size paper—from a business card to a large architectural blueprint.

You can choose from both 2-D and 3-D CAD programs. Use 2-D CAD for more "traditional" drafting tasks, such as the elevation on a house or landscaping plans. With 3-D CAD software you can draw an object in all three dimensions. Obviously, it still looks flat on the computer screen, but the PC will let you rotate the object to see it from all angles. You can even draw two related objects and see how well they fit together—all without ever making a real model.

Graphic Arts

Graphics programs let a professional design a logo, or let the kids design a card.

If you're a graphic artist, or need to draw, illustrate, or do paste-up work, you can benefit from PCs, too. In the same way that a personal computer can help an architect with drafting work, it also can help a graphic artist create images of a less mechanical nature. Using the computer as canvas and palette, you can create all sorts of images that aren't possible with other media. Generating artwork with a computer may not be for everyone. But just as some artists prefer watercolor to acrylic, some have found the PC an indispensable tool.

We've all seen computer-generated graphics on television at some time; for example, in the opening titles for a news program or in commercials. These are images that might not have been possible to achieve through any other means. Each picture in a sequence is created individually by an artist or group of artists and saved on film or videotape, one frame at a time, much the way that animated cartoon cels are made. When shown at full speed, some spectacular effects are possible. Professional television graphics are usually done with more sophisticated computers than the average PC, but even a personal computer can produce some wonderful effects.

NEW WORD: Computer-aided graphic arts programs let you draw on the computer screen with thousands of colors. You can also touch up and edit existing pictures or photographs.

Computer graphics are also useful for other, less glamorous, businesses. A column of figures in a quarterly report can quickly be jazzed up with a multicolored pie chart or an interesting graph. You can electronically "paste" charts and graphs into your printed reports, overhead transparencies, or presentation slides for an extra-special effect.

You say you're not good at drawing? Don't worry, your PC can help you there, too. You can "scan" a drawing or photograph from another source and have it appear on your computer screen. Or you can buy collections of pictures, graphics, and logos ready-made for your PC (called *clip art*), like those shown in Figure 1-5. And, just as with word processing or CAD programs, you can experiment, adjust, and modify to your heart's content before you commit any graphic to film or paper.

Communications

When you want to share information with someone far away, you can write a letter or talk on the telephone. The telephone has the advantage of being instantaneous and allowing two-way communication. Over the years, the telephone has become a universal appliance. Most of us would feel isolated without a telephone nearby. (Others pay extra for vacations with exactly that distinguishing feature.)

Connect your computer to a modem and let your PC do the dialing—to anywhere in the world.

Computers can exchange information in a simple, efficient manner over great distances too. How do they do it? They talk on the telephone! Any computer can use the telephone lines to communicate with another computer, if they've both got the right equipment. Sometimes a PC will have a phone jack right in it. More often, the telephone connection is an optional piece of equipment called a *modem*. The word *modem* is an abbreviation for modulator/demodulator, a technical term that describes how it works but not what it does. A modem simply allows your computer to talk on the telephone with other computers. A computer-to-computer link is illustrated in Figure 1-6.

NEW WORD: A modem is a device that lets a computer talk on the telephone with another computer (and another modem).

Sample of
ready-made
graphic art
Figure 1-5.

When you have a modem and a communications program, your
computer can dial the telephone by itself, wait for another computer to
answer, and begin a "conversation" with the computer at the other end.
What kind of information the computers exchange is entirely up to you
and the other computer's owner (they're not going to talk behind your
back). The electronic dialogue consists mostly of high-pitched beeps
and squeals that only other computers can understand. Computer talk
is not harmful to your local or long-distance telephone lines, and is
billed at the normal person-to-person rate.

NOTE: Modem is both a noun (the modem is purple) and a verb (to
modem something to someone). Make sure to pronounce it
"*mode* 'em."

When you send information from your computer to another computer,
you are *uploading* data. Information that's sent from another computer
to your computer is *downloaded*. You might want to download stock

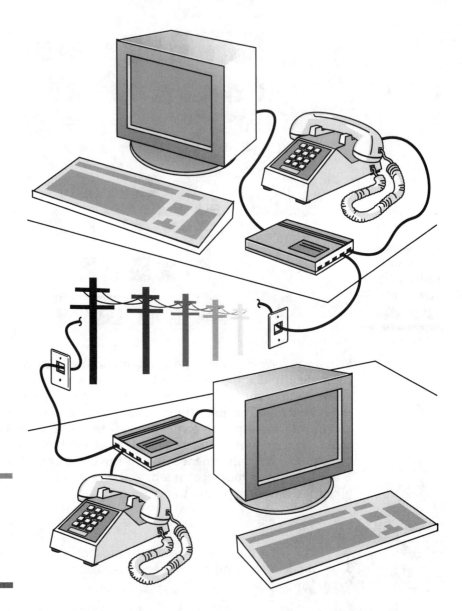

A pair of modems can link any two computers worldwide
Figure 1-6.

quotations from a large computer across the country, or upload a new recipe to your friend across town. There are hundreds of thousands of computers all over the country, large and small, that you can reach through the telephone. Some carry stock prices, world news, games,

1

classified ads, free software, to name a few. Often, the only cost to access these computers is the cost of the telephone call.

NEW WORD: Uploading and downloading are two words that describe sending information between two computers. You upload from your computer to another, and download from another PC to yours.

Music

Even though the keyboard on a computer is quite different from a musical instrument's, you can use a computer to compose and play music. Most PCs come with a small speaker, normally used for warning beeps. It can also play little tunes, though the sound is pretty tinny. (The Amiga computer from Commodore and the Apple IIGS are two notable exceptions. Their sound is quite good.) Using the computer as a composition tool and playing the music on equipment that is better suited to it, however, works well.

Today, many electronic musical instruments, especially keyboards, come with a special connector specifically for connecting to a PC. This is called a *MIDI* port, for Musical Instrument Digital Interface. Unfortunately, not all computers have a corresponding connection, but you can add one. With a MIDI connection and the proper software, your computer and your electronic instruments can communicate.

NEW WORD: MIDI is an acronym for Musical Instrument Digital Interface. That means that a musical instrument like an electronic keyboard can talk directly to a PC, and vice versa.

NOTE: Even without a top-quality electronic keyboard or other instrument, it's possible to play music and sound effects from your PC. Lots of Apple Macintosh computers have special sound electronics already in them. Some even have a built-in microphone.

An electronic keyboard sends musical tones to your computer in electronic form. The computer can then alter the sound in almost any imaginable way and send it back to the keyboard. Or you can work the other way around. You can synthesize sounds on the computer and then send it to the instrument to play. Record pieces of music in electronic form and store them in your computer's memory indefinitely; later, you can restore them, alter them, and play them again.

Games

Computers make some of the best game-playing partners. They are patient, willing adversaries with sly moves and inscrutable motives. You can't bluff them and they never get bored or lose their concentration. That isn't to say your PC is unbeatable; just good; very good.

There are PC games to appeal to just about everyone.

There are all kinds of computer games. You can choose traditional games, like chess, checkers, mah-jongg, and dominoes. A typical PC today can beat any human opponent at chess, except for a few remaining grand masters. But it can also train a beginner, or play at an intermediate level. There are also hundreds of new games that can only be played with a computer. These include exciting simulations that put you in the cockpit of an F-16 fighter jet (as in the Falcon 3.0 game, shown below); role-playing games, where you take the place of your favorite character; complex strategy games that let you command Allied forces invading Normandy; fast-action, shoot-em-up games, where the fate of the known universe depends on your aim with a laser cannon; or interactive fiction games, where you take the lead part in a story of imagination and fantasy. Nearly anything is possible, even things that aren't.

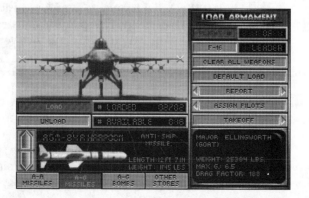

Computers are also good at card games like poker—maybe because they can calculate odds faster than any human player could (or maybe they're just good at bluffing).

More, More, More

The examples provided in this chapter are only the beginning of possibilities open to you with a personal computer. You can use a computer for all kinds of applications in all kinds of places. Today, PCs can read books to the blind, respond to spoken commands and take dictation, control your home lighting and appliances, plot the course of planets and stars, and receive cable television right on the screen. What about tomorrow?

Personal computers are only a small part of the broad spectrum of computers that are used around us every day. Smaller computers called *microcontrollers* are used in appliances, air conditioners, thermostats, refrigerators, and automobiles. Look at any late model car and you'll find a small computer under the hood.

NEW WORD: A microcontroller is a tiny device that acts like a miniature computer. They're used in all kinds of everyday appliances.

Bigger computers are used in business, manufacturing, and universities. These large computers are used for basic research in mathematics, physics, astronomy, and chemistry. Engineering companies use large computers to simulate the physical effects of stress, airflow, heat, and vibration before prototypes are constructed. Banks, of course, use their computers to track accounts, calculate interest, transfer funds (using a modem), and print statements and bills.

In this chapter you've seen some of the things that a personal computer can do for you. There are lots and lots of other uses for PCs too numerous to mention. As you have seen, all of these different tasks are controlled by software: different task, different software required. Sometimes, additional hardware is required, too. For more in-depth information on special software, refer to Chapters 8 and 11. In the upcoming chapters, you'll look at the different components of a personal computer system, beginning with the hardware.

CHAPTER

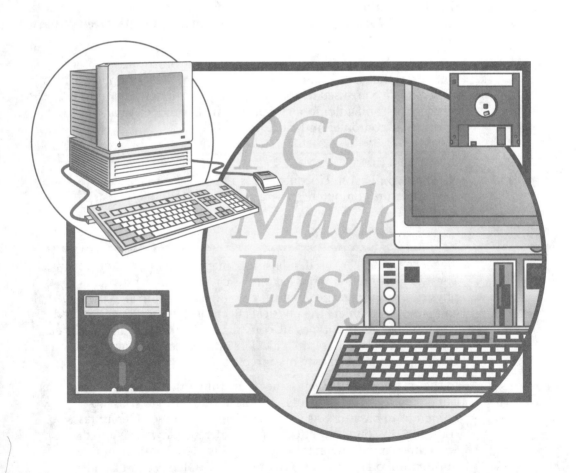

2

WHAT ARE ALL THESE PARTS?

In this chapter, you'll find out about the main parts of a personal computer. You'll look at different kinds of computers and each part will be discussed individually. You'll also learn something about what each piece does and how it works. For more in-depth information, you can also read Chapter 13.

Anatomy

A personal computer is made up of many separate pieces. The combined pieces make a personal computer *system*. For some computers, you pick out and buy the pieces separately, like the components of a stereo system. For others, most or all of the necessary pieces come already assembled. The all-in-one approach isn't any better or worse than the a la carte method of building a computer. You may prefer the convenience of an assembled system. Or you may like selecting your components separately to build a system that's tailored to your needs.

NEW WORD: System is a much-overused word. A computer system usually means a basic computer box plus some additional equipment like the keyboard and a display monitor. Just for fun sometime, try to find a computer company that doesn't have the word system in its name.

Desktop Systems

Figure 2-1 shows a good example of the a la carte style of computer, made up of various pieces of related equipment that are connected. This one is a fairly typical model of an IBM compatible PC. The original IBM PC, XT, and AT models all look very similar. Another very popular arrangement is shown in Figure 2-2. It may not look like it, but this is exactly the same kind of computer as in the previous figure, tipped up on its side. This arrangement is known as a *tower configuration* or just a *tower*. Shorter versions are called *mini-towers*.

By contrast, Figure 2-3 shows an early Apple Macintosh computer, like the Mac Classic. This is an all-in-one type of computer, making it more compact and, if you're so inclined, easier to carry. More recently, though, Apple started making the Macintosh more like the PC, with separate pieces connected by wires. You can see a more typical Macintosh in Figure 2-4. It doesn't look remarkably different from the IBM computer in the earlier figures (or is it the IBM that looks like the Apple?).

There are also some "consolidated" types of PCs like IBM's ValuePoint, Compaq's ProLinea, and Apple's Performa series. These have *almost* everything in one box with just the keyboard detached. These are nice

2

Your typical
PC-style
computer
system
Figure 2-1.

A PC in a
tower-style
configuration
Figure 2-2.

Early Apple
computers were
the all-in-one
type
Figure 2-3.

The modern
Macintosh
comes in
separate pieces
Figure 2-4.

for home offices where desk space is limited. Figure 2-5 shows one example.

Laptop Computers

2

Finally, Figure 2-6 shows off some of the current advances in miniaturization and compactness. In this machine, all of the necessary components have been squeezed into one small package that you can hold on your lap. These small *laptop* computers run on batteries and weigh anywhere from 2 to 12 pounds. This computer even has most of the features and capabilities of the full-size computers. Laptops are very popular with people who take their computers traveling, even if there's no convenient source of electricity. Laptop computers can be used on an airplane, in a car, on boats, or on desert islands.

NEW WORD: A laptop computer is one that's small enough to—you guessed it—rest in your lap. It also means that the computer runs on batteries. Otherwise, what would be the advantage?

Many PCs come in compact low-profile cases
Figure 2-5.

A computer to
take with you
everywhere
Figure 2-6.

The Apple PowerBook computers are one example of a portable
battery-operated laptop computer that doubles as a full-function
desktop computer. You can insert the laptop computer into a "docking
station" on your desk. The docking station includes a full-size color
screen, more storage, and a bigger keyboard.

Let's take a closer look at each of the individual components of the
system. You can refer to the figure that looks most like your computer,
if you want.

Display Screen

Your personal computer's display screen is, of course, the part of the
computer that you'll look at most frequently. The screen is where you'll
see your letters, numbers, and maybe pictures appear as you work;
where the computer will display your answers; where diagrams, charts,
and pictures might appear; and where your computer might ask you
questions.

2

The computer display screen has many names—monitor, CRT, terminal, VDT, or just plain tube. Although there are fine technical distinctions between these terms, they are all acceptable. Generally, you'll see the words *screen* or *display* in this book.

NOTE: For your technical trivia collection, CRT stands for cathode ray tube, and VDT stands for video display terminal. Both of these terms are a little pretentious for the average user, but you can impress people at the computer store, if you like.

Some screens can display in different colors, some only in black and white. You can also find green or amber screens if you look around. It used to be that you had to give up picture clarity for color. That is, the black-and-white screens gave sharper pictures, but the color monitors had, well, color. That isn't the case anymore. The screen for a normal desktop computer is made from thick glass, like a television set. Obviously, that's too big and heavy for a tiny laptop computer, so they use something called an LCD or an ELD. The *LCD* (liquid crystal display) screens are usually gray (as on a digital watch), but some are blue. The *ELD* (electro-luminescent display) screens glow reddish-orange. Some laptop computers use an *active-matrix* display. These are like the LCD versions, but active-matrix screens work in color.

Most computers can display *graphics* on their screens. This means that your PC can display pictures, pie charts, graphs, symbols, and other things. A few computers can only display numbers and letters, like a typewriter does. If you're shopping for a new computer, you should consider the graphics feature and a color display. All Macintoshes can display graphics on their screens and most IBM-style computers can, too.

NEW WORD: In the computer world, graphics means pictures, lines, charts, or drawings—something besides letters and numbers. It's anything that you can't make with a typewriter.

Screen Size

Usually, the screen size and choice of color or black and white is simply a question of what you prefer. Other times you don't get a choice, as with a laptop computer or some of the Macintosh models. But most PCs let you choose what screen you like best.

A larger monitor doesn't always mean a better picture. A bigger screen, like a bigger television set, doesn't let you see more, it just lets you see it bigger. After a certain size, larger monitors can be pretty expensive. And no, you can't use your television as a monitor.

Screens show a fixed number of characters per line. A bigger screen means bigger characters, not more of them.

Cursor

A *cursor* is a little mark on your computer screen that shows where you are typing. Normally, it is a small blinking square or an underline. The cursor, which comes from the Latin word for *runner,* moves around the screen as you type, marking the spot where the next letter, number, or symbol that you press on the keyboard will appear. Figure 2-7 shows a display screen with text and the cursor.

The cursor shows you where you're typing
Figure 2-7.

2

You can move the cursor around the screen before you type, if you want to, so that the next thing you type will appear exactly where you want it to on the screen. This is kind of like rolling paper up or down in a typewriter or moving the carriage left or right to get to a particular spot. With your computer, you can move the cursor with either the arrow keys on your keyboard or with a mouse. The arrow keys are described in the next section, and the mouse in the section following that.

Keyboards

The keyboard is one of the most important parts of any personal computer system. Normally, the keyboard is how you communicate with your computer, and you need to become very familiar with it. That is not to say that you have to be good at typing, though. Far from it. You are free to use the "Eagle Method" (circle twice, then dive) if you are comfortable "typing" that way.

Keyboards differ slightly depending on the type of computer you have. Different computer manufacturers and models often have different keyboards. Some have more keys than others, and sometimes those keys are arranged differently on different keyboards. Fortunately, there are many features that all computer keyboards share.

IBM-Style Keyboards

Figure 2-8 shows a close-up view of the keyboard of an IBM PC XT (the type of system that was in Figure 2-1). This keyboard is fairly typical of IBM's early computers, as well as most other companies' earlier PCs. It has the standard typewriter-style keys, plus a few extras. Now look at

An early
IBM-style
keyboard
Figure 2-8.

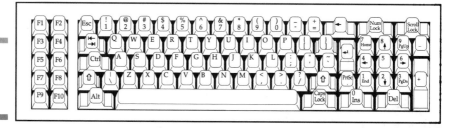

the keyboard in Figure 2-9. It's a bit larger and it has more keys. This is called an *extended* keyboard, and it's standard with IBM AT-class computers and nearly all PC clones today. Let's take a look at both keyboards, section by section.

NOTE: An extended keyboard, once an oddity, is *de rigueur* these days. Also called a 101-key keyboard, it is the most popular kind, supported by most new programs. Besides, it has some nice features, like separate arrow and editing keys and two extra function keys (more on these later).

Main Keyboard Keys on IBM-Style Computers

If you are a touch typist, you'll recognize the keys shown here. Even if you're not, the arrangement might be familiar. Computer keyboards use the standard *QWERTY* typewriter layout found throughout English-speaking countries for the last 100 years. You can get keyboards that are larger or smaller than the standard size, or with keys that click, or even one that has a solar-powered calculator built in. If you are so inclined, a Dvorak keyboard, which has the keys rearranged for efficiency, is available for most personal computers as an extra-cost option.

NOTE: It's called *QWERTY* because of the first six keys. They're arranged that way for a reason. On the earliest mechanical typewriters the keys were deliberately mounted in this pattern to discourage rapid typing—which they do admirably—because it made the keys jam.

An extended or 101-key keyboard from most newer computers **Figure 2-9.**

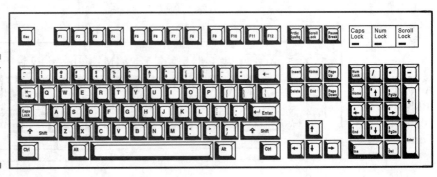

2

Your computer will wait as long as it takes you to press the right keys, so don't worry about your typing speed. In fact, computers are far more tolerant of sloppy typing than the average typewriter, because the computer allows you to back up and edit your typing until it's right. Beyond the standard typewriter-like keys, there are some extras, listed below.

Escape   The key in the upper-left corner of the main section of the keyboard is labeled Esc. This is called the Escape key. You won't find this key on a typewriter, but almost all computers have one. The origins of the Escape key's name are murky, and its usefulness is not well-defined either. Generally, Esc is used as an "undo" button. If you are operating your computer and you tell it to do something and then change your mind, often you can undo your error by pressing Esc.

Apart from the standard typewriter keys, all computer keyboards have some special keys too.

Tab   The key just to the left of the letter "Q" with the two arrows pictured on it is the Tab key. When you are typing, press Tab to move several spaces to the right, or to the next tab stop. Pressing Shift and Tab together will usually tab backwards, to the left. Note that the funny double arrow symbol is an IBM design feature and does not appear on all PCs.

Control   Below the Tab key is a key labeled Ctrl. This is the Control key, which is a lot like a Shift key on a typewriter. By itself, it doesn't do anything. But together with another key, it can do a lot.

You use the Control key to give commands to your PC. Exactly what it does depends on the software you're using at the time. To use Ctrl, hold it down and press one of the letter or number keys. For example, you can hold down Ctrl and then press the letter C to produce Ctrl-C. Pressing *control characters* is a common requirement for most personal computers. Computer manuals usually abbreviate control characters by using a caret (^) followed by the letter. The notation for Ctrl-C would be ^C for instance, while Ctrl-Z would be ^Z. You might also see it abbreviated, as in Ctrl-Q.

Shift   Just below the Ctrl key (for XT-style keyboards), or just above it (for extended keyboards) is one of two Shift keys. Note that the big upward-pointing arrow on this key is another IBM symbol. Not all computers' Shift keys look like this. This key does just what you would expect it to. Hold it down as you type a letter and you get an uppercase letter instead of a lowercase one. There's a [Shift] key on the right side of the keyboard, too.

Alternate   If you look either below the left-hand [Shift] key or to the right of it, you'll find the Alternate key, labeled [Alt]. The [Alt] key is like the [Ctrl] or [Shift] key. By itself, it doesn't do anything. When you hold it down and type something else, however, you get an "alternate" function. This special key isn't used as much as the Control key, but you ought to be aware of it.

Caps Lock   Sitting near the [Shift] key is the Capitals, or [Caps Lock] key. Yours might be either on the left or on the right, depending on your keyboard. The newer extended keyboard uses the preferred placement, which is on the left between the [Tab] and [Shift] keys.

The [Caps Lock] key works pretty much like the Shift Lock key on a typewriter—you press it once and everything you type after that is in uppercase. The [Caps Lock] key only works on letters. It won't give you the characters at the tops of the number keys, such as !, @, #, and $. Pressing [Caps Lock] a second time turns it off. On some computers this key will "click and stick" when you press it, as on a typewriter. Other keyboards have a little light that comes on to tell you that [Caps Lock] is turned on. On other PCs, you can't tell if it is on or off until you start typing and see all your letters come out as capitals.

Print Screen   Here's a funny one. Every IBM-style keyboard has a Print Screen key somewhere. Look next to the right-hand [Shift] key or past the [F12] key. It should be labeled [Prt Sc] or [Prt Sc]. As its name implies, this key is used to print a paper copy of what is displayed on the computer screen, but it doesn't always work. If it does, you'll have to hold down the [Shift] key to use it; otherwise you'll simply get an asterisk.

Enter   The big key at the right side of the keyboard is the [Enter] key. It is located where the carriage return key would be on an ordinary typewriter. It is a very important key on a computer and one that is often misunderstood.

On a typewriter, you must press the carriage return key at the end of every line. If you don't, you'll type past the margin and off the edge of the paper. There is no such danger with a computer. As you type, your

You'll find the [Shift] and [Caps Lock] keys in different places on different computers.

The [Enter] key is also called the Return key.

words just continue on the next line down. Although the (Enter) key is located in the same place as the carriage return key, it has a function very different from placing your words on a new line. On a computer, you must press (Enter) after every command that you type. This tells the computer that you have finished typing the command and that you want it to begin working now.

NOTE: The (Enter) key on your keyboard is also called the Return key. Be aware that many people use either term, but it's really the same thing. You might also hear people talk about the "carriage return." That's a real throwback to the typewriter, but it, too, means the same as the (Enter) key.

When radio operators and pilots communicate, they finish their conversations by saying "over." Until the listener hears "over," he or she can't be sure whether the speaker has finished or not. Similarly, your computer can never be sure that you've finished typing until you press (Enter), which is the electronic equivalent of saying "over."

Use the (Backspace) key to fix your little typing mistakes.

Backspace   Placed above the (Enter) key is the (Backspace) key. Pressing (Backspace) erases the last character you typed. It also moves your cursor back one space to the left, into the space you just erased.

Function Keys on IBM-Style Computers

On an IBM XT or compatible keyboard you will find ten keys on the far left-hand side of the keyboard labeled (F1) through (F10). The AT, PS/2, and most newer models have (F11) and (F12) keys as well, and they're all located across the top of the keyboard, above the numbers. These are your *function keys*. They are also called soft keys, programmable keys, or simply F-keys. Function keys have no fixed meaning. Each one performs a different function depending on the program you're using. For instance, the (Q) key always types the letter "Q," but there's no telling what the (F7) key will do. Each individual program you use will tell you what the function keys are used for when that program is running. For example, a spreadsheet program might allow you to use the function keys to total a column, calculate a percentage, or convert fractions to decimals.

Numeric Keypad on IBM-Style Computers

The far right-hand side of your keyboard holds 15 or so keys arranged like the numbered keys on a calculator or adding machine. This is your *numeric keypad*. Underneath some of the numbers on the keys is a different label, like [Home] or [Pg Dn]. Ignore those for now; they'll be covered in the next section, "Number Lock." To the right of the number keys are an extra plus key, minus key, and a decimal point. If you have an extended keyboard, you've also got a multiplication key (marked with an asterisk), a division key (marked with a slash), and even an extra [Enter] key. These are conveniently placed for entering figures.

Frequently, the add, subtract, multiply, and divide keys are gray, not white like the others. Every once in awhile, a program might ask you to press the "gray plus key," or something similar. Now you know what they're talking about.

Number Lock   At the top of the numeric keypad is the Number Lock key, labeled [Num Lock]. This is similar to the [Caps Lock] key. It operates like an on/off switch. If you press [Num Lock] once, the ten numbered keys on the right (*not* the ones across the top) can be used to type numbers.

If you press [Num Lock] again, the numeric keypad becomes a *cursor control pad*. This means that instead of the [8] key typing a number 8, it works as an [↑] key. Your cursor will follow the arrow printed on the [8] key, moving up one line on the screen. The [2] key will move you down a line, and the [4] and [6] keys move left and right, respectively. The [0] key acts like an Insert key, used to insert new words at the cursor, and the decimal point acts like a Delete key, erasing the text at the cursor.

The [Home] and [End] keys are less well-defined. Their exact function depends on the software you're using. Typically, they move your cursor to the top and bottom of the screen. The two keys labeled [Pg Up] (Page Up) and [Pg Dn] (Page Down) are similarly flexible. For instance, they might move the text on your screen up or down by several lines.

When the number/cursor keys are being used to move your cursor, you cannot use those keys to type numbers. If you need to type numbers, you can do one of three things:

Some keyboards have two sets of number keys — one across the top and another when [Num Lock] is turned on.

+ Use the number keys across the top of the keyboard instead.

+ Press [Num Lock] again to return the keys to number pad mode.

You can use the [Shift] key to turn [Num Lock] on and off.

✦ Hold down the [Shift] key. Pressing one of the [Shift] keys reverses the meaning of the [Num Lock] key until you release the [Shift] key.

If the keypad is in cursor control mode, you can hold down the [Shift] key and type a few numbers on the keypad before letting up on the [Shift] key. Conversely, you can temporarily use the cursor control keys the same way, if the keypad is in number mode.

Scroll Lock   The [Scroll Lock] key is usually located next to the [Num Lock] key or close by. Like [Num Lock] and [Caps Lock], this key is an on/off switch. You normally use it with word processing software to control how the words on the screen scroll up and down. To *scroll* up means to move all the text on your screen up, making room for a new line of text at the bottom, while the line that was displayed at the top disappears. Scrolling down does the reverse. The line at the bottom disappears, and a new line is displayed at the top.

NEW WORD: When you scroll something on the screen, you make it move up or down. The term harks back to ancient parchment scrolls, when the reader unrolled the bottom and rolled up the top while reading.

Macintosh-Style Keyboards

Macintosh computers use three different keyboards, depending on the particular model. They're all very similar, of course, but there are some differences. You may want to take a moment to look at your particular Mac to find out which keyboard you have. There are three basic kinds: the basic keyboard, the Apple keyboard, and the extended keyboard.

Basic Keyboard   Figure 2-10 shows what a keyboard for the Macintosh Classic and Macintosh LC computers looks like. If you have one of the original Macintosh computers, your keyboard may have fewer keys than the one in the figure. As you can see, the Macintosh keyboard is not too different from the XT keyboard mentioned earlier. The major difference is the lack of special function keys on the left-hand side. This is not a major drawback, because most Macintosh programs draw their function keys right on the screen!

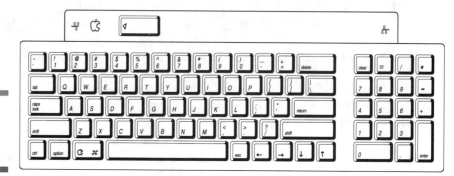

Macintosh "basic" keyboard
Figure 2-10.

Apple Keyboard In Figure 2-11 you can see the Apple keyboard. What makes this one an Apple keyboard? Nothing special, really. That's just what Apple calls it. Compare the Apple keyboard with the basic keyboard in the previous figure. Can you spot the differences?

Although they're very slight, the differences between the two keyboards can be enough to drive a touch typist crazy if you're not aware of them. For example, look at the key in the upper-left corner of the keyboard. On the basic keyboard, it has the tilde (~) character, but on the Apple keyboard it's labeled Esc. Now check the lower-left corner. The basic keyboard has a Ctrl key, while the Apple keyboard puts the Caps Lock key there. There are about a half-dozen differences in all.

Extended Keyboard Figure 2-12 shows an example of the Macintosh extended keyboard. You can tell that this one looks significantly

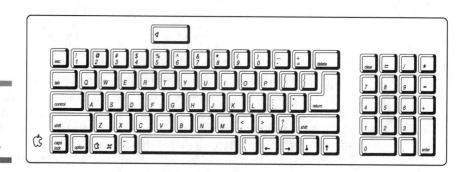

Macintosh "Apple" keyboard
Figure 2-11.

2

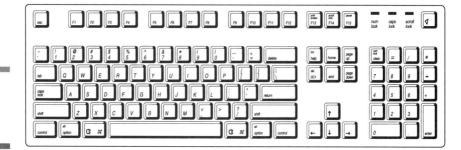

Macintosh
"extended"
keyboard
Figure 2-12.

different from the other two. For one thing, it's larger. For another
thing, it has a whole new row of keys across the top. This is the
keyboard of choice for all of the newer Macintosh models, like the IIci,
IIcx, IIsi, and so on. If you've just recently bought your Mac, you
probably have one of these.

Main Keyboard Keys on the Macintosh

The ⌜Tab⌟ and ⌜Shift⌟ keys are in their familiar locations, and the ⌜Return⌟ key
is on the right-hand side, as expected. No changes have been made to
the normal typewriter keys.

The ⌜Option⌟ key
signals your
computer
that a
command is
coming next.

Option Key   On the bottom row, near the left side, you'll find the
⌜Option⌟ key. It has a picture of an apple on it (the company's logo, by
coincidence). You use it like a ⌜Shift⌟ key—hold it down while you press
one of the other keys on the keyboard. Instead of typing the letter or
number that you pressed, the computer performs some command.
Exactly what it does depends on the program that you're running at the
time. Different programs use the ⌜Option⌟ key to perform different
functions.

NOTE: The ⌜Option⌟ key is sometimes called the "open apple" key.
That's because the old Apple II computers (not the Macintosh II)
had two special option keys. One was marked with a dark, filled-in
apple, called the "closed apple" key, and the other had a light, outlined
apple, called the "open apple" key. The new ⌜Option⌟ key looks a whole lot
like the latter one.

Command Key   Next to the [Option] key is the [⌘] key, emblazoned with what looks like a daisy (or for those with a different point of view, a splat—that's why it's also known as the "splat" key). The [⌘] key is very much like the [Option] key, but you use it more often. Its function also depends on the software that you happen to be using. If you're using a word processor, for example, pressing the [⌘] key and the [J] key together might justify the paragraph that you're typing. Pressing the [⌘] key by itself doesn't do anything.

Using the arrow keys is sometimes more handy than the mouse.

Arrow Keys   On the bottom row, to the right of the [Spacebar] are four keys, each marked with a directional arrow, like this: [←], [→], [↓], [↑]. These keys are used to move things around on your screen. On the extended keyboard, the four arrow keys are by themselves, set a little bit apart from the other keys. This is called an "inverted-T" arrangement.

Numeric Keypad on the Macintosh

All three styles of Macintosh keyboards have a separate numeric keypad. On the right-hand side are 18 keys arranged like the keys on a calculator or adding machine. These are here as a convenience. If you look, you'll see most of the same keys elsewhere on the keyboard. Having them grouped together like this can be helpful when you want to enter lots of numbers for financial or statistical work.

You can change a Macintosh keyboard just by plugging in a new one.

If you enter a lot of numbers, as in accounting work, you'll appreciate the extra number keys. It's much easier than using the number keys across the top of the keyboard. If you have a Mac with the Apple keyboard, pay particular attention to the placement of the [+] and [−] keys on the number pad. They're reversed from the other two keyboards.

Enter   At the lower-right corner of the keypad is a second Return key; this one is labeled [Enter]. The [Enter] key usually does the same thing as the [Return] key, but having one next to the number pad is convenient.

Clear   The [Clear] key is located in the upper-left corner of the numeric keypad. Unlike the other keys in this section, the [Clear] key only appears in the numeric keypad. There isn't a second [Clear] key. Press this key to clear, or undo, the number you typed if you made a mistake and want to start over.

2

Power-On Key

The great big funny-shaped key at the top of your basic or Apple keyboard, and on the right-hand side of your extended keyboard, is called the power-on key. The power-on key has a triangle marked on it.

If you have one of the Macintosh II models (IIcx, IIsi, and so forth), this is how you turn your computer on. On the Macintosh Classic, this key has no function (the power switch is located on the back of the computer).

Extended Keyboard Keys on the Macintosh

The extended Macintosh keyboard has a bunch of extra keys that the other keyboards don't have. Also, some of the keys that they do have in common are labeled differently. If you've got an extended keyboard with your Mac, you should read over the next few sections.

Function keys are extra buttons that your computer can use for anything.

Function Keys   The extended keyboard has an extra row of keys across the top of the keyboard. These are labeled F1, on the left, to F15, on the right. These are called function keys (as they are on IBM-style keyboards).

The function keys are another special kind of key, like the Option and ⌘ keys. The function keys do things, but what they do depends on the program you're using. The F4 key, for example, doesn't necessarily do the same thing all the time. You'll need to read the instructions that come with your program(s) to learn just what each function key will do.

Special Editing Keys   If you look just above the "inverted-T" where the arrow keys are, you'll find six special editing keys. They're between the Return key and the numeric keypad. The six editing keys are labeled Help, Del, Home, End, Pg Up, and Pg Dn.

These keys are usually used when you're doing word processing. If you have a word processing program for your Macintosh, it will tell you when and how to use these. For example, you might be instructed to press the Del key when you want to erase (delete) a word.

Second Labels   You might have noticed that many of the keys on your extended keyboard are labeled twice. Once, in the normal way, and a second time, with smaller writing. What you are seeing is the evidence of the power of the IBM-style PC over personal computers today.

If you compare the keys on the extended keyboard (Figure 2-12) to the IBM AT-style keyboard from Figure 2-9, you'll notice many similarities. That's not an accident; Apple planned it that way. It's one of the ways they've tried (with some success) to get people to move away from the IBM-style PCs over to Macintosh. By making the keyboards more similar, and calling the keys by the same name, people might be a little bit more inclined to switch.

Figure 2-13 shows some of the Macintosh extended keyboard keys. Notice that the F13, F14, and F15 keys are also called Prt Sc, Scroll Lock, and Pause, respectively. These are the names given to the keys that occupy a similar location on the IBM-style keyboard. There are even three green lights (called LEDs) that light up when you press the correct key, the same as on the IBM-style PC.

Mouse

A mouse is an optional piece of equipment on some computers; it is mandatory on others (the Macintosh in particular). A *mouse* is a small

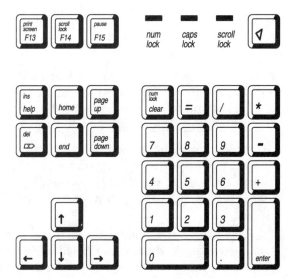

The extended
keyboard
includes some
extra keys
Figure 2-13.

2

More About Mice

There are two species of mouse, optical and mechanical. They both do the same thing, but in different ways. You can tell them apart because an optical mouse requires a special shiny mouse pad to work, while the mechanical mouse doesn't.

Underneath an optical mouse are two little lights and two matching light sensors ("electric eyes"). One light is red and the other one is ultraviolet. The ultraviolet light is invisible, so it won't look like it's turned on, but it is. When you place the mouse on its special mouse pad, both lights reflect off the shiny surface and into the light sensors. When you move the mouse around, the red and blue stripes on the pad temporarily block the reflection of the red and blue lights. When the light sensor "sees" the light blink off for a short time, it knows that you have moved it across one stripe. The red light (and the red stripes) measure vertical movement, and the invisible blue light measures horizontal movement.

A mechanical mouse is even simpler. It has a small steel and rubber ball inside it that rolls around kind of loosely inside the mouse. Inside the mouse are two small wheels that press against the ball. One wheel rolls left to right, the other one, forward and backward. When you move the mouse around on your desk, the ball rolls underneath your hand and that makes the two wheels spin. Every time a wheel turns, it knows that you've moved the mouse left, right, up, or down.

Some people prefer one kind of mouse over the other. A mechanical mouse works on any desk, even a cluttered one, without a mouse pad taking up space. On the other hand, an optical mouse doesn't pick up dust and debris from the desktop like a mechanical mouse can. That can clog the works after awhile, and may mean a trip to the veterinarian, uh, computer store.

thing that looks a little like a bar of soap with a wire attached to it. There's always at least one button on the top that you can push. It might have only one button, but some have two or three. Some people love using a mouse with their personal computers, and others hate it. If you use a mouse, you'll find that it is useful for many different functions.

NEW WORD: A mouse is a device that you hold in your hand to control the computer. You move the mouse around on your desk and the computer does things. The small wire that attaches it to the computer looks like a mouse's tail, hence the name.

The mouse was developed the by Xerox Corporation at the Palo Alto Research Center (PARC) in California for their computer called Star. The mouse was, and still is, intended as a supplement to a computer's keyboard. It helps you to do things that normal computer keyboards aren't well suited for.

The most common use for a mouse is to move your cursor around on the screen.

The idea behind a mouse is very simple. You roll it along your desk, in any direction you like, and your cursor follows it on the screen. If you move the mouse to the right, your cursor moves toward the right of the screen by the same amount. The farther you move the mouse, the farther the cursor goes. Moving the mouse down (that is, toward you) moves the cursor down toward the bottom of the screen. Diagonal moves are possible, as are backward slants, circles, and curlicues. A household computer mouse is shown in Figure 2-14.

Using a Mouse

To use the mouse, hold it in your hand, as shown in Figure 2-15. Rest a few fingers on the top. Get comfy. It doesn't matter whether you use

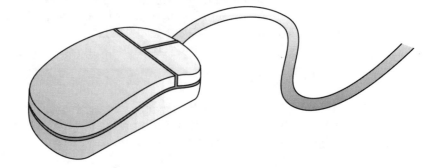

Typical
electronic
mouse
Figure 2-14.

2

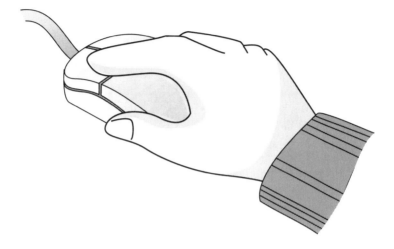

*Practice and
experiment
with your
mouse. Have
some fun. It's
easy once you
get used to it.*

your right hand or your left hand. The only important thing is that you hold it with the cord away from you. You may find it most comfortable to rest the ball of your hand on the table top and just move the mouse around by bending your wrist.

If you have a mouse that uses a mouse pad, make sure the mouse is resting on the pad, not on your desk. Also check that the pad is right side up. Obviously, the shiny side is supposed to be up, but what's not so obvious is that the mouse pad has a definite left and right to it. Look carefully at the red and blue lines on the shiny side of the mouse pad. The red lines have to go side-to-side, so that the blue lines go up and down. Otherwise, your mouse will get confused and the cursor will move the wrong way.

If your mouse doesn't use a mouse pad, you still have to make sure that you hold it "right side up." Keep the mouse's "tail" pointing away from you. If you hold the mouse crooked, as in Figure 2-16, you'll find that the mouse's idea of left, right, up, and down is a little confused.

If all of this sounds like a lot of trouble, relax. It may sound complicated, but it comes naturally to most people. Reading about it is kind of like reading about how to breathe. Once you get the hang of it, you'll be able to do it without thinking.

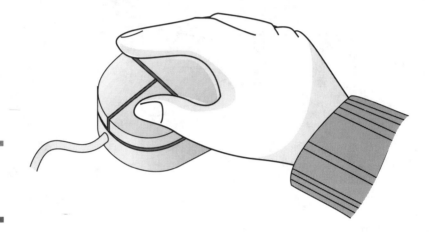

How *not* to
handle your
mouse
Figure 2-16.

What's a Mouse For?

A mouse is a great substitute for typing tedious commands or remembering which function keys to press.

Using a mouse is handy for rapidly positioning the cursor just where you want it to be before typing, for example, when you're word processing. Some people find it easier to move the mouse around than to press the keyboard's ⬆ key several times, followed by several ➡ presses, for example.

You can also use the mouse instead of the keyboard to carry out commands. For example, if your computer screen is displaying several options or choices and waiting for you to choose one, you can point to your choice by positioning your cursor on it with the mouse, as shown in Figure 2-17. Then you press the mouse button to tell the computer to do it, just like pressing the Enter key to tell it when you're finished typing. This "point and click" operation is easy to get used to, especially if you don't really enjoy typing. The Macintosh uses this method a great deal. In fact, you can operate a Macintosh without a keyboard but not without a mouse!

For the Macintosh and Amiga computers, the mouse is necessary to operate the computer. Almost all the programs available for these machines assume that you already have a mouse. For the Apple II family and IBM-style PC family, a mouse is optional. You can add one

2

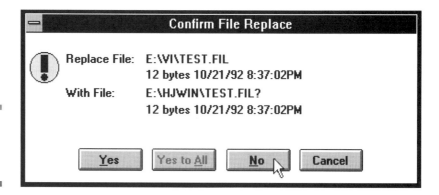

to these computers if you like. Some programs for these computers can use a mouse if you have one, but it's not required. Other programs aren't designed to use a mouse at all, and will ignore it even if it's attached.

Instead of a Mouse

If you think you might like to use a mouse, but just can't find one that you're happy with, consider one of the alternatives: a trackball or a tablet.

NEW WORD: A trackball is an alternative to a mouse that takes up less space on your desk. Trackballs also are easier to use with portable laptop computers because they don't need a flat desk top to work.

A *trackball,* like the one shown in Figure 2-18, is nothing more than an upside-down mouse. Instead of moving the mouse around to make the ball inside roll, you roll the ball around inside the mouse. What's the advantage of this? First of all, you don't need to have as much clear space on your desk. You just set a trackball down and it stays put. A mouse needs "running room" so you can move it around. Also, some people prefer the trackball because they don't have to move their hands away from the keyboard as much. Finally, if you have a little

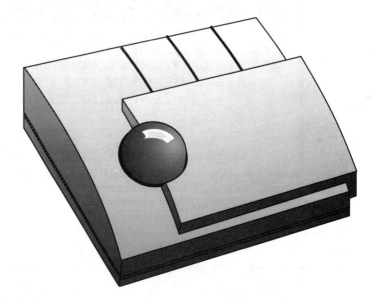

Trackball: an
alternative to
the mouse
Figure 2-18.

*A trackball
works exactly
like a mouse.*

battery-powered laptop computer that you like to take on airplane trips, you might be hard-pressed to find enough space on your tray table for a mouse. In fact, you can get trackballs that are specially made for laptop computers, like the ones in Figure 2-19.

Another mouse alternative is a *tablet*. This is a little like a magical slate that you draw on with a special stylus. As you draw on the tablet, the movement of your stylus is reflected in the movement of the cursor on your computer screen. This is terrific for graphic arts kinds of applications, where nothing beats the feel of drawing with a pen.

A tablet is usually about the size of a spiral notebook and is made of plastic. It has a thin wire that connects it to the rest of your computer system. It usually comes with a special stylus that looks like a thick pencil, paintbrush, or ball-point pen. The stylus may or may not have a wire attached to it, too. Underneath the smooth surface of the tablet is a crisscross matrix of tiny wires that sense the position of the stylus as you draw. That information is sent to your computer through the connecting cord so the computer can draw what you are drawing.

Portable
trackballs
Figure 2-19.

The tablet's smooth surface lets you lay a picture onto it and trace over
it with the stylus. You can use that to copy an artist's hand drawing
into the computer for editing, for instance, or to include it in
something you are publishing, like a brochure. Architects use tablets
to copy landscape drawings into the same PC that they use to design
the building.

Disks

A disk is where your PC stores its information. Disks are a computer's
file cabinet, if you will, where it saves everything when it's not running.
Without a disk, your computer would forget everything you've stored
in it every time you turned it off. It would also forget its programming,
or how it works. Disks are covered much more in Chapter 4, but a
summary is included here.

As Figures 2-1 and 2-2 at the beginning of this chapter might have
suggested, disks come in two basic types—floppy disk and hard disk.
Floppy disks are also known as removable or flexible disks, and hard
disks are sometimes called fixed disks or Winchester disks. Figure 2-20
shows a system with one floppy disk and one hard disk. Floppy disks

are more common and less expensive. Hard disks can store more information and they work faster. Practically every PC has at least one floppy disk and most have a hard disk, too.

Actually, what Figure 2-20 shows are two disk *drives,* not really disks. A *disk drive* is the device inside your computer that spins the disk so it can store and retrieve information on it. The disks themselves are what you put into the disk drive, just like putting a CD into a CD player. In fact, terms like "disk player" or "disk recorder" would probably be more descriptive than disk drive.

NOTE: Early microcomputers had no disks; they usually used cassette tape recorders. Before that, computers used punched paper cards. And even before that, patient computer operators had to flip rows of switches carefully and tediously to retrain the computer every time it was turned on, a procedure that took several minutes, and was very prone to errors.

Disk drives (and therefore, disks) come in two popular sizes. There's the 5 1/4-inch size, and the 3 1/2-inch size. Both sizes are used worldwide. If you take a look at Figure 2-21, you'll see samples of each kind. There is no real difference between the two sizes, except, well, their size. The

Hard disk drive (*a*) and floppy disk drive (*b*)
Figure 2-20.

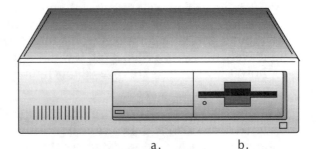

a.   b.

2

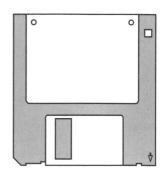

Get to know
your disks
Figure 2-21.

5 1/4-inch disks don't work any differently than the 3 1/2-inch disks. For the most part, you take whatever comes with your computer. For example, the Apple II family uses only 5 1/4-inch disks, but Macintoshes use only 3 1/2-inch disks. IBM-style machines use both kinds. The IBM PS/1 and PS/2 computers use only 3 1/2-inch disks. Other manufacturers, like Commodore, Atari, and Tandy are similarly split. Just so you know, the trend is toward smaller and smaller disks. Before the 1980s the most common size was 8-inch diameter. Before that, it was 14 inches!

Lately, a third kind of disk has come on the scene. This is called a *CD-ROM*, and it's nothing more or less than a CD player right in your PC. It takes real CDs just like a floppy disk drive accepts floppy disks. Some PCs can even play the music!

NEW WORD: A CD-ROM is a type of disk drive that uses compact discs (CDs). The ROM part stands for read-only memory. Not a very helpful term, but it is technically accurate. A CD stores information, so that makes it a memory device. And you can't write new information on a CD, only read what's already stored, so that makes them read-only.

Normally, you wouldn't want to use a computer with a CD-ROM drive to play your musical CD collection. Instead, you can buy prerecorded data CDs with large databases of information already stored on them. Because a CD can store an enormous amount of information—much more than floppy disks or even most hard disks—and because you can't accidentally erase a CD, it makes the perfect medium for an encyclopedia, atlas, telephone directory, or other large database. There are even new games that only come on CD.

Some computer CD-ROM drives can play music as well as data.

Right now, CD-ROM drives are not common, but the time is coming when they will be. A CD-ROM player can fit right into your PC, as shown in Figure 2-22. But they have their drawbacks, too. For one, they can be used only to read prerecorded CDs. You can't use one to store your own files. Second, they are fairly slow, at least compared to hard disk drives. Last of all, CD-ROM drives are expensive. But for use in a library or similar information bank, a CD-ROM can be a terrific help.

Computer with
CD-ROM drive
Figure 2-22.

Expansion Ports

Even with as much equipment as your computer has (keyboard, mouse, disk drive, and so on) the day may come when you'll want to add more to it. Maybe you'll want to add another disk drive, or a new mouse, or a high-quality printer. How will you attach that equipment to your computer?

External Expansion

Almost all personal computers have a way to add new equipment and capabilities. Usually there are special connectors on the back of your machine into which you can plug new equipment. The connections are called *expansion ports, adapter ports,* or *I/O ports*. I/O is an abbreviation for input/output, and it means that information sometimes goes into the computer, and sometimes out. Figure 2-23 shows the back of an IBM-style computer, highlighting the I/O ports. The back of a Macintosh, in Figure 2-24, looks pretty similar.

NEW WORD: An expansion port is a place where you can plug in new equipment in the future. It's called a port because it allows information to enter and leave your computer, like ships from a harbor.

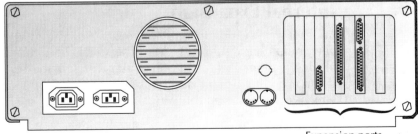

I/O ports on the back of a PC

Figure 2-23.

Expansion ports

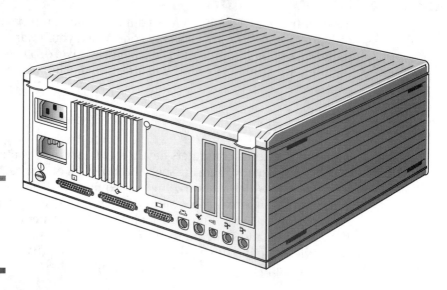

A Macintosh includes many expansion options
Figure 2-24.

As you can see, not all I/O ports look the same. There are different kinds of ports for different kinds of needs. If you look around your home or office you'll see different kinds of ports, too. Ports for electricity, telephone hookup, and cable TV, for instance. The expansion ports on the back of your PC have names like serial, SCSI, floppy, ADB, parallel, and worse things. Don't worry about the particular names for now. They'll be made clearer in Chapters 4, 10, and 11.

Internal Expansion

Your computer's expansion capabilities let you grow for the future.

Another way to add capability to your personal computer is to put the new equipment right inside. Many personal computers have room left inside the main unit for add-on equipment. Obviously, this works only if you're adding on something relatively small. Printers and display screens can't be added this way.

If you remove the cover of a computer, like the one shown in Figure 2-25, you may find room for expansion. This machine has several *expansion slots* where you can add small electronic circuit boards called *expansion boards* to your computer, enhancing its capabilities.

2

Remove the
cover of the
computer to
look for
expansion slots
Figure 2-25.

NEW WORD: An expansion board is an electronic circuit card you can buy to plug into your PC. It fits into a reserved space in the computer called an expansion slot. Different computers have different kinds of expansion slots. Some don't have any at all.

Cables and Cords

Often, the back of a personal computer can look like the back of an audiophile's stereo system—a tangle of wires and *cables*. You probably need at least one cable to connect your keyboard to the main computer unit and another one to connect your display screen to the main unit (unless your screen is built in). You'll also need to use an electrical cord to plug your computer into the wall socket. If you want to add an external disk drive, printer, or other piece of outside equipment, you will need cables for each of those, too.

NEW WORD: Computer cables are nothing more than wires covered in a protective plastic wrapper. Some are no different than a lamp cord. Other cables hold a complicated collection of separate wires.

Cables come in different lengths, sizes, and styles, just like the I/O ports they plug into. All of the necessary cables should be provided by your computer's manufacturer or come with any equipment that you purchase.

Internals

This last section will take a quick look at some of the electronics that make your computer go. These are the components that you never see from the outside, but in a very real sense, they *are* the computer.

There are many parts inside your computer—like inside your car—that you'll never see.

The inside of every personal computer is made up of dozens, and sometimes hundreds, of tiny electronic components called *integrated circuits,* or ICs for short. They are also more popularly known as *chips.* The ICs contain microscopically small squares of silicon (not silicone, which is something different), packed inside little black plastic rectangles about 1-inch long and 1/4-inch wide. To the untrained eye, each of these chips looks pretty much the same. It takes a specialist to tell them apart. There are thousands of different kinds of them, and each kind performs a different function within your computer.

Each chip is connected to its neighbors by thin copper wires. You can't see the wires because they're buried inside a green fiberglass board. This type of board is called a *printed circuit board,* or PCB for short. The board is made by stacking layers of copper wire between layers of fiberglass. The whole thing is glued together and sprayed with a green coating to protect it from damage. The main PCB in your computer is called the *motherboard* because it holds all of the most important chips on it. Any smaller boards that may be added to it are called *daughterboards.*

NEW WORD: The motherboard is the heart of your computer. It holds all of the most important electronic components inside your PC. On some computers, you can remove the motherboard and replace it with a newer, faster one.

There's no need to become an expert on the chips inside your PC, or even to be on speaking terms with them. This section is only presented so that you can have a basic understanding of what's in there when it comes time to describe a problem or talk to a computer salesman.

2

Microprocessor

The biggest and most important IC in your PC is the one called the *microprocessor*. Microprocessor is sometimes shortened to processor, or CPU (for Central Processing Unit). The microprocessor is the brain of a PC. It is the chip that evaluates and executes each and every instruction of your computer's software. The rest of the ICs within your computer are there only to assist the microprocessor.

NEW **WORD:** A microprocessor is a big, expensive silicon chip that makes your computer run. Every PC has exactly one. It's like the motor in a car; the bigger and faster it is, the faster (and more expensive) your computer is.

A microchip is what those in the know prefer to call an integrated circuit, or IC.

Each type of personal computer uses a particular type of microprocessor chip. The type of microprocessor has a lot to do with how fast your PC will run, and it also determines what software you can and can't use. Each type of microprocessor understands a different computer "language," and you have to choose software in the correct language for your PC's processor. That's not as hard as it might sound, though. There are really only two or three basic choices, and the programs at the computer store are very clearly marked.

Most kinds of microprocessors don't have names. Instead, they use enigmatic three- to five-digit numbers, like 8086, 68030, or 486. Microprocessor chips are rated by their size (measured in bits), and by their speed (measured in megahertz). For the average user, these terms aren't really all that important. If you want to know more, it's all in Chapter 15.

Memory

Another kind of IC is the *memory* chip. If the microprocessor does the thinking, then you could say the memory chips do the remembering. Some number of memory chips is required in any personal computer; a typical machine might have 16. The more memory your computer has, the more advanced and powerful the work it can do. This is because the computer will have more room to remember the instructions it is supposed to follow, and more room to remember the information you've given it. Don't confuse the memory function of the memory chips with the storage function of a disk. Memory is used while the computer is turned on and running; disks are used to save your work while the computer is turned off.

NEW WORD: Memory chips come in two basic kinds, called ROM and RAM. ROM stands for read-only memory, while RAM means random-access memory. Admittedly, these are technical terms. The RAM chips, in turn, come in two sorts called SRAM and DRAM. These stand for static and dynamic RAM, respectively. No need to memorize these words; they are covered in more detail in Chapter 3.

The capacity of a computer's memory is normally not measured by the number of memory chips it contains, but in *bytes*. This term is another engineer's whim, because it means a "bite" of something intangible. A byte is a unit of information, or memory. One byte is enough to "remember" one letter of the alphabet. (That's not the technical definition, but it's close enough for our purposes.) One byte is also enough to remember small numbers. Larger numbers, or words more than one letter long, require multiple bytes of memory to store. Each instruction in a computer program takes three or four bytes. Naturally, half a byte is called a *nybble*.

NEW WORD: A byte is a unit of measure, like inch or gram. A byte measures how much information something can store. One byte's worth of storage is about equal to one letter of the alphabet. For example, it would take eight bytes to store the name Caroline.

Having a few bytes of memory is about as valuable as having a few cents of money. It isn't very useful, so you'll hear people talk about *kilobytes* and *megabytes* more often than just bytes. The prefix *kilo*, the Greek word for one thousand, makes a byte around 1000 bytes. (Actually, for obscure technical reasons, it's exactly 1024 bytes.) A megabyte is a thousand times greater, the prefix *mega* being Greek for one million. A megabyte is a kilo-kilobyte, or 1,048,576 bytes—enough to store the entire text of this book two times over.

NEW WORD: A kilobyte means about 1000 bytes. A megabyte is equal to about 1 million bytes. Kilobyte is usually abbreviated as K, and megabyte as MB.

In this chapter, you have seen what all of the major components of a personal computer are and what they do. You should now be able to recognize and identify the various parts of any personal computer system. Two sections that were passed over rather quickly were memory and disks. That shouldn't lead you to believe that these are unimportant parts of your PC. On the contrary, they are two of the most important features of your computer, which is why they are covered in detail in the next two chapters.

CHAPTER

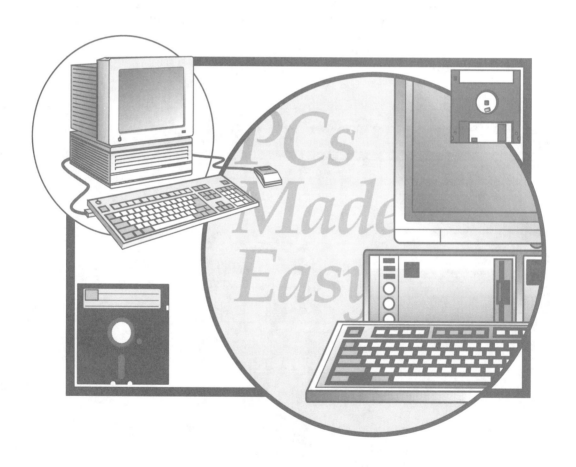

3 WHAT IS MEMORY?

Anyone who's ever watched late-night science-fiction movies knows that computers have something slightly ominous called "memory banks." The memory bank usually holds something vitally important and difficult to get out. It is the hero's task to either keep something in or get something out of the computer's memory bank.

The item in question here is an important part of every personal computer, although the word "bank" is outdated. Today, you would just talk about your computer's memory and everybody (at least, everybody who had read this book) would know what you meant.

Memory is a term that has several different meanings in the computer world. In the beginning of this chapter, we'll look at what memory means and the different kinds of memory that you should be familiar with. In the second half of the chapter, we'll cover some more in-depth information for more advanced (or just curious) computer users.

Your Computer's Workspace

Memory—you can't see it, but it has a big effect on how your computer works. It governs how fast your computer can run. It determines what programs you can and can't use. It controls how many programs you can use at once. And it significantly affects the price of your computer. All of this—from a part of your computer that you normally don't even see.

Imagine that you are sitting at a desk working with a lot of papers. You have a pencil and eraser and your job involves writing lots of notes on the papers. If you have a big desk, you can spread the papers out so you can see them all and write on them from time to time. Or, you can erase notes from other pages without having to shuffle them around.

The more memory you have in your PC, the easier it is for your computer to work with big programs and projects.

On the other hand, if you have a small desk, one where you can only lay out a few papers at a time, your job becomes much harder. You have to find a place to stack most of the papers out of the way so that you have a clear space to write on. You also need to shuffle through the stack often, searching for the papers you need. Every time you pull out a new paper you have to make room for it on the desk by taking one off and putting it in the stack.

In this imaginary world, the desk represents your PC's memory, while you stand in for the microprocessor. You could even extend the analogy and say that the desk drawers represent the PC's disks (but let's save this for the next chapter.) The point is, memory is your computer's workspace. The more room you give it to work, the more easily it can work for you.

The only technical thing you need to know about memory is how to measure it. As you read in the previous chapter, memory is measured in bytes. Pushing the desktop analogy a little, you could say that the

3

number of bytes of memory in your PC corresponds to the number of square inches of desk space. The more you have, the better for you.

Memory is only temporary storage; remember to save your work on a disk.

The amount of memory you have is not always fixed forever. Just about any PC can have memory added to it. If you're buying a new computer, it might make sense to buy it with a minimum amount of memory to save money, and then add some later. Another constant in the computer world is that memory always gets cheaper. Prices have been dropping steadily for 25 years, and there's no indication that this trend will stop anytime soon.

Memories Aren't Forever

Another important fact to remember about your computer's memory is that it needs electricity to work. Once the power goes out, so does all your information. That doesn't mean that you can never turn your computer off, only that you must remember to save your work onto a disk from time to time. (Disks are covered in the upcoming chapter.) Once you understand that memory is temporary and only works while the computer is running, many other concepts will suddenly become easier to understand.

How Much Is Enough?

You've probably figured out by now that the most important thing you need to remember about memory is that more is better. But how much is enough? That depends on what you want to use your computer for. To some extent, the more memory you have, the broader your choice of programs will be. But after a certain point, having more memory doesn't buy you much. The trouble is, that point keeps moving upward.

It's easy to add more memory to most any PC. Adding some to yours may let you run new programs.

In 1980, having 32K of memory was a big deal (but then, so was having a personal computer at all). In 1990, having 1024K of memory (1MB) was no big deal.

There's been a kind of memory "arms race" ever since Apple and IBM-style computers started finding their way into the marketplace. The more memory the computers had, the more advanced the programs got. The more advanced the programs got, the more memory they used. So, computers got more memory, and the programs got bigger, and computers got more memory, and it's still going on today.

TIP: To find out how much memory you really need, look at the programs you want to run. Ask at the computer store or check the box that the program comes in. It will usually say on the outside, "512K required" or something similar. Then double that. Software companies want to sell software, after all, so they typically underrate the amount of memory required to use their products.

Memory, Macintosh Style

If you want to find out how much memory you already have, that's easily done. For the Macintosh, you just pull down the Apple menu in the upper-left corner and select the first choice, "About the Finder...":

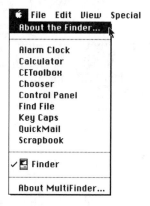

Depending on what version of the Apple software you have, you will get a display like this:

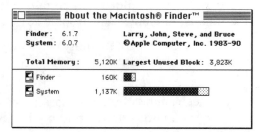

Notice that it tells you how much memory you have altogether, plus how much it's actually using at the moment. Watch the display for a little while; the bars should change. If you have a lot of white space showing at the right-hand end of the bars, you've got nothing to worry about. If the bars are looking pretty dark, it may be time for some more memory.

Memory, IBM PC Style

On an IBM-style PC, it's a little more difficult to discover just how much memory you have because the PC doesn't come with a handy program to tell you. The closest thing is a program called CHKDSK (that's supposed to stand for "check disk"). In addition to checking your disk, it reports how much memory it thinks you have. Trouble is, it's not very accurate.

Type **CHKDSK** to run the program.

```
C:\>CHKDSK
```

Now look at the last two lines of the display:

```
C:\>chkdsk

Volume DRIVE C      created 07-26-1992 6:07p
Volume Serial Number is 1D7D-19CE

  46514176 bytes total disk space
  12640256 bytes in 5 hidden files
     92160 bytes in 35 directories
  33466368 bytes in 1160 user files
    315392 bytes available on disk

      2048 bytes in each allocation unit
     22712 total allocation units on disk
       154 available allocation units on disk

    655360 total bytes memory
    488448 bytes free

C:\>
```

It is telling you how much memory you have and how much you aren't using. If you get a number under about 650,000, CHKDSK is probably reporting your total memory accurately. (Remember, a kilobyte is really 1024 bytes, not 1000, so amounts like 512K don't come out as round numbers.) If you get a value of 655,360, you might appear to be getting short-changed. You may actually have more.

The CHKDSK program is not able to count any higher than 640K, which is 655,360 bytes. If it reports this much, you might actually have this much, or you might have a lot more. There's just no easy way to tell.

If you're lucky, you may have another program on your PC called MEM. If you run this program it will tell you if you have any additional memory. You can type **MEM** to run this program.

```
C:\>MEM
```

If you do have the MEM program, and it works, you might want to refer to the expanded/extended portion of this chapter to decipher what the MEM program is trying to tell you.

Technical Stuff

Memory chips come in two basic types called *RAM* (random-access memory) and *ROM* (read-only memory). RAM chips are the kind you will be most interested in, but the ROM type will be covered first to get them out of the way.

ROM Memory

ROM stands for read-only memory, and you pronounce it (if you ever need to) just like it looks. There are probably one or two ROM chips in your PC and they hold a program that is absolutely, positively necessary for your computer to work. It's so important, in fact, that it isn't stored on a disk or in "normal" memory, but in these special ROM chips. The ROM chips can't be erased—that's why they're called read-only memory—so your program is safe. The program itself is called the *BIOS,* and you won't hear any more about it in this book.

NEW WORD: The BIOS is a special program that is stored as a permanent part of your computer. BIOS stands for Basic Input and Output System, and it helps your computer run.

3

Figure 3-1 shows you what a ROM chip looks like, should you ever be called upon to identify one. They often travel in pairs. For more information about ROM chips you can flip ahead to Chapter 13.

RAM Memory

The other kind of memory chip is the RAM chip. Most of the time, when computer people talk about memory, they mean RAM. Throughout most of this book, when you read about memory at all, it will be RAM memory.

Memory chips usually come in sets of eight because there are eight bits in each byte.

RAM stands for random-access memory. They're called that because read-write memory would spell "RWM" and that's hard to pronounce. But that's exactly what RAM chips are, read-write memory. They're the opposite of ROMs. A ROM chip can't be erased and reused, but RAM chips are erased and reused all the time— about 5000 times per second, as a matter of fact.

Each RAM chip in your PC can hold a fixed amount of information, like a one-quart bottle. The more of them you have, the more you can store. Your PC might have eight or sixteen RAM chips, or more. (They usually come in multiples of eight, like hot dog buns.) You can usually add more RAM chips to your computer later on, if you want to. Figure 3-2 shows what a typical RAM chip looks like.

Most people get all nervous and uncomfortable if they have to add chips to their computer. It's not an easy procedure for the beginner and there's plenty of opportunity to damage something. Besides, if RAM chips always come in packs of eight, why not make it so that you can install all eight at once?

ROM
(read-only
memory) chip
Figure 3-1.

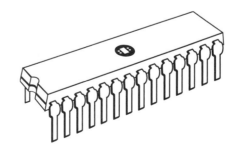

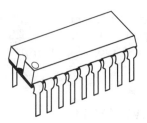

RAM
(random-access
memory) chip
Figure 3-2.

Most personal computers today (and this goes for Macintoshes as well as IBM-style PCs) keep their RAM chips on little things called *SIMM* modules. SIMM stands for single in-line memory module, which you don't need to remember. The good part is, the SIMM modules hold a complete set of RAM chips and they (the modules) are relatively easy to install. Figure 3-3 shows you how they differ from the single RAM chips in the previous figure.

More About RAM Chips

There's even more you can learn about RAM chips. First of all, they come in two basic kinds, *dynamic RAM* and *static RAM*. The difference is highly technical and doesn't affect your computer (or you) one way or the other. Suffice it to say, about 95 percent of all PCs use the dynamic type instead of the static type.

NEW WORD: Dynamic RAM is usually abbreviated DRAM, while static RAM chips are called SRAMs. For no apparent reason, both words are pronounced with the first letter, like "dee-ram" and "ess-ram." Don't say "dram" unless you're an apothecary.

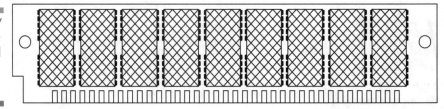

SIMM memory
modules make
it easier to add
RAM chips
Figure 3-3.

The other thing to know about RAM chips is that they each have a speed rating. That is, some RAM chips can "remember" faster than others. Generally speaking, the faster the RAM, the better. The faster RAM chips are also more expensive (naturally). The speed of a memory chip is measured in nanoseconds. For those who have forgotten their Greek, the prefix *nano* comes from *nanos,* the word for dwarf. Accordingly, a *nanosecond* is a very short period of time. It is exactly 0.000000001 second, or about the time it takes light to travel 6 inches. A typical RAM chip will have a speed of about 80 nanoseconds. The lower the number, the better.

Faster memory chips are necessary to keep up with faster computers.

3

Finally, not all RAM chips store the same amount of information. They come in different sizes, like cereal boxes. About every three or four years, the world's chip makers find a way to squeeze four times as much information into a RAM chip as before. (The increases always come in leaps of four; just because.) For example, there are chips that store 1 *megabit* of data, or 4 megabits, or 16 megabits. The only reason this might be relevant to you is if you want to increase the memory capacity of your computer someday. You may be called upon to answer some difficult questions about the kind of memory that you have and what you want to upgrade it to.

NEW WORD: A megabit is approximately one million bits of information. That's bits, not bytes. A bit is an even smaller measure of storage than a byte is. There are exactly 8 bits to a byte, so 1 megabit makes 128 kilobytes. Got it?

Different Classes of Memory

In the IBM-style PC world (and that includes the XT and 286, 386, and 486 computers), there are three classes of memory. "Class" refers to the way that your computer uses the memory. There's nothing different about the memory chips themselves. The difference is what your PC does with the memory and what programs are able to use it.

The three classes of memory are conventional, expanded, and extended. Pay particular attention to the latter two, because it's awfully easy to get them confused. Every PC has some of the first kind—conventional. Your PC may or may not have either of the latter two kinds. A really top-notch computer will have all three.

Conventional Memory

When the first IBM PC was released into the world, it had 64 kilobytes (64K) of RAM. This was the basic memory that the PC used for just about everything. All of your programs (software) had to fit within this 64K space. Your data had to fit within the same 64K, too, so if your spreadsheet program used 60K, you only had 4K left to work in. Of course, you could still store as much information on disk as your disk could hold. But your spreadsheet program could only *work on* 4K of data at a time.

Later, the IBM PC was updated to allow you to double your memory size, to 128K. The IBM XT came with 256K of memory, doubling it again. You could expand that to 512K if you bought extra memory chips. And, for the real "power user," the maximum amount of memory was a whopping 640K of memory. For a long time, 640K of RAM was the limit.

All PCs have conventional memory. This is the first 640K. The next 384K is reserved by the PC maker.

The limit of 640K is an arbitrary one, but one that we all have to live with. It's there because of the way IBM engineers designed the original PC, way back in 1981. At that time, most personal computers of the day (in fact, practically all of them) had less than 64K of memory. Most had about 16K or 32K. Nobody anticipated using more than that much memory, but IBM played it safe and designed the PC to use *ten times* that much, just in case. Little did they know that five short years later, 640K would seem ridiculously low.

Figure 3-4 gives you a chart of memory sizes. Memory starts at the bottom of the chart and grows toward the top. The very top of the chart represents 1024K of memory, or 1 megabyte (1MB). About two-thirds of the way up is the "640K barrier." This is how much memory the IBM PC and XT could use.

The space above the 640K line was reserved by the IBM engineers for other things. Even though the PC *could* have used that much memory, it was not allowed to. Today, the memory below the 640K mark is called *conventional* memory.

The extra 384K of space between the 640K mark and the 1MB mark is used by the expansion boards in your PC. You may have one or more of these expansion boards plugged into your computer already. There's probably one that controls your video display, and another one that controls your disk drives. Each of these expansion boards has a little bit

3

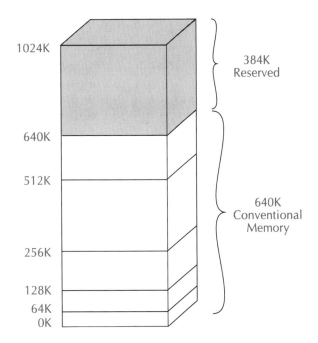

The first
megabyte of
memory
Figure 3-4.

of memory on it. For example, a video board needs memory so it can
"remember" what to display on your screen. The better your display
screen, the more memory your video adapter board has.

That memory is not used by your programs in the normal way. IBM
needed to reserve that 384K area for future expansion boards, like video
boards with greater memory requirements or fancy network adapter
boards. The whole 384K space is practically never all used, though.
There's always some wasted room, and that's aggravating to PC users
who need more than 640K of memory.

Expanded Memory

The fabled "640K barrier" was finally broken shortly after the IBM AT
came out in 1985. The AT used a new microprocessor chip called the
80286 (or just 286, for short). The 286 chip could use more memory

than the earlier microprocessors in the original PC and XT computers. However, there were still technical barriers in the way. Namely, if the AT used more memory than the PC and XT did, then all of the PC's and XT's programs wouldn't work anymore.

Expanded memory is one way to increase your memory capacity beyond 640K.

The solution came not from IBM, but from three other companies working together. They figured out a way to use the "empty spaces" between 640K and 1024K that weren't already being used by expansion boards. Their scheme allows you to increase your memory size in 64K chunks. So instead of having 640K of memory, you might be able to use 704K, or 768K, or even more.

The three companies that worked out this system were Lotus Development Corporation (of Lotus 1-2-3 fame), Intel (the company that made the 80286 microprocessor), and Microsoft Corporation (which created some of the most important PC programs). Together, they created the *Expanded Memory Specification,* often abbreviated as *EMS.*

NEW WORD: The Lotus-Intel-Microsoft Expanded Memory Specification (or LIM EMS, if you prefer) was the first step to letting IBM-style PCs use more than 640 kilobytes of memory. Since that time, there have been more enhancements, and now PCs with thousands of kilobytes of memory are commonplace.

To use expanded memory, you need two things: a memory board and the EMS software. Just about any PC is able to use expanded memory once you have these two things. The first step is to start with a "full load" of 640K of memory. After all, there's no point in increasing your PC's memory beyond 640K if you aren't even up to 640K yet!

For the memory board, make sure it's one that supports expanded memory. There are some that won't work with expanded memory, but these are getting fewer and farther between. The only other thing you need is the expanded memory software. This is quite often included with the memory board when you buy it. In that case, you will get instructions on installing the memory board in your PC and directions on using the EMS software. If not, you'll have to buy the EMS software separately.

The Lotus-Intel-Microsoft EMS specification has been changed and updated a few times, so there are different versions of the so-called LIM EMS. Version 4.0 is the most widely used, so most computers, memory boards, and programs are compatible with that system.

Extended memory works like expanded, but faster. Most high performance PCs use extended memory.

Extended Memory

3

Now it's possible for you to go the expanded memory system one better. If your PC has a 386 or 486 microprocessor in it, you can use a newer method called *extended* memory. Like expanded memory, extended memory lets you use more than 640K of RAM. The advantage that extended memory has over expanded memory is that it's faster.

Installing and using extended memory is no different from adding expanded memory. In both cases you need a memory board and memory manager software. Obviously, you need to use a memory expansion board that can support extended memory, but they're not hard to find these days. Your memory board should also come with the software required to make it run smoothly. If it doesn't, don't worry, you may have the software already.

NEW WORD: Extended memory is handled using an extended memory manager, called the XMS. It's a standard, like the expanded memory (EMS) manager is.

If you are using the PC software called DOS 5.0 or DOS 6.0, you already have the extended memory manager software. It is called HIMEM, and your DOS manual explains how it works. Other programs from other software companies also support extended memory boards. Programs like QEMM and 386MAXX are two examples.

Turning Extended into Expanded

Even though the extended memory scheme is better and faster than expanded memory, not every program can use it. In fact, there are a lot of PC programs that can use expanded memory but not extended memory. If your favorite program doesn't use your added memory, there's not much point in having it.

To solve this problem, there are programs that make your extended memory "look like" expanded memory. By fooling your computer in this way, you can really enjoy the best of both worlds. You have extended memory when you want it, and expanded memory when you need it.

The DOS 5.0 software includes one such program for free. It is called EMM386.SYS, and your DOS manual explains how to use it. If you have another kind of memory management software, like QuarterDeck Office Systems' QEMM program, you can use QEMM to "convert" your extended memory to expanded. The QEMM program will work on demand, automatically switching between extended and expanded memory while you work.

Funny Memory Terms

After conventional, expanded, and extended, there are still more memory terms cropping up. Like the others, you don't need to become an expert in these, but they're bound to appear, and you're likely to see them yourself before too long.

Upper Memory Block

In the never-ending struggle to squeeze more memory out of your PC, somebody has developed the concept of Upper Memory Blocks, or UMBs. The UMB principle only works on 386 computers or better; that is, 80386, 80486, and higher. If you've got an older PC you can skip over this part.

With UMB you take back a small part of the 384K reserved area.

UMB is a part of your computer's memory between the legendary 640K barrier and the 1MB line. Earlier, you saw that this area is off limits to most programs. That space is reserved for the memory on your add-in expansion boards like the video board, disk controller, and so on. It turns out, though, that not all of the memory is really used. The whole 384K area is reserved (1024K minus 640K), but most of it is still free.

With the proper software, your PC can make use of this space to store small programs. Even your PC's main operating software, called DOS, can be stored there. The net benefit is, you have that much more conventional memory free for your favorite programs.

High Memory Area

With the right memory-management software you can squeeze every last byte from your PC.

The so-called High Memory Area (HMA) is really just another name for the first 64K of your extended memory. For obscure technical reasons, the first 64K of a block of extended memory is usually never used. If you have a computer with extended memory, you might be able to utilize this space better.

This requires, of course, that you have a PC with some extended memory. That, in turn, implies a PC with a 386 microprocessor or better. Then you need the extended memory manager software, and last, but not least, the extended memory itself.

Cache

If you're familiar with Robinson Crusoe, he hid his most valuable tools and food up in a tree, in a *cache*. In the same way, your PC might have a special private area of memory where it stores its most precious information.

NEW WORD: A cache is a special area of super-fast memory that speeds up your PC. If you have a PC with a cache memory, say it like "cash."

A cache memory—if your PC has one—is completely separate from all of the other kinds of memory discussed so far. It's not a part of conventional, expanded, or extended memory. It's another thing entirely and it makes your PC run faster.

Cache memory uses special extra-fast memory chips. The chips are faster than normal memories, so they cost more, too. A PC with a cache memory will usually have somewhere between 16K and 256K of cache. There's no memory management software required, and usually you can't add more cache to your computer. In fact, you can forget about it entirely, secure in the knowledge that it's working for you, making your PC go just a little bit faster.

CHAPTER

4

WHAT IS A DISK?

Disks are an important part of your personal computer system. They are your computer's permanent storage—where it "remembers" everything you've taught it and where you save your work when the computer is turned off. Disks also store programs that you buy; the program instructions are kept on a disk until your PC needs them. With disks, you can conveniently move information from one computer to another. This book, for example, was written on a computer and then stored on disk and mailed to the publisher, where it was read, edited, and typeset using other personal computers.

This chapter will explore different kinds of disks and how they work. You'll learn what they can and can't be used for and how to take care of them. Chapter 5 will discuss disks from a different point of view, including ways to arrange your information on disk and how to protect your valuable data.

What Do I Use a Disk For?

You use disks for permanent storage. They are your computer's file cabinet. Software programs and other kinds of data are stored on disk until you need them. When you stop working you can store your work on disk until you're ready to resume it. Disks also make your data tangible. When you store information on a disk you can lock it in a drawer for security, or duplicate it and share it, or mail it to another computer user.

Disks give you storage like a file cabinet.

Let's say that you're going to write a company memo, but you only have enough time to get halfway through it before quitting time. With a typewriter, you insert a sheet of paper, type as much as you can, then take the paper out and file it away until tomorrow.

With your PC, when quitting time comes, you "file" your half-finished memo on a disk and turn your computer off. If you forget to save your work on a disk, you'll lose it, and it won't be there when you come in tomorrow. But once it's saved, it can be retrieved any time. Every time you turn your computer off, its memory is erased. However, anything stored on disk is safely filed.

You could also give the disk to somebody else to finish the memo for you. Or, your co-workers might want to use it to save time if they were writing similar letters. You could use the same disk again and again, as a sample for company memos. Reading information does not remove it from the disk, any more than watching a video tape erases the movie.

Disks and Memory

If you recall from the previous chapter, your computer uses its memory to store information that it's working on. Memory is the desktop to the disk's file cabinet. Only some of the information goes into memory, where it's being actively worked on; the rest of it is stored on disk for another time. Your computer moves information from disk to memory and back to disk all the time—sometimes without your knowing about it.

REMEMBER: Your PC can't edit or alter the data stored on disk directly. It has to read it from the disk into its memory, alter it there, and then write it from memory onto the disk.

4

Both computer memory and computer disk capacities are measured in bytes. The more disk capacity you have, the more information you can store. There's no particular relationship between the amount of memory in your PC and the amount of disk space. Typically, you'll have about 10 to 100 times as much disk space as memory space.

Disks Versus Disk Drives

Before going too much further, you need to understand the difference between two terms: disks and disk drives. These are not the same thing, but they are closely related. Don't be confused if you hear people use both terms interchangeably.

A *disk* is a small, flat, plastic or vinyl square that you use to store information. The *disk drive* is the part of your computer's machinery that reads and writes information onto a disk. The relationship between disk and disk drive is the same as between, say, a CD and CD player or paper and typewriter.

Your computer might have one or two disk drives, but you can accumulate as many disks as you like. Like building a record collection, you can build a data collection, with disks.

Different Disks and Disk Drives

Figure 4-1 shows three different kinds of disk drives that hold different kinds of disks. The two on the top are floppy disk drives, where you can remove the disk. The one on the bottom is a hard disk drive. Unlike the

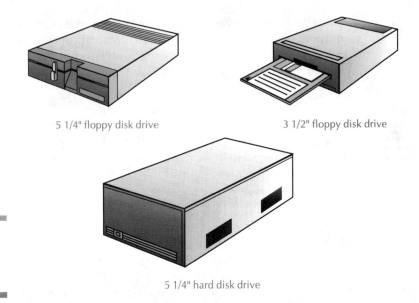

5 1/4" floppy disk drive · 3 1/2" floppy disk drive

5 1/4" hard disk drive

Disk drives come in two basic types
Figure 4-1.

other two, the hard disk drive has no slot to insert a disk. That's really all you need to know to use your disks, but let's look at them in more detail.

Floppy Disks

Floppy disks, which are also called *removable disks* or *diskettes,* are used in all personal computers. It is a rare PC that is without a floppy disk drive. Floppy disks are small, convenient, inexpensive, and let you store nearly limitless amounts of information, because the more floppy disks you have, the more information you can store.

Floppy disks are portable storage.

Figure 4-2 shows the two different sizes of floppy disks: 5 1/4-inch and 3 1/2-inch. As you can see, they look similar except for their size. A 5 1/4-inch floppy disk must be used with computers that have 5 1/4-inch floppy disk drives, and a 3 1/2-inch disk must be used with 3 1/2-inch drives. The amount of material you can store on a disk may vary from computer to computer and from disk to disk, but it has nothing to do with the actual size of the disk.

4

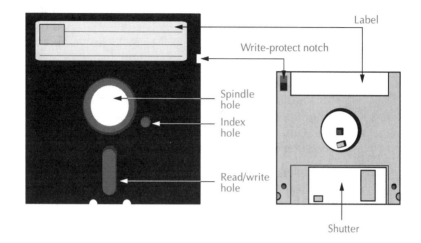

How to
recognize
floppy disks
Figure 4-2.

If disks are supposed to be flat and round, why are these floppy disks
square? To answer that question, you need to look inside a floppy disk.
Figure 4-3 shows a 5 1/4-inch floppy disk after it's been peeled open.
(Don't try this at home!) Now you can see that there really is a round
disk in there after all. The square exterior is merely a protective cover.

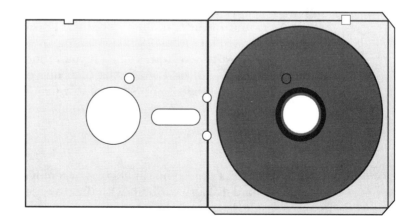

What's inside a
5 1/4-inch
floppy disk
Figure 4-3.

The disk itself is very thin and flexible (hence, "floppy" disk). The inside is usually dark brown in color. The material used to make floppy disks is exactly the same material used to make audio and video tapes.

A floppy disk is a cross between a CD and a cassette tape. It looks like a CD (sort of), but it's made of the same stuff used for tapes. A floppy disk spins around like a record or a CD, but it's actually recorded using the same principle as a tape recorder. Information is converted to magnetic pulses and stored on the surface of the disk (like the tape). The same recording can be read again and again, until the recording is erased.

The new 3 1/2-inch floppies are a bit sturdier than the 5 1/4-inch variety.

The disk in Figure 4-3 is a 5 1/4-inch floppy; a 3 1/2-inch floppy disk looks the same inside. The biggest difference between them (other than the size) is on the outside. The protective cover on a 3 1/2-inch disk is hard plastic instead of thin vinyl. That makes the smaller disks less "floppy" than their 5 1/4-inch counterparts. It also protects the recording surface inside better than the thin vinyl on a 5 1/4-inch disk. There are also no exposed holes on a 3 1/2-inch disk. Instead, a small aluminum *shutter* at the edge of the disk is automatically moved aside, exposing the recording surface when you insert the disk into a disk drive. The shutter closes by itself when you remove the disk. Another nice feature of 3 1/2-inch disks is that they fit very nicely into a shirt pocket.

Technically speaking, neither disk is superior to the other. Surprisingly, both store a similar amount of information, despite their size differences. However, 3 1/2-inch disks seem to be growing more popular over time. In the end, the choice of disk size is probably not up to you; it is dictated by the size of the disk drive in your personal computer. Don't worry about this detail if you're shopping for a computer. Buying a PC based on the size of its disk drives would be a little like buying a car based on the size of its wheels.

Hard Disks

Unlike a floppy disk drive, you can't insert or remove disks from a hard disk drive. A hard disk drive is built with the disks permanently mounted inside. Each hard disk, or *platter,* is mounted one above the other, on a vertical spindle. The disks themselves are similar to floppy disks, except that they are made from aluminum or glass instead of thin plastic. The disks, the spindle, and all the electronics that go with them are sealed inside an airtight box. Hard disk drives are manufactured in ultra-clean rooms by workers wearing masks, gloves, and pressurized suits, like astronauts. The inside of a hard disk drive is *thousands* of times cleaner than a hospital operating room could ever be.

NEW WORD: A platter is a hard disk, like a metal CD, that spins around inside a hard disk drive. Most hard disk drives have more than one disk, or platter.

4

Why do they take such elaborate precautions to manufacture a disk drive? Why mount all of the disks inside? Why not make the disks removable? Why would I want one of these things in my computer, anyhow? The answers to these questions can be summed up in two words: speed and storage.

Hard disks have two big advantages over floppy disks: they're faster and they store a lot more. They're faster because they are built as precision instruments, like fine watches. They store a lot more because there is more than one disk inside each drive unit, and each disk can hold much more than a floppy can. The net benefit to you is that you can have more of your information at your fingertips (or your computer's).

Hard disk drives are also called *fixed* disk drives or sometimes *Winchester* disk drives. Winchester is often shortened to just "Wini" and a little Winchester disk is a "mini Wini."

NOTE: Winchester comes from the Winchester Repeating Rifle Company, makers of firearms in the Old West. Much later, in the 1970s, a prominent Silicon Valley firm was developing a hard disk drive that could hold 30 megabytes of data and access it in 30 milliseconds. It became known as the "30/30"—the same name as the popular Winchester rifle.

Nearly all PCs now have a hard disk drive. Only the earliest IBM and IBM-compatible PCs, and the first Macintosh models could make do without one. One hard disk is normally enough; but it's not uncommon to have two or more. Even small battery-powered laptop and notebook computers have hard disks in them. They're just too useful to pass up.

Using only floppies, you might have to swap diskettes in and out of your disk drive, searching for the information you want. A hard disk can hold as much as 500 floppy disks and access it all instantly. With floppies, you run the risk of losing or misplacing your disk. With a hard disk drive in your PC, the data is always handy. Loading a large amount of information from floppies may take five or ten minutes, and several disks, while a hard disk can load as much in seconds. When you add the speed advantages of a hard disk drive to its greater storage capacity, you begin to understand the tremendous appeal of hard disks.

If you copy information from your floppy disks onto a hard disk you can have it all accessible in the same place.

The scrupulously clean manufacturing procedures are what give hard disk drives their technical superiority. The drive's moving parts must be built to precise tolerances to work properly, and any dust or other contaminant in the works will ruin them. Also, the magnetic recording surfaces of the hard disks must be kept clean and ultra-smooth. Even a tiny fingerprint on the surface of a hard disk platter would destroy the delicate recording heads inside.

Fortunately, all of these elaborate precautions are invisible to you, the computer user. No unusual maintenance or care is required. Indeed, since the hard disks are not removable, you normally don't have access to the hard disk drive at all. It is often buried inside the computer, and it is sometimes difficult to tell whether a PC has a hard disk in it or not. The only clue you might get is a small blinking light or a soft whirring sound to tell you that it's working. As a precaution, you should avoid jarring a computer with a hard disk drive, or you risk damaging some of its sensitive internal workings. Treat a hard disk drive as you would an expensive watch.

Special Disks

There are other kinds of disks that you might see in your work with computers, or you might even have one yourself. If you're preparing to buy a PC, you might want to consider one of the following special-purpose disks.

CD-ROM

The newest kind of disk in the PC world is called the *CD-ROM* (compact disk read-only memory). This is an exciting blend of the computer and stereo worlds. A CD-ROM is, quite simply, a compact disk for a computer. While your stereo CD player plays music, your computer can use a CD to "play" software.

The music CD has taken the music and recording world by storm. A CD can hold more music in a smaller package than a 33 1/3 LP record. But the real difference is in the quality of the sound. While a record can get scratched or warped, a CD is nearly indestructible. Plus, the sound is recorded more accurately to begin with. Rather than relying on the size and width of tiny grooves cut in vinyl, a CD records sound "by the numbers."

A CD-ROM is a good choice for very large storage needs.

CDs store music exactly the same way that a computer stores data. The recording on a CD is nothing more than a string of numbers, or measurements. The numbers tell your stereo system how to move the speakers. That's all. Simply by moving a speaker back and forth in precisely measured amounts, a CD player can make you hear music—or any other sound.

Since a CD stores numbers, why not use it in a computer? That's exactly what has happened. While you *could* use your PC to play stereo CDs, CD-ROMs are usually used for something a bit more businesslike. A CD-ROM disk can store in the neighborhood of 600 megabytes (MB) of data—that's about 150,000 typed pages, or 100 dictionaries, or five complete *shelves* of reference books!

It's no wonder, then, that CD-ROM disks are being used to store huge databases like telephone directories, postal code lists, almanacs, and financial records. They can also hold a complete illustrated encyclopedia, word atlas, photographic library, or super-advanced games. And here's where the other advantage of CD-ROMs shows up—the "read-only memory." They can't be erased or edited. That makes a CD-ROM particularly valuable for storing important archival information or sensitive business records. They can't be tampered with, and they can't be erased by accidentally pushing the wrong button.

4

Removable Hard Disk

You read earlier that hard disks can't be removed from the hard disk drive, and that's true—most of the time. There are some hard disks that are removable, and they fulfill a special purpose.

If you're willing to make do with a little less disk storage capacity and a little bit slower operation, you can have a hard disk drive that lets you remove the disks whenever you want. Why would you want to do this? There are a couple of reasons.

A removable hard disk is good for safe storage, but not as efficient as a normal hard disk drive.

Some people like removable hard disks because they can carry large amounts of data around, for example, from building to building in a big company. Others like them because they can physically take the disk out and store it in a safe or in a fireproof box to protect their data from accidents. Still others like the convenience of storing several megabytes of data on what is essentially a super-duper floppy disk.

Normal hard disks have to be sealed into the disk drive to keep them clean so they work reliably. With a removable hard disk, the disk is sealed in its own little safety chamber. When you remove the disk, you're really removing the disk plus the air around it! Like the cover on a floppy disk, the box protects the disk inside from dust, dirt, and fingerprints.

Even with the protective cover, removable hard disks can't be kept as clean and well-balanced as normal hard disks. They have to spin a little slower, and their read/write heads can't fly quite so closely. The net result is, the removable hard disk can't store as much, and it can't run as fast. But if the benefits outweigh the drawbacks, a removable hard disk may be for you.

Using Your Disks

Much of learning how to use your PC is learning how to use your disks. Once you feel comfortable handling, inserting, removing, and storing your floppy disks, you're well on your way to managing your entire PC.

Inserting a Disk

It's important that you know how to insert a diskette into your PC, and how to remove it when you want to. This is a trivial skill—and it will become second nature after the second try—but if this is your first time, be sure to get it right. Start a good habit now, and you'll never have troubles later.

Floppy disks must never be bent or creased. Use care and a gentle touch when handling.

First, it depends on whether you're using a 3 1/2- or 5 1/4-inch diskette. That part's easy, right? Let's start with the 3 1/2-inch kind. Take a look at your diskette and decide which side is the front and which is the back. (Hint: The back has the round disk hub in the middle of it.) Hold your diskette with the metal shutter away from you, as illustrated in Figure 4-4. Now you have to locate your disk drive. On most PCs and Macintoshes, the disk drive lays "flat," that is, with the slot running side-to-side, as in Figure 4-5. If your PC has the disk drive mounted vertically (up-and-down), skip ahead a couple of paragraphs.

4

Take your diskette and insert it *slowly* into the slot in the disk drive. The shutter end goes in first. When you get it about halfway in, use your thumb to press it in the rest of the way. Again, go *slowly*. When you get it all the way in, the diskette should drop just a little bit and fall into the drive. You may hear a little click when this happens. If any part of the diskette is still hanging out of the disk drive slot, or if it pops back out at you, you haven't got it all the way in yet. Push it in again.

How to insert a
3 1/2-inch disk
Figure 4-4.

A typical PC,
with disk drives
mounted
horizontally
Figure 4-5.

REMEMBER: There's only one right way to insert a disk into a disk drive, but there are a lot of wrong ways. Trying to put a disk in the wrong way can damage your disk or your disk drive. The disk drive is more expensive, but the information on the disk is probably more valuable.

If you have a vertically mounted 3 1/2-inch disk drive, you need to decide if it's laying on its left side or its right side. (Most PCs lay them on their left side, but yours might be the exception.) How do you tell? Look for the pushbutton and/or the light on the front of the disk drive. These are always at the bottom of the drive. So if your drive looks like the one in Figure 4-6, it's laying on its left side. Turn your diskette to the left, too, and slide it in just as described above.

4

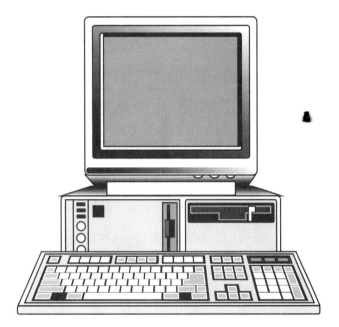

Computer with
3 1/2-inch disk
drive mounted
vertically
Figure 4-6.

If you have 5 1/4-inch disks, start by carefully removing the diskette
from its jacket. (That's the loose paper sleeve the square diskette is in,
not the disk cover itself.) You should be holding the disk near the top,
where the label is (or where it would go if it had one). If you've got it
right, the oval hole should be away from you, as in Figure 4-7.

A 5 1/4-inch diskette has a front and a back, too, but it's not always
easy to tell which is which. Here are two clues: If you're holding the
disk properly, with the oval read/write hole away from you, then the
write-protect notch and index hole should be on the right side (see
Figure 4-7 again). Or, if you're holding it upside-down, you will be able
to see the seams around the edge of the diskette. Turn it over so it is
right-side up.

You need to open the disk drive door, if it is not already open. (This is a
step that 3 1/2-inch disk users don't have to worry about.) The drive
door may differ depending on exactly what brand of PC you have, but
most of them look like the one in Figure 4-8. They have a handle or

How to insert a
5 1/4-inch disk
Figure 4-7.

lever that is across the disk slot when the drive door is closed. To open the drive door, turn the handle one-quarter turn. It may click when you do this. Now, insert the diskette *slowly* into the disk drive. Gently slide it in all the way. On some computers, you may feel a little spring or resistance for the last quarter of an inch or so. When the diskette is all the way in, you might hear a click, and there should be nothing sticking out. Don't press too hard; remember, these are *floppy* disks.

After the disk is in, turn the handle back the other way to close the drive door again. If you don't close the door, your computer won't be

Typical 5
1/4-inch drive
with latch
Figure 4-8.

able to read the disk. It's like lowering the tone arm on a record; it won't work until it's all the way down.

NOTE: If you are inserting a brand new disk for the first time, you may need to prepare your disk with an additional step called formatting. Formatting is covered later in this chapter.

4

Removing a Disk

Fortunately, removing a disk is a lot easier than inserting one—with fewer chances for error. It's especially easy with a Macintosh. It removes the disk for you!

To pop a disk out of your Mac, you drag the picture of the disk to the Trash icon on the screen. This procedure is described much more completely in your Macintosh manual, but the basic procedure is shown in Figure 4-9. When the disk hits the trash, the Mac ejects the real disk from the disk drive.

Another method is to pull down the File menu, shown here, and select the Eject command:

⌘	**File**	Edit	View	Special
	New Folder	⌘N		
	Open	⌘O		
	Print			
	Close	⌘W		
	Get Info	⌘I		
	Duplicate	⌘D		
	Put Away			
	Page Setup...			
	Print Directory...			
	Eject	⌘E		

This works, but the Trash method is preferred. As you can see from the File menu, you can also press the ⌥Option⌅ and Ⓔ keys on the keyboard to eject the disk.

NOTE: If none of these methods works, you can force a diskette out of your Macintosh with a paper clip. Don't try this unless you are desperate. Bend a paper clip so that an inch or so is straightened out. Gently stick the end of the paper clip into the tiny hole just below and to the right of where the diskette goes in. Push the paper clip in until your disk comes out. Reset your computer or turn it off and restart it.

To remove a 3 1/2-inch disk from an IBM-style PC, simply press the button on the front of the disk drive, and the disk pops out. You should see a little red or green light on the front of the disk drive, not far from the button. Always check that the light is off *before* you press the button and remove the disk. The light tells you whether the computer is using the disk or not. *Never* remove a disk when that light is on. If you do, you'll most likely ruin some of the data on the disk, and you might even ruin the entire disk drive.

CAUTION: Never remove a disk from the disk drive until the drive light goes out. Removing a disk too early can result in lost data and damaged diskettes.

Removing a 5 1/4-inch diskette is just the reverse of inserting one. After the light on the front of the disk drive goes out, you turn the handle or lever one-quarter turn and the disk should pop out for you. Hold it gently at the top end and replace it in its protective sleeve right away. Don't let your disks sit out where they can collect dirt and fingerprints.

Writing a Label

It's better to write a label with a felt-tip pen than with a ball-point.

On every floppy disk there's a place to stick an adhesive label. You can write anything you want on the label. It makes the most sense to write down what the disk holds and when you stored it. Then you can always find your data again later on. All disks look pretty much the same without labels on them.

An important rule to remember is to always write out the label *before* you stick it onto the disk. This is especially important for 5 1/4-inch disk users. If you put the blank sticker on first, and then write on it, you run the risk of damaging the disk with your pen.

Storing Your Disks

After you've stored your data on a disk and properly labeled it, you need a place to store the disk. You can store your disk just about any place you want to, but there are some guidelines you should follow. Most people simply place their diskettes back into the box they came in, and that works fine. But be careful where you put the box after that.

Treat your disks with care. Store them in a cool dry place.

Tapes are vulnerable to heat, records are vulnerable to dropping, CDs are vulnerable to harsh cleaners, and floppy disks are vulnerable to magnetic fields. Since the data on your disk is stored magnetically, you need to protect the disk from magnetic fields. These are more common in your home or office than you might suspect. For example, most telephones use a magnetic bell for the ringer, so keep your disks away from the telephone. Fluorescent lamps also produce strong magnetic fields, especially when they're turned on. Refrigerators, heaters, photocopiers, fans, and other large appliances almost always have electric motors in them that can damage your disks if you place them too close.

One of the most convenient, but worst places to put your floppy disks is on your computer's video display screen. There it is, right in front of you; but not only does the monitor produce a strong magnetic field, it's warm, and may warp your disk.

Disk Anatomy

Let's take a look at some other parts of the floppy disk that have been mentioned but not explained. You might want to refer to Figure 4-10 as you read the next sections.

Spindle Hole

In addition to their square exterior, both disks have in common a large *spindle hole* in the center. On the 3 1/2-inch diskette, this hole has a metal plug in it and is only visible on the back of the diskette. This is where the disk drive grabs the diskette to spin it around. Most floppy disks spin at about 300 RPM.

NEW WORD: The spindle hole is the large hole in the center of every diskette. The motor inside the disk drive uses the spindle hole to spin the disk when it's inside the disk drive.

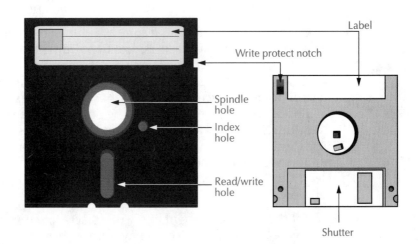

Anatomy of a
5 1/4-inch and
3 1/2-inch
floppy disk
Figure 4-10.

4

Index Hole

On the 5 1/4-inch disk, the small hole just off the large central hole is called the *index hole*. There is a small matching hole in the round disk inside the square cover. Your disk drive shines a light through this hole to tell if the disk inside is spinning properly or not. The 3 1/2-inch diskettes do not have index holes. Instead, the central metal hub has a notch cut out of it, which the 3 1/2-inch disk drive uses to count revolutions.

Data Protection

Near the upper-right corner of the 5 1/4-inch floppy you will see a notch cut out of the cover. This is called the *write-protect notch*. Usually, when you buy a box of disks, they come with black or silver adhesive stickers for each diskette. These are your *write-protect tabs*.

NEW WORD: You can write-protect a floppy disk to guard it against accidental erasure. Different disks use different methods for write protection.

If you take one of these tabs and fold it over the notch and stick it down, your computer won't be able to erase anything off the disk. It won't be able to store anything new on that disk, either. If you change your mind and decide you want to add something or erase something, just peel the tab back off.

REMEMBER: On a 5 1/4-inch disk, tab on, your disk is protected. Tab off, you can erase or write on the disk again.

Always use the silver or black tabs provided with your diskettes for write-protecting. You can't use household transparent tape for this purpose. Why not? Because your disk drive looks for the write-protect tab by shining a light through the notch, not by "feeling" for the sticker. Since cellophane tape is transparent, it doesn't work.

You don't use stick-on tabs to protect 3 1/2-inch disks. Instead, each disk has a special protection "switch" built right in. Flip a 3 1/2-inch disk over and look at the back. In the upper-left corner you should see a little black plastic square that moves up and down in a groove. (You might have to use a paper clip or your fingernail to get it to move.) This is your write-protect tab.

When the square is pushed down, the disk can be erased and new data can be stored. When you push the tab up, you should be able to see through the hole it was covering. Now the disk is protected. Nothing can be erased and nothing more can be added.

REMEMBER: On a 3 1/2-inch disk, tab up (window open), your disk is protected. Tab down (window closed), you can read, write, and erase your disk.

Read/Write Hole

The long, oval hole in the 5 1/4-inch disk's protective jacket allows the magnetic recording heads inside your floppy disk drive to touch the disk surface. This is your floppy disk's Achilles' heel, since it is the only place where the actual recording surface is exposed to the outside. Never touch the surface of the disk with your fingers or another object. The oil from your fingers can damage the disk inside, and sharp objects like paper clips or pencils can make permanent creases.

REMEMBER: Never touch the exposed surface of a disk that shows through the hole. It can damage your disk, and you might lose your data.

On 3 1/2-inch disks, the read/write hole is covered with a metal shutter. The shutter is drawn back automatically when the disk is inserted into a disk drive. It closes again when you take the disk out, providing built-in protection for your disk. You can slide the shutter back with your finger if you're careful, but make sure you avoid touching the insides.

Label

All disks look alike. Don't forget to label yours.

The label is the only part of the disk that's completely for your benefit, not the computer's. All diskettes have room on them for a small adhesive label. You can, of course, use the label for anything you like, but most people indicate the contents of the data stored on the disk and the date. For example, you might write "Memos, Feb. through Sept." on your label, or "Word Processor, Version 3."

4

As mentioned previously, to avoid damaging the disk, it is strongly recommended that you write out your label first, and stick it on your diskette afterwards. Writing with a ball-point pen directly on a diskette can make creases on the surface of the floppy and permanently damage your data. If you must write on a label that's already attached to the disk, use a felt-tip pen and write very gently.

Disk Anatomy II

Like most aspects of computers, disks have special terminology describing their various parts or functions. You might want to browse through the following sections to familiarize yourself with some of these terms. Then you will be prepared when your manual says something like, "Park head in landing zone."

Track

Both floppy disks and hard disks have a lot in common with records and CDs. The music on a record is cut into a spiral groove that runs around the record's surface. There is only one groove on each side of the record. It starts at the outside edge and works toward the center. For comparison, Figure 4-11 shows how the information on a disk is arranged. The diagram happens to illustrate a floppy disk, but hard disks work exactly the same way. Unlike a record that stores information in a single continuous spiral, a disk is divided into a series

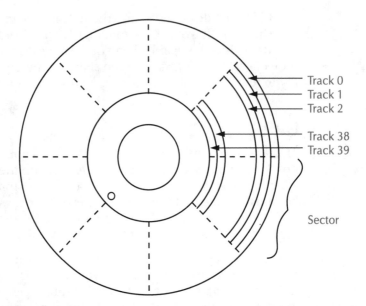

Track 0
Track 1
Track 2

Track 38
Track 39

Sector

Disk tracks and sectors
Figure 4-11.

of concentric rings, like ripples on a pond. The rings do not overlap, and there is nothing stored in between the rings.

Each of these rings of information is called a *track*, and tracks are numbered from the outside, going inward. In the figure, the outermost track is Track 0, and the innermost is Track 39, making a total of 40 tracks. (Computer engineers just *love* to number things starting with zero.) Different kinds of computers fit different numbers of tracks on a disk. For a floppy disk, 40 to 80 tracks is about average. Hard disks may have 300 tracks, or 1000, or even more.

Cylinder

A disk *cylinder* is almost the same as a disk track. A cylinder is a collection of all the like-numbered tracks. That is, Cylinder 0 means Track 0 from the top surface of the disk, plus Track 0 from the bottom of the disk. If you have a hard disk drive, and it has more than one disk inside (which it probably does), then Cylinder 0 also includes Track 0 from the top of the second disk, plus the bottom of the second disk, and so on, down to Track 0 from the bottom of the last disk. As an example, if your hard disk drive has three disks in it, Cylinder 0 would consist of six Track 0's.

Granted, this is technical esoterica, but you'd be surprised how often you might need to know this later on, when you're loading new software for the first time.

Sector

To help your computer locate a particular area on the disk, each track is subdivided into *sectors*. Sectors are pie-shaped wedges of the disk's surface divided by imaginary lines radiating outward from the center of the disk. Like tracks, different computers divide a disk into different numbers of sectors. Between 8 and 16 sectors is about average for a floppy, with 20 to 30 sectors the norm for a hard disk. The disk in Figure 4-11 is divided into 8 sectors.

4

Head

Phonograph records are recorded on both sides. To play the other side, you flip the record over. Disks are also recorded on both sides, but you don't ever have to turn them over. In fact, you're not supposed to turn them over. (The write-protect notch and index hole would be on the wrong side if you did.) Instead, disk drives are designed to read the bottom of a disk at the same time as the top. This works for both hard disks and floppies.

The device that does the actual reading and writing to your disks is called the *head*. It's designed to convert your computer's electrical signals into magnetic fields and vice versa. There's one read/write head for each disk surface. A floppy disk drive has two heads, one for the top of the disk and one for the bottom. A hard disk drive has two heads for every disk it contains, usually from 6 to 16 heads.

Landing Zone

Landing zone applies only to hard disk drives. When the drive is running, the disks spin at 3600 RPM—as fast as the motor in a sports car. Compare that with a floppy disk's 300 RPM rate, or 33 1/3 for an LP record. At 3600 RPM, the outside edges of the disks are whipping around at several hundred miles per hour—nearly the speed of sound! All that spinning makes quite a breeze inside the disk drive chamber. It's supposed to. In fact, this is called the *Bernoulli Effect,* and it's critical for the proper operation of your hard disk drive.

In order for the drive's read/write heads to work, they have to be very, very close to the surface of the disk. But if the hard disks are spinning at a hundred miles an hour, how do the delicate little heads keep from smearing themselves across the disk? Simple—they fly!

NOTE: On floppy disks, the heads actually do touch the surface of the disk. Floppy disks spin much slower than hard disks do, and the read/write heads are much tougher.

A hard disk drive's read/write heads are very carefully shaped and balanced so that they literally fly on a thin cushion of air over the spinning disk surface. This is one reason why hard disk drives are built under such stringently clean conditions. Any imperfection or roughness on the disk's surface, or dust speck in the airflow, would crash the heads into the disks. This is called a *head crash,* and it's about the worst thing that can happen to a hard disk drive. When the head crashes, all of your data is lost for good. But what happens when the disks slow down?

Disk drives don't run when you turn your computer off. The floppy drives and the hard drives wind down to a halt. For floppy drives, this is not a problem. (You should make it a habit to take your floppy disk out of the drive first, anyway.) For hard drives, it is vital that the delicate heads not skid across the disk once they lose their cushion of air. To save the heads, most hard disks have designated several of the innermost tracks as a landing zone. The *landing zone* is a special area that doesn't store any data. Instead, it's lubricated and reserved as a "runway" for the heads to land on. Most hard disk drives automatically place their heads over the landing zone when they're turned off. On others—particularly on old PCs—you have to tell your computer to do it (check your manual for a command called *PARK* or *SHIPDISK* or something similar). This is called *parking the heads,* and it is recommended before moving the computer around.

Access Time

Your computer has to move the read/write heads over the disk before it can read or write information. It has to place the heads over the correct track and then wait for the disk to rotate to the correct sector. The mechanism is very much like the tone arm on a record player placing the needle into the groove. Some disks can move the heads back and forth faster than others. The time it takes is called the *access time* or *seek time*. These times are measured either track-to-track (meaning the amount of time it takes to move between adjacent tracks on the disk) or as an average seek time (over all the tracks).

4

The more you use your PC, the more you'll appreciate a fast hard disk drive.

Because a disk is not very big around, and because the mechanism that moves the heads is very quick, a drive's access time is measured in thousandths of a second, or milliseconds (ms). For a hard disk drive, an average (overall) access time of 10 to 30 ms is typical.

Should you worry about a few one-thousandths of a second for a disk drive? You don't have to, of course, unless you're interested in buying a faster computer. A few milliseconds aren't going to make a big difference, but over the life of your computer they really add up. For example, the difference between a 15-ms access time and a 25-ms access time is 60 percent, which means one disk will fetch your information 60 percent faster than the other. Over a few years, that can add up to a few hours of time spent waiting for your PC.

How Much Can a Disk Hold?

Because disks are your computer's primary means of storing programs, data, and all forms of information, it's only natural to wonder "how much can a disk store?" The answer is "it depends." Different disks have different storage capacities. Over the last decade, disks have become smaller and smaller, yet they store more than ever. Even different computers can store different amounts of data on the same disk, depending on how they go about it.

Floppy Disk Capacity

Floppy disk capacity rarely goes above 2MB, and floppies that store under 1MB are the most common. The actual capacity depends on the computer that's using it. Different computers store their data in different ways, and some are more efficient than others. Capacities of 360K, 720K, 1.2MB, and 1.44MB are common.

To measure capacity, you must first know whether you are talking about 5 1/4- or 3 1/2-inch disks. Then, you have to consider what kind of computer is doing the storing, Macintosh or IBM-style PC, and how old it is. All of these factors affect how much data you can store on any one disk.

Floppy Disks on a PC

Let's start with the IBM PC and its clones. First off, the original PC and XT only used 5 1/4-inch disks. It wasn't until after the IBM AT came out that PC clones started using 3 1/2-inch diskettes. For either size disk, there are two common storage formats, or *densities,* that affect how much data will fit: low density and high density.

NEW WORD: Disk density refers to how much data a computer can fit onto a floppy disk. The more the computer can fit, the more "dense" the data is. Words like single, double, and quadruple are used to describe density.

As Figure 4-12 shows, a low-density 5 1/4-inch disk holds 360K. That's about 90 pages of typewritten text. After a few years, IBM and the other companies made improvements so that you could store 1.2MB on the same diskette (about 300 pages). That's a healthy fourfold increase.

NOTE: Historically, IBM-style PCs have used a lot more than just the two different disk formats. At first, PC disks held only 160K. Later, that increased to 180K, then 320K, 360K, 720K, and finally, 1200K (or 1.2MB) on a disk.

Today, the 360K format is called *double density,* and the 1.2MB format is called *quadruple* (or quad) *density,* or *high density*. There is a much older storage format called *single density* that isn't used anymore. If your PC stores data in single density, it's probably worth more as a museum piece than a computer.

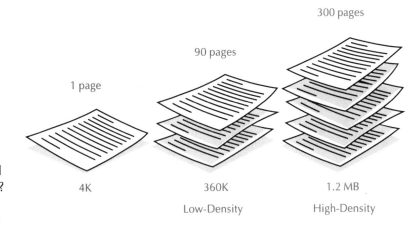

	300 pages
90 pages	
1 page	
4K	360K	1.2 MB
	Low-Density	High-Density

How much will fit on a PC disk?
Figure 4-12.

One floppy disk will let you carry a dictionary in your pocket.

Let's move on to 3 1/2-inch disks. These have gone through density changes, too, so there are lower- and higher-density 3 1/2-inch disks. Low-density holds 720K per disk; high holds 1440K, or 1.44MB—twice as much. As with 5 1/4-inch disks, the lower-density format is called double density and the higher-density format is called quad or high density. There apparently never was a single-density 3 1/2-inch disk format.

Floppy Disks on a Macintosh

The Macintosh line of computers has never used 5 1/4-inch disks, so there's one less thing to worry about. However, Apple has changed the amount of information that the Mac can safely store on each disk. There are two basic formats, the 800K and the 1440K, or 1.4MB. Figure 4-13 shows how the two stack up. Even the 800K disk can hold the equivalent of 200 typewritten pages.

As you might have guessed, the older Macs can fit "only" 800K on a disk, while the newer ones use the 1.4MB format. What's funny is that not all of the newer Macs can use a disk that has been used by an older Mac. Many Mac disks are labeled so that you don't try to use them in

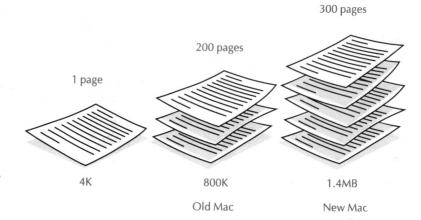

300 pages

200 pages

1 page

Macintosh
floppy disk
storage capacity
Figure 4-13.

4K
800K
1.4MB

Old Mac
New Mac

The Microfloppy

The 3 1/2-inch diskette almost didn't happen. Beginning around 1980 several floppy disk companies were competing for the new, smaller-sized disk drive market. Some companies were offering the 3 1/2-inch diskette that we know today, but others were pushing a 3 1/4-inch size. The 3 1/4-inch disk looked just like a miniature 5 1/4-inch version, with a square black plastic cover and a little hole in the center.

It wasn't until 1984 when Apple Computer selected the 3 1/2-inch diskette for the brand-new Macintosh that the industry settled on one over the other. Apple picked the 3 1/2-inch size for two reasons: its tough plastic shell and the protective shutter over the disk.

an older model. They carry a "No 800K" logo, warning you that you shouldn't try to use them as low density disks.

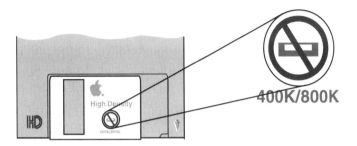

4

Telling the Disks Apart

Now that you know there are at least two disk densities for each disk size, how do you tell them apart? Here's the secret. For a 3 1/2-inch diskette, look in the upper-left corner of the disk (that's if you're looking at the front of the disk, with the shutter down). If there is a little square hole there, you have a high-density floppy. If there's no hole, it's a low-density disk. The density hole looks just like the hole for the write-protect tab, except that it doesn't have a slider inside it. Another thing to look for are the stylized letters "HD" printed near the lower-left corner.

For your 5 1/4-inch disks, the job is a little bit tougher. To tell the truth, you often can't tell. You just have to try them out and see how much your PC will store on it. But here are some clues. If your diskette has a manufacturer's sticker or label in the upper-left corner, it might say something like "Double Sided," "Double Density," "High Density," or "PS/2 Compatible." Ignore "Double Sided"; all disks are double-sided these days. (It means that it's okay for your PC to read and write on both sides of the disk.) You can also skip over things like "Double Track" or "96 TPI." If it says "Double Density," you're looking at a 360K disk. If it says "High Density," it's iffy, and could go either way. Words like "Quad Density," "IBM/AT," or "PS/2 Compatible," mean it's a 1.2MB disk.

Hard Disk Capacity

As a rule, hard disks can store much, much more than floppy disks. A normal hard disk drive in a personal computer might store from 40MB to 400MB. Hard disk drives are even available in larger sizes, but they're too expensive for most computer users. Since a megabyte is 1,048,576 bytes, and a byte is about enough to store a single letter of the alphabet, 40MB is about enough to store an entire dictionary four times over. Because hard disk platters cannot be added or removed from a hard disk drive, the drive's capacity is fixed. Of course, the greater the capacity of the disk, the more it will cost.

CD-ROM Capacity

A CD-ROM holds a lot more than any floppy disk and most hard disks. How much more? Well, a lot more. It's hard to make specific claims, because CDs are not as standardized as other disks are. In most cases, each CD uses a different storage format, and therefore can squeeze different amounts of information onto its shiny surface. A number in the 500MB-to-800MB-range is about right.

You can buy programs and databases on CD-ROM, but you can't store your own data there.

A CD-ROM is a special kind of disk. If you are lucky enough to have one, you know that each CD can hold many hundreds of megabytes of information. That's more than almost any hard disk drive can hold. The drawbacks of a CD-ROM drive are that it's slower than a hard disk drive, and you can't erase information from the disk. That's why it's called CD-ROM—for read-only memory. Read-only means no writing, editing, altering, and no erasing, either. All the data that's on a CD-ROM is put there when it's manufactured.

This is also the advantage of a CD-ROM. You can use it for your most vital information, and you don't have to worry about it being erased accidentally. The bottom line is, whatever you have stored on a CD-ROM is there to stay, for better or for worse.

When a Disk Gets Full

When a disk gets full, or almost full, you can erase old, unwanted information from it. The freed-up space can then be used for something else. You can erase and reuse portions of a hard disk or floppy disk as much as you like. There's no limit to the number of times you can erase and rewrite information. You can also erase the entire disk if you want to. However, instead of erasing information from your hard disk, and losing it forever, you can copy it to one or more floppy disks. Then you can free up the space on your hard disk, while keeping an archival copy of your data on floppies, in case you need it later.

Formatting Disks

4

When you buy new diskettes they are completely blank. (The exception is when you buy a new computer program. That will come on a set of disks, too.) Blank diskettes are like blank audio or video tapes. Unlike the tapes, though, computer disks must be specially prepared before you can use them for the first time. You have to do this yourself. This special preparation is called *formatting* on a PC and *initializing* on a Macintosh.

When you format or initialize a blank disk, you write invisible track and sector marks onto it. (Tracks and sectors were covered previously, under "Disk Anatomy II.") Then each sector is numbered, going around each track, from the outside track working in. Each sector gets a unique sector ID so that your computer can remember the spot where it will store your information. Without the formatting, your computer would wander aimlessly about looking for data on the disk.

NEW WORD: A disk format is a computer's way of invisibly dividing up a diskette into small, usable chunks called sectors. Each sector is magnetically numbered and from then on, your PC will use those numbers to remember where it stored your data.

To format a disk on a PC running DOS software, use the FORMAT command. Rather than explain it all here, it's probably better if you look up the FORMAT command in your PC's DOS manual. If your PC is running Windows, you can use the Windows Format Disk command by pointing to it with the mouse. From the File Manager window, pull down the Disk menu and select the "Format Disk..." option.

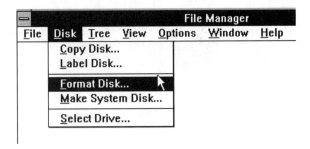

Your PC will start to format your blank disk. Formatting only takes about a minute.

NOTE: You can't format a diskette that has been write-protected. When you put the write-protect sticker on (for 5 1/4-inch disks) or slide the button to the "protect" position (for 3 1/2-inch disks), the disk is protected against erasing—and that includes formatting.

On a Macintosh, you simply put a new, blank diskette into the floppy disk drive. Your Mac will discover on its own that the new disk isn't initialized. Then it will ask you if you want to take the disk back out or if you want to initialize it.

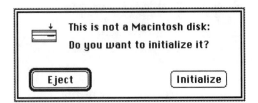

If you select the Initialize button, your Mac will start initializing the new disk. It only takes about a minute.

When to Format

Formatting only needs to be done once for each disk. In fact, you should *only* do it once. Formatting or initializing a disk after you've already used it will erase everything on the disk. It won't damage the disk at all, it just erases all the old data to make room for the new.

CAUTION: You can format hard disks, too. If you format your PC's hard disk by mistake, you'll lose everything. Pay special attention to the warning messages when you format a disk.

4

Also, it's a good idea to format new disks on your own computer, not somebody else's. This isn't *really* important, just a helpful hint. Even though all PCs store data the same way, and all Macs store data the same way, there are inevitably tiny differences between one disk drive and another. There's a small chance that if you format your disks on one computer, but use them on a different computer, you might have trouble reading the disks in the future.

After a disk is formatted, it is ready to hold whatever information you choose to put on it. It might hold software that you've purchased, backup copies of old information, or your work in progress. In the next chapter, we'll explore just what it is that disks hold, how information is stored and retrieved by a computer, and how to organize that information so that both you and your computer can find it again.

CHAPTER

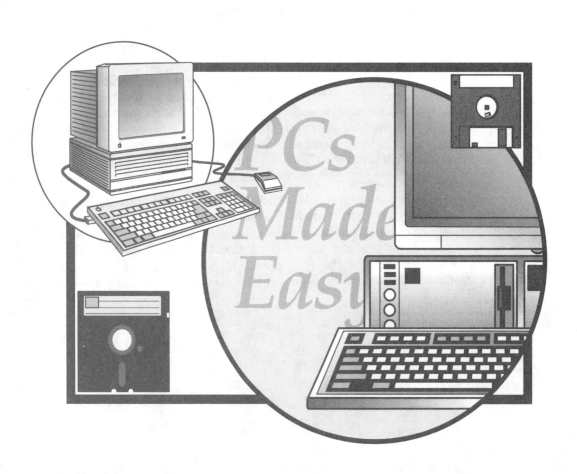

5

WHAT IS A FILE?

This chapter will explore more about disks and how to store your information on them. You'll also see ways you can organize your information so that you can find it easily. Because your data is so important, we'll also look at ways to protect it, and finally, this chapter will offer some tips on managing your disks, with specific information about buying diskettes.

What Are Files?

In the previous chapter you learned that your computer stores information, or data, on disks. They can be floppy disks or hard disks or both. This section examines in greater detail just how your information is stored on disk, and it also describes some ways you can use your disk storage most efficiently and conveniently.

Several files will all fit on one disk, like more than one song on a CD.

Unless you're storing a very large chunk of information (like an entire telephone directory), you probably won't use up an entire disk. Instead, your data will occupy just some of the space on the disk, as shown in Figure 5-1. The rest of the disk will still be available to store more information. You can store as many different, unrelated collections of information as you like, so long as their combined size does not exceed the disk's total capacity.

The information that you store in your computer isn't just thrown haphazardly onto the disk, like you might throw receipts into a shoe box. Instead, your computer enforces a certain amount of organization on you. You'll need to store your "computerized" information in a regular fashion. If you're an orderly person by nature, this will come naturally. If you're a pack rat, you'll need to develop some new habits.

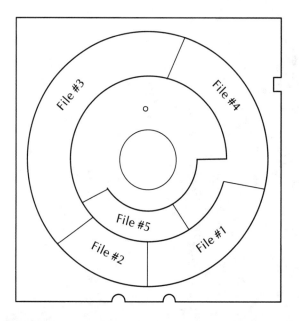

Your information can be scattered all over the disk
Figure 5-1.

Your computer is fairly clueless about what information you're storing and why. If you keep things somewhat organized, you—and your computer—can find them again. For example, financial records should be kept separate from business letters, which need to be kept apart from graphics or games. It's a bit like keeping all your things organized in drawers, or in a file cabinet. A place for everything, and everything in its place.

Organize your files now so you can find them later.

That doesn't mean there's only one way to store your information. On the contrary, there are as many ways to organize information as there are people to organize it. There's no "right" way to store your data. The point to remember here is that your PC won't store it all in one big pile. Everything is divided into distinct piles—or files.

A computer *file* is a collection of related information. For example, you might create a file to hold your household budget for a month, or for a year, if you prefer. Another file might hold the contents of a letter to your aunt, while yet another file would hold the contents of a similar letter to your cousin. Files may be large or small, and you may have thousands or just a few. There's usually no limit to how many different files you can create. At least, not until you run out of disk space to store them all!

5

NEW WORD: A file is a place on a disk where you have a collection of related information stored. It works just like a hanging file in a filing cabinet. The file can grow as you add more information to it, or shrink as you erase information. You can move files from disk to disk or erase them entirely.

The word *file* describes pretty accurately how your data is stored. Like papers in a filing cabinet, each file is separate from the others, even though they're all stored together. Some may be short one-page memos while others are long multi-part contracts. You might file pictures, or letters, or inventory records all in the same filing cabinet. To help you organize better, you might want to group similar files into file folders. Finally, each file probably has a label or name written on it so that you can find it again.

Filenames

Just as in a paper filing system, every file you store in your computer must have a name. The name is there so that you can remember what information is in the file. You pick a name every time you store new information on a disk for the first time. From then on, you can refer to the collection of information in that file by its *filename*.

NEW WORD: A filename is just that, a file's name. Different computers have different rules for naming files, but every file must have a unique name so that you can tell your computer what file you want.

Use filenames that are easy to remember.

Normally, you'll want to give your files names that describe what kind of information is stored in the file. It is important to pick names that you will remember later on. Like storing old receipts in the closet or leftovers in the refrigerator, it doesn't do you any good if you don't write labels, or if you pick labels that won't mean anything to you a week from now.

Different kinds of personal computers have different rules about what you can and cannot name your files. Some make you use short names, and some let you create long names. Some computers will even make up part of the name for you depending on what kind of information is stored in the file. As an example, the Apple II computers (like the IIc, IIe, and IIGS) are quite flexible in this matter. They let you make up filenames that are 64 *characters* long.

NEW WORD: A character is any letter of the alphabet, or a digit (0 through 9), or a punctuation mark (such as a comma, period, space, or hyphen).

Sixty-four characters allow you to name a file containing a business letter something like "Price Quotation to Mr. Baumann, Aug. 14, 1993." This is completely descriptive, and therefore immediately recognizable when you look for it later on.

No matter what type of computer you have, each file stored on a disk must have its own unique name. If, for instance, you have stored a dozen files on a single floppy disk, each one must have a different name. If you have a lot of floppy disks, there's nothing to stop you from giving two files the same name, as long as they are stored on different disks. Your computer is not going to confuse a file on a disk it's actually reading with another file of the same name on a disk that's lying on the table.

Every file has a name and each name can only be used once per disk.

Filenames for IBM-style PCs

The IBM PC family of computers is fairly restrictive about filenames. Filenames can only be eight characters long at most. The entire name must be in uppercase letters. You are not allowed to use some punctuation marks in your filename, either. In particular, periods, commas, and spaces are forbidden, but you can use the pound sign, tilde, dollar sign, and a few others.

In the IBM PC world, this eight-character name is called the file's *primary filename*. After you pick your file's primary filename, your PC will add a period (dot), and a three-character *extension* name. Between the two, your file will have an eight-character "first name" and a three-character "last name." Together they make the file's complete name. The following list shows you some of the possibilities.

```
QUOTE.DOC
J-LETTER.DOC
BUDGET92.BAK
BUDGET93.DBF
Q1-93-JT.WKS
TIGER-1.PIC
YODA.PIC
VOLVO.TXT
```

Everything is uppercase, limited punctuation is allowed, and nothing is longer than eight characters.

The PC's restrictive naming rules mean you may have to be a little creative when selecting names for your files. You might name your files QUOTE.DOC, CAROLINE.PIC, or something similar. IBM-style personal computers do not make a distinction between uppercase and lowercase letters in filenames. All filenames are treated as though you had typed them in uppercase letters, whether you really did or not.

Your PC will generally pick a three-character extension that suggests the nature of the file's contents. For example, some common extensions are DOC for documents (like business letters), DBF for database files, PIC for pictures, BAK for backup files, and so forth. Some file extensions (like EXE, COM, and SYS) have special meaning for the PC, and are reserved for its own internal purposes.

Filenames for the Macintosh

The Macintosh doesn't rely so much on filenames because you usually pick a file by pointing to it, not typing its name.

Compared to the PC, the Macintosh gives you a thousand times more freedom in naming your files. Your files can have names up to 32 characters long, and you can use mixed upper- and lowercase letters. You can also have spaces in filenames, effectively allowing you to use more than one word to name a file.

Because the Mac allows you to use both upper- and lowercase letters, you might not discover right away that you can give two different files almost identical names. This can be a problem if you're not careful. For example, you might name one file "Quantity Pricing for September, 1993" and name another file "Quantity pricing for September, 1993." These are not the same file, because they have slightly different names (in the first one, the *P* in *Pricing* is uppercase; in the second it is lowercase). As far as your Mac is concerned, these are two completely different and unrelated files. Computers are picky about this kind of thing; most people aren't.

NOTE: If your computer does treat upper- and lowercase letters differently, try to come up with a standard pattern, or you'll forget what your files are called.

It's also important to pay attention to spacing. If you put two spaces between words in a filename, that's not the same as typing the same name with only one space between words. Again, most people wouldn't notice this kind of thing if they were typing it on a file folder label, but your Mac will pick it up right away. That's the price you have to pay for being able to use nice long filenames.

Program Files, Data Files, and Temporary Files

Data files hold the ingredients; program files, the recipe.

Files that you create to store your own information are called *data files*. Your computer can also create short-term files on its own that it uses as a kind of "scratch pad" while it's working. These temporary files are normally small, and are automatically erased when their work is completed.

Program files are another kind of file. These files store your computer's operating instructions, or software. A word processing program, for example, will be stored in one or more program files. (The next chapter has more information about program files.) On your disk you'll have the word processing program files, plus all the data files that you create.

You won't be creating any program files unless you decide that you want to learn to write your own computer software. (See Chapter 6 or Chapter 12.) Instead, you will use existing program files written by other people to operate your computer.

5

What Do Files Look Like?

Before going any further, let's see just what a file *looks* like. It will help you to follow the upcoming sections if you have an idea of what a file is and how your computer shows it to you. We'll look at two different computers and three different ways they use to show files. The two computers are, of course, the Macintosh and the IBM-style PC. The three ways depend upon what software you have on the computer—your operating system software. Chapter 7 explains more about operating systems.

PC Files with DOS

You can't actually see your files stored on disk, but your PC has a way of showing you a list of those files, if you know the right command. The command is DIR, and you can type it anytime, for any disk, and your PC will tell you what files are on that disk. DIR is short for directory, and the list of files is called a *file directory*.

The example in Figure 5-2 shows what a sample file directory looks like. The files are listed from top to bottom along the left side of the directory. Notice that the directory listing doesn't show the mandatory period (dot) in between the primary filename and the extension. Instead, it places the names in two columns. Files are not listed in any particular order.

A directory listing shows you a lot of information about your files.

After each filename is a number. This is the size of the file measured in (what else?) bytes. Some files are very small while others are quite large. After the file's size, the date and time that the file was last modified are listed. At the very bottom of the file directory, your PC tells you how many files it just listed. Then it tells you how much disk space is taken up by those files, and finally, how much disk space is left over.

File Modification Date

The date item requires a little extra explanation. Nearly all PCs have a "clock" inside them that keeps track of the date and time. Normally this

```
A:\>dir

 Volume in drive A is PCSMADEEASY
 Volume Serial Number is 4226-1BF9
 Directory of A:\

ASSIGN   COM     6399 03-16-87   8:53p
CV       COM      716 06-21-84   8:53p
DOSHELP  BAK     5651 04-09-91   5:00a
DOSKEY   COM     5883 11-23-92   8:51p
EDIT     COM      413 04-09-91   5:00a
FIND     EXE     6770 04-09-91   5:00a
LOADFIX  COM     1131 04-09-91   5:00a
MORE     COM     2618 11-23-92   8:51p
RAMDRIVE SYS     5873 04-09-91   5:00a
        9 file(s)      35454 bytes
                      322560 bytes free

A:\>
```

IBM-style PC disk directory
Figure 5-2.

clock has to be set when you first buy the computer, and from then on it keeps accurate time. Whenever you create a new file, your PC writes the current date and time onto the disk next to the file. This is called the *creation date*—the date that shows up in the directory listing. If you ever change the contents of the file, either by adding new information, removing existing information, or just editing what's already there, your PC will write the date and time again. This is called the *modification date,* and it replaces the creation date in the directory listing. Reading from a file doesn't alter the date or time at all.

NOTE: The built-in clock inside most PCs is called the "real-time clock," or RTC, because it keeps track of the "real time." It runs on battery power so it keeps accurate time even when your PC is turned off.

5

Why would you want to know any of this? Because sometimes it is important to know which of two files is newer. Say, for example, that you have a copy of a contract stored on disk and that you update it from time to time. Let's say you also make copies of this contract on other disks. Somewhere along the line, you forget which copy of the contract, on which disk, is the latest copy. No problem, just look at the modification date on both disks, and use the newer one.

PC Files with Windows

Windows attaches an icon to each file to show you what type of file it is.

If your PC is running software called Windows, your file directories look a lot different from those described in the previous section. PCs with Windows look and act very differently than PCs without Windows. Some people prefer it this way; some the other.

Along with listing your files by name, Windows represents each file on your disk with a picture. The picture is meant to represent what kind of file it is (data file, program file, and so forth). These pictures are called *icons.* Figure 5-3, which shows the File Manager window, gives you an idea of how a PC with Windows lists your files.

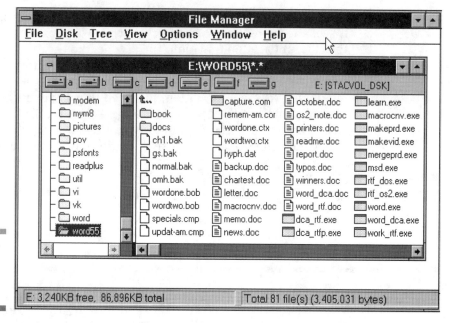

The Windows
File Manager
disk directory
Figure 5-3.

NEW WORD: An icon is a small picture or a figure that your computer uses to represent something. Pictures of a sheet of paper can represent a file. A picture of a floppy disk represents the disk itself.

If Windows can't tell what is in a data file, it shows a generic document icon that looks like a blank sheet of paper with the corner folded over. If Windows can tell what you have stored in a file, it draws lines across the icon to represent writing in the file. Program files are represented by a rectangular icon with a bar across the top. Some other icons shown in Figure 5-3 are folder icons, which represent directories.

Notice that next to each icon is the name of the file (or directory), just as in the DOS file directory. That is because Windows doesn't change the basic nature of your PC. You still have to follow the PC naming rules for files (up to eight characters in the first part, with three characters in the extension). Windows just lets you display the file directory in a little more friendly way.

Macintosh Files

The Macintosh and Windows file directories can look very much the same.

The Macintosh also has a friendly way of showing you what you have stored on your disk. It creates an icon of a piece of paper to represent each file. Underneath the icon is the name of the file. The "paper" is always the same size no matter how big or small your file is.

Sometimes, if your Mac can tell what kind of information is stored in a file, it will draw a slightly different sheet of paper. If it knows that you have some kind of writing (a letter, contract, or document) stored in a file for example, it will draw a special kind of icon to represent it. Normally however, the paper is blank, representing a "generic" file that the Mac can't identify. If a file is a program file, the Mac will draw the program's logo for an icon.

Figure 5-4 shows what a typical Macintosh file directory looks like. The file icons are not displayed in any particular order. You can have the

5

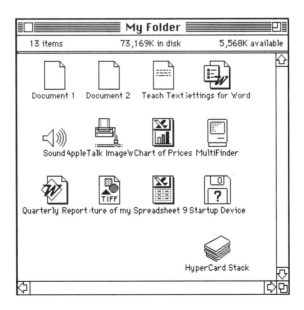

Macintosh disk directory
Figure 5-4.

Macintosh show them in order by size, by kind (data, program, and so on), or alphabetically by name if you want, as in Figure 5-5.

After each icon in the list comes the name of the file. If the file has a particularly long name, only the first two dozen characters or so are listed. After the name comes the size of the file, the kind of file it is (if the Mac can tell; otherwise it's a "document"), and the date and time the file was last altered. You can make your Mac hide some of this information if you're not interested in it.

Working with Files

Because all of your information will be stored on disks at one time or another it is important to become familiar with disks and what they can and can't do. Managing your information efficiently will make your time with your computer much more productive.

Creating Files

When you store new information for the first time, you must select a disk to store it on and create a new file on the disk. You also must

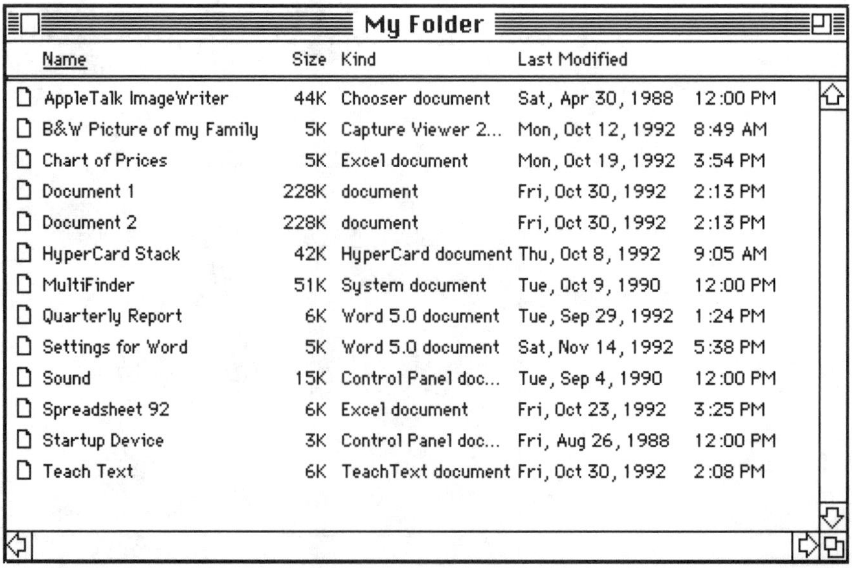

Name	Size	Kind	Last Modified	
AppleTalk ImageWriter	44K	Chooser document	Sat, Apr 30, 1988	12:00 PM
B&W Picture of my Family	5K	Capture Viewer 2...	Mon, Oct 12, 1992	8:49 AM
Chart of Prices	5K	Excel document	Mon, Oct 19, 1992	3:54 PM
Document 1	228K	document	Fri, Oct 30, 1992	2:13 PM
Document 2	228K	document	Fri, Oct 30, 1992	2:13 PM
HyperCard Stack	42K	HyperCard document	Thu, Oct 8, 1992	9:05 AM
MultiFinder	51K	System document	Tue, Oct 9, 1990	12:00 PM
Quarterly Report	6K	Word 5.0 document	Tue, Sep 29, 1992	1:24 PM
Settings for Word	5K	Word 5.0 document	Sat, Nov 14, 1992	5:38 PM
Sound	15K	Control Panel doc...	Tue, Sep 4, 1990	12:00 PM
Spreadsheet 92	6K	Excel document	Fri, Oct 23, 1992	3:25 PM
Startup Device	3K	Control Panel doc...	Fri, Aug 26, 1988	12:00 PM
Teach Text	6K	TeachText document	Fri, Oct 30, 1992	2:08 PM

My Folder

Macintosh files sorted by name
Figure 5-5.

create a new file when you begin a database or start a new spreadsheet. Remember, anytime you need to create a new disk file, you must give it a unique filename.

The procedure for creating a new file depends on your computer and on the software you're running. Usually, you just type in the filename and press (Enter) when your computer asks you to. Then your PC knows where to save your work, whether it's document editing, financial calculations, data entry, or some other type of information.

Adding to Files

If you want to add more information to a file created earlier, you can do that too. This is called *appending* data to a file. For example, you append information to a file whenever you use your word processor to add a few words to an existing letter, or you append quarterly results to a spreadsheet that keeps running totals. For the most part, you'll probably append data to existing files more often than you'll create new ones.

 NEW WORD: When you append information, you're adding new information to what's already in a file. Technically, appending means adding data to the end, but you can add data anywhere in the file.

When you add information to an existing file, you don't have to create a new file or a new filename to hold the additional information. Your computer simply enlarges the existing file. The filename stays the same, but it takes up more space on your disk. Of course, you can't expand a file beyond the storage capacity of the disk it's on. Aside from that limitation, you can add as much as you want to an existing file as often as you want. Data files can also be made smaller by removing information.

Deleting Files

When you no longer need the information you have stored in a file, you may erase it completely from your disk. When a file is deleted, all of the information previously stored in that file disappears. The disk space that the file used to take up becomes available to store other files. Also, the name of the file is removed from the disk, and you can use the filename again for a new file.

REMEMBER: Once you delete a file, it may not be possible to get the information back, so delete files with caution.

On a PC you can delete a file with either the ERASE command or the DEL command. You simply type the command, followed by the name of the file you want to erase, and press the `Enter` key. If your PC is running Windows, you can point to the file you want to erase (use your mouse here) and then use the menu across the top of the screen to find the Delete... choice. On a Macintosh, simply drag the icon that represents the file to the Trash icon.

Copying Files

Sometimes it is convenient to have the same file in more than one place. If you have a computer at home and one at work, for instance, you may want to have some of your data files available at both locations. Data files and most program files can easily be copied from one disk to another.

You can make as many copies of a file as you like.

Copying a computer file is basically the same idea as copying a "real" file using a photocopier. Copying a file to another disk does not harm or alter the original file (or the disk) in any way. The file is not "moved" off one disk and onto another. Instead, an identical copy is made onto a second disk.

The disk that the original file is coming *from* is known as the *source* disk. The disk that you are copying your file *to* is called the *destination* or *target* disk. Any files that are already stored on your destination disk will be unharmed (with one exception, noted in the next section). A new file will simply be added onto the destination disk (see Figure 5-6). Obviously, there must be enough space left on the destination disk to hold the additional file. If not, you will get an error message. The new file on the destination disk will have the same name that it had on the source disk.

5

NEW WORD: Source and destination are two words that are used a lot when copying files. The source disk is where the file is now, and the destination disk is where the copied file will go.

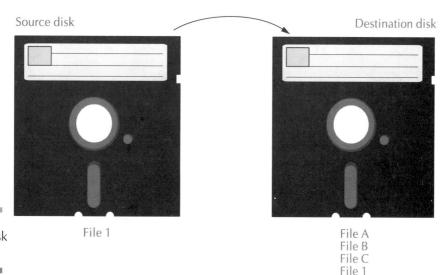

Source disk   Destination disk

Copying a file
from disk to disk   File 1   File A
Figure 5-6.   File B
                                                          File C
                                                          File 1

Files with the Same Name

When you copy a file from one disk onto another you end up with two identical copies of the same file. They contain the same information and they have the same name. But if there's already a file with that name on the destination disk, what happens?

The answer depends on your particular computer. On an IBM-style PC, the new file will *replace* or *overwrite* the existing one with the same name. This means that the file on the destination disk will be destroyed, just as if you had deleted it, and be replaced with the file from the source disk that has the same name. It doesn't matter if the two conflicting files are related or not. If they have the same name, the file on the source disk will automatically replace the file on the destination disk.

Sometimes this is exactly what you want. If you want to update an old copy of a file with a newer version from another disk, copying the newer file "over" the older one leaves you with two up-to-date copies of your file, and no old ones.

If your PC is running Windows, or if you have a Macintosh, you'll get a warning before any of this happens. Both of these computers are designed to keep you from accidentally erasing a valuable file that just happens to share its name with another file you're trying to copy.

Trying to put two files with the same name on one disk will erase one of the files.

If you don't want to copy over the existing file after all, simply select the CANCEL option with your mouse, and the copy function won't take place. This gives you a chance to change the name of one of the files and try making the copy again.

Copy-Protected Files

Some files can't be copied at all. In order to protect their investment, some software companies store their program files on diskettes in a special way so that they can't be copied. You can use the software normally, but the files that contain the program's instructions cannot be copied onto another disk. That means you can only have one copy of the program at a time.

Copy protection is intended to prevent people from making unauthorized duplicates of software. Computer programs are copyrighted just like books and movies are, and writing computer software involves a considerable investment in time, talent, and money, just like movie-making or writing does. Many software authors (programmers) are understandably concerned about their products being duplicated and distributed for free. They lose sales. Most state laws prohibit the unauthorized duplication of program files, unless you are making them strictly for your own backup purposes. Making backups is covered later in this chapter.

It is illegal to copy a program and give it to someone else unless you get special permission.

5

Renaming Files

If you want to change a file's name, you can. Changing the name of a file is a good idea if the original filename you picked isn't an accurate description of the file's contents anymore. You might also rename an important file to avoid losing it when you make a copy, as described previously. To deal with this problem, you could do one of two things:

✦ Rename the source file before you copy it to the destination disk.

✦ Rename the destination file that would be overwritten before you copy the source file to the destination disk.

Organizing Your Files

When you have collected several programs for your PC that are useful or store a lot of data, chances are that you'll need several diskettes to store them all. After you accumulate more than three or four diskettes' worth of data, you may find that locating the program or data file that you want is more difficult. Creating, storing, retrieving, and managing information is what personal computers are all about, but that won't do you much good if you can't find your correct file!

The following sections deal with some of the ways you can organize your information. Not only will this make it easier for you to find what you want, but it may make it easier for your computer as well.

Grouping Your Files

When you go to the library to look for a book about French cooking, you expect to find it with other cookbooks. Grouping books with similar themes seems an obvious way to organize them. It helps you to find what you want, and it also encourages browsing for related topics. Similarly, one of the best ways to organize your PC's files is to group similar contents together on a diskette.

If you do a lot of writing, typing, or editing with a word processing program, you can group all of your letters, documents, and manuscripts on one disk. That way you always have access to related work files on a single disk. Perhaps more importantly, your computer can then access any one of your work files without making you change the disk all the time.

Spend some time planning how to group your files to save effort later on.

Your financial or statistical spreadsheet files can all be stored on another disk. If your work files grow too large or too numerous to be stored all on one disk, you may need to narrow your grouping criteria. Perhaps first-quarter financial statements could be stored on one disk, second-quarter on another disk, and so on. When the files get too big for this arrangement, you can go to one disk per month.

You can copy your files from one disk to another, as much as you like, until you're happy with their organization. Program and data files do not deteriorate after copying the way that cassettes or video tapes do. The one hundredth copy of a file is just as fresh and reliable as the first.

You might want to group your program files the same way, if a particular arrangement appeals to you. If you have more than one database program, for example, you could put them on a single disk and label it "Database Programs." Programs are often either too large or include too many files to allow grouping them on a disk. Of course, it's perfectly all right to store only one file on a disk and leave the rest of the space unused.

About Subdirectories and Folders

When you store papers in a file cabinet, they're seldom thrown in haphazardly. Instead, most people maintain some filing system for their information, categorizing and subdividing files into useful groups. A file drawer can be divided, with portions allocated to particular subjects. Manila folders group related papers. Hanging file folders collect associated files into a single group.

There is another similarity between paper files and electronic data files. You can group files that are already stored on a disk into smaller groups, creating a disk within a disk. If a disk is like a file drawer, then a group of related files within a disk becomes a folder.

Creating a *folder* of files on a disk allows you to segregate your files into whatever arrangement suits you best. The word *folder* is usually used with Apple computers. For IBM-style computers, the term *subdirectory* is generally preferred.

5

NEW WORD: A subdirectory, or folder, is a group of files stored together on a disk. You can group files into subdirectories any way you like, or not at all. Using subdirectories allows you to keep related items together.

Creating and using folders is purely optional. You will find, however, that using them can be helpful, especially if you have a hard disk. Hard disks store so many files compared to floppies that some organizational method is necessary just to keep all your files straight.

Creating and using disk subdirectories, or folders, doesn't use any extra space on your disks. It doesn't save any space, either. It really only affects how your file directories look. Instead of always showing *every* file on a disk, your computer will only show you the files that aren't included in a folder. The folder "hides" the files that are "inside" it.

Subdirectories on a PC

Previously, you saw how your PC can display a file directory using the DIR command. If you create no subdirectories, every file on that disk will be listed in the directory. But if you do create a subdirectory, only the files that are not part of the subdirectory will be shown—not the

Subdirectories let you make groups of files on one disk.

individual files that are in that folder. Look at Figure 5-7 and see how it compares to the previous example in Figure 5-2, which had no subdirectories.

Note that the two subdirectories are marked with the message "<DIR>" in place of the file size. The subdirectory itself has no size, because it's not a file. Subdirectories have to be named, just like files do. A good name is one that describes what all the files in the group have in common.

If you have a PC running Windows, and you have a color monitor, the subdirectory will appear as a yellow manila folder. Windows also shows how each folder relates to the overall arrangement of files on the disk.

Folders on a Macintosh

When you look at a Mac file display, the icon for a folder appears right alongside the file icons. The folder's name is displayed underneath the icon, also like files. If you point to the folder with your mouse and press

```
A:\>dir

 Volume in drive A is PCSMADEEASY
 Volume Serial Number is 4226-1BF9
 Directory of A:\

ASSIGN   COM      6399 03-16-87   8:53p
CV       COM       716 06-21-84   8:53p
DOSHELP  BAK      5651 04-09-91   5:00a
DOSKEY   COM      5883 11-23-92   8:51p
EDIT     COM       413 04-09-91   5:00a
FIND     EXE      6770 04-09-91   5:00a
LOADFIX  COM      1131 04-09-91   5:00a
MORE     COM      2618 11-23-92   8:51p
RAMDRIVE SYS      5873 04-09-91   5:00a
LETTERS       <DIR>      03-16-87   8:54p
PERSONAL      <DIR>      03-16-87   8:54p
       11 file(s)        35454 bytes
                        320512 bytes free

A:\>
```

A PC disk directory with subdirectories Figure 5-7.

the mouse button twice, your Mac will "open" the folder and show you the files that are grouped "inside" it.

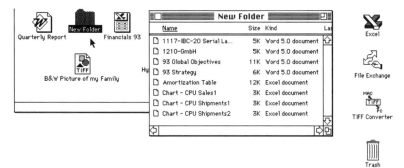

Creating a Folder or Subdirectory

Creating a folder on a disk is similar to creating a file. The most strenuous part is thinking up a name for the new folder. The rules for naming a new subdirectory or folder are the same as for naming a file.

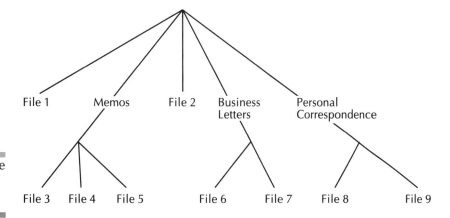

Disk with three subdirectories

Figure 5-8.

5

If you are running DOS, you use the MKDIR (Make Directory) command to create a new subdirectory. Windows has a Create Directory... menu option under the File Manager's File menu, shown below. With a Mac, you can use the New Folder menu item.

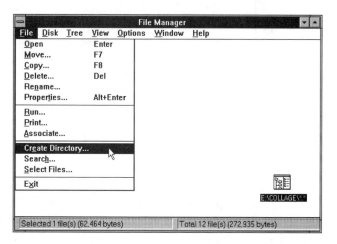

If your disk contains word processing data files, you might want to create separate subdirectories for memos, business letters, and personal correspondence. Within the limitations of your particular machine, you might be able to name the three of them just that. Figure 5-8 shows an abstract diagram of how your files would be stored. The top of the diagram represents the main disk, with the folders below. The files are arranged like an organizational chart, or an inverted tree.

NOTE: When a disk is divided into groups of files using subdirectories or folders, it is called a hierarchical file system. That's because you've created a "hierarchy," where some files are higher in the organization than others, like a business organization chart.

When a folder is first created, it is empty. It contains no files. You must deliberately copy your files into a folder after you create it. You copy files from folder to folder the same way you copy from disk to disk. On a PC, you use the COPY command. On a Mac, you drag the icon of the file to the icon of the folder.

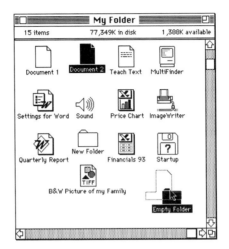

Subdirectories can even be created as part of other subdirectories, letting you create groups within groups. There is no real limit to how many times a subdirectory can be further subdivided. For example, your subdirectory for business letters could contain more subdirectories for each company with which you regularly correspond. Those subdirectories could, in turn, be divided into subdirectories for quotations, referrals, and invoices. The resulting directory tree of *nested* subdirectories would look like the one shown in Figure 5-9.

Nested
subdirectories
Figure 5-9.

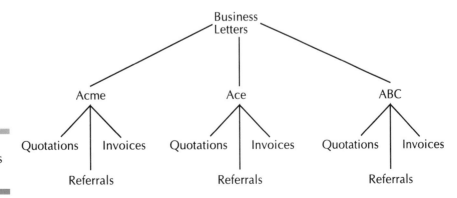

Protecting Your Data

The greatest fear that most PC users have—and rightfully so—is of losing their data. Nothing is as frustrating as working all day typing a report or performing financial wizardry on a spreadsheet only to lose it all when the computer malfunctions. These occurrences are rare, but they do happen. Stories about events like this are enough to make anyone hesitate before using a computer to do important work. Fortunately, there are a few very simple habits you can cultivate to practically eliminate the possibility of losing your work to a mechanical or electrical failure.

Save Your Work Often

When you're working on your computer, your work is kept in the computer's memory, not on disk. Your computer can't work on disk files directly. All information must be copied into memory before your computer can use it. When your work session is done, you must save your work back to disk. With many older computers and computer programs it was easy to forget to save your work before turning the computer off. Most newer programs warn you in no uncertain terms if you try to finish without saving a file that you might have altered. Saving your work is usually as simple as typing a command or pointing at a menu.

Saving your work only takes a few seconds; re-entering lost data can take hours.

If your computer gets turned off by accident, unplugged, or experiences even a brief power failure, every bit of information in its memory will disappear. Of course, all the information stored on disk will be safe. To avoid these mishaps, the trick is to get your important work onto a disk as often as possible.

Develop the habit of saving your work to disk regularly, not only right before you finish working, but while you are working as well. If a local power outage occurs six hours into your eight-hour project, you would lose most of a day's work. But if you're in the habit of saving your work to disk every half hour, you can never lose more than a half hour's worth of work.

REMEMBER: Never wait longer to save your work than you would be willing to spend redoing it.

Make Backup Copies

The single biggest cause of lost work is from not saving files onto a backup disk. Even after your work is saved it is not totally safe. Should something happen to the disk it's stored on, you'll lose all your work. In fact, if your disk contained several files, you could lose several days' or weeks' worth of work.

Making duplicates of your important files protects you against damage and accidents.

The safest and easiest way to protect your information is to make duplicate copies of your files. You should have at least one backup copy of every important file. Copying a file takes only a few seconds. Copying an entire diskette may take as much as a minute; copying a hard disk may take 30 minutes. But having a backup copy can save days of tedious labor. Lost data may be impossible to reproduce.

Businesses usually back up their important files once a week, at a minimum. The backup copy (or copies) are transported off-site, to be kept in another office, a safety deposit box, or in a vault. Keeping the backup copies separated from the originals is important. A fire can destroy floppy disks just as quickly as it can paper records.

Write-Protect Your Disks

Sometimes valuable information is lost not through mechanical or electrical failure, but because of human error. If disks are not carefully cataloged and labeled, an important disk or file may be erased accidentally. Don't keep your disks with your important files in the same box or stack as your new, blank disks.

5

As you read in Chapter 4, both 5 1/4-inch and 3 1/2-inch diskettes have a way to protect the contents of the disk from being altered. On a 5 1/4-inch disk, you place a write-protect tab over the write-protect notch. On a 3 1/2-inch disk you slide the write-protect tab to the protected position. In both cases, your computer will enforce the following prohibitions:

✦ No new files can be added.

✦ No new folders or subdirectories can be created.

✦ No file can have its contents altered.

✦ No files can be erased.

Write-protection is your best guarantee that a disk won't be tampered with.

A write-protected disk can be used only to read data. If you want to alter a file on a write-protected disk, you must either remove the write protection or copy the file from the write-protected disk to a nonwrite-protected disk.

Take Care of Your Disks

No safety procedure can help you if you don't take care of the disks themselves. Floppy disks are fairly rugged little devices, but they can be ruined by seemingly harmless (and mostly invisible) forces. Hard disks are not immune to physical abuse either. Chapter 4 covers the physical hazards to disks in detail, but here are some reminders.

✦ *Do not fold, spindle, or mutilate* Disks should never be folded or bent. Do not even curl a disk slightly to insert it into a shipping tube. Use a diskette mailer instead. They are made of stiff cardboard, resist attempts at bending, and have space for addresses and postage. Obviously, you cannot fold a hard disk, but it can be damaged if the hard disk drive is dropped or jarred, especially when it's running. If you plan to transport a hard disk drive, you should always turn your PC off first and give it a minute or so to spin the disks down to a standstill.

✦ *Do not expose to heat, fire, or flame* Leave a 33 1/3 RPM record out in the sun and it will curl and warp like a potato chip. Floppy disks will do the same, but the final results are usually worse. You can still play a warped record if you really want to. A warped floppy disk cannot be read by your computer at all, and the information on it is not always so easily replaced.

✦ *Avoid magnets* Magnets and magnetic fields spell silent death for your recorded information. Digital computer data is stored on your disks by the magnetization of tiny spots on the surface of the disk. The coating on the disk's surface can maintain these magnetic spots almost indefinitely, "remembering" the pattern that was laid down by your computer. Magnetic fields can be disturbed only by other magnetic fields, and unfortunately, there are many magnetic devices at home and in the office. Take care to keep your disks away from televisions, radios, telephones, video display screens, and speakers, for example.

✦ *Do not write on your disks* When making a new label, fill it out before sticking it on. If you're updating it, you can either peel off the old one or stick the new one on over the old label. If you must write on a diskette, use a felt-tip pen, never a pencil or ball-point pen.

✦ *Never force a disk into a disk drive* If the disk doesn't slide in easily, something's wrong. Check your drive carefully—a disk may be in there already.

✦ *Avoid spilling food or drinks onto a disk* Spills may not ruin your disk, but they will never improve it.

Caring for your disks is mostly common sense. Make a habit of protecting your disks and keep your data safe.

5

Exchanging Disks Between Computers

There's good news and bad news about exchanging disks between computers. The bad news is, not all computers store information on a disk in the same way. A disk file created by one kind of computer may be completely incomprehensible to another computer. Disk size is no indication of file compatibility, either. Four different computers with 5 1/4-inch disk drives may store information in four different ways. The disk might fit, but an incompatible computer will treat it as blank or defective. This can make it difficult for you to exchange data files between computers.

The good news is, the problem is mainly only between IBM-style PCs and Macintoshes. Transferring from PC to PC, or from Mac to Mac, is not too bad. If you remember from the discussion of disk formats in

Chapter 4, IBM went through several generations in disk storage, and not every computer can read or write every different format. Today, there are (only!) four commonly used disk formats. For 5 1/4-inch disks, there's the 360K and the 1.2MB format. For 3 1/2-inch disks, PCs use the 720K and the 1.44MB formats most often. Once you decide what size of disk you want to use, you're only left with two choices. As a general rule, you're safer with the lower-density format (360K or 720K). You are more likely to find a new computer that will read and write the old format, than an old computer that can read the newer disks.

Macintoshes have the same problem as PCs, in that Apple has used two different disk formats. Fortunately, they have stayed with just one disk size. Older Macs use 800K disks, while newer ones use 2MB disks. When in doubt, use the lower-density format.

The real excitement comes in trying to transfer files between a PC and a Mac. That's like mixing oil and water. Until fairly recently, you couldn't do it at all. That was partly because Apple and IBM didn't want you to; they were each trying to protect their customers from intermingling with the "other side."

Now it's fairly easy to transfer files from a PC to a Macintosh; it's harder to go the other way. Many Macintosh models have a special floppy disk drive called the "SuperDrive." What makes it "super" is that it can read and write IBM-style disks. There are no IBM-style PCs with this feature. Even with the SuperDrive-equipped Macintosh, you need to have special software to make sense of what's on the disk.

You see, there's more to transferring files between a Mac and a PC than just getting the disk to work. Once the data is transferred, your Mac might not "understand" what it is. Data files created on one kind of computer aren't necessarily usable on computers of another kind. Don't expect to transfer your spreadsheets or word processing documents freely between computers. Program files don't transfer at all. Don't bother.

In the next chapter, we will take a closer look at one important kind of disk file, the program file. As you will see, the programs are what make your computer work. We'll examine the concept of a computer program, or software, and briefly discuss how software works.

CHAPTER

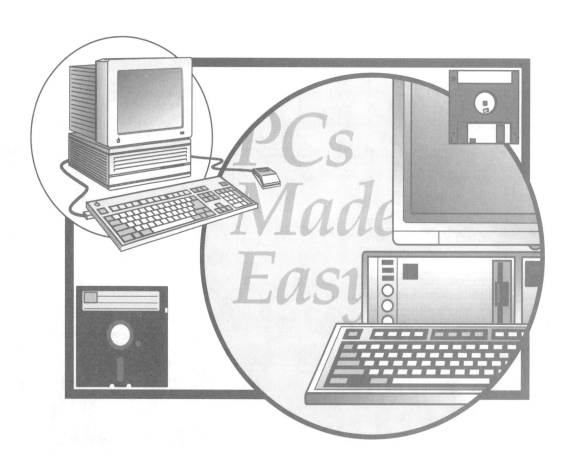

WHAT IS A PROGRAM?

Nobody needs to become an expert in computer programming to use a personal computer. Learning the mechanics of a car won't necessarily make you a better driver, but it may help you when something breaks. And it will certainly come in handy when "talking shop" with others. Let's look at what computer programs are, and how much you might want to know.

A computer program determines exactly what the computer will do and how it will do it. A step-by-step

Your
computer
needs
software like
a car needs
gas.

program describes each action the computer must take to reach the desired goal. That goal may be adding two numbers together, looking for a particular file on a disk, or drawing a 3-D picture of a new car on the screen. Whatever the task is, your computer cannot do it by itself. Programs make computers work. Hardware requires software.

This chapter explores just what a computer program really is. If you understand the concept of a program you will better understand your personal computer and be able to use it more effectively. You'll see how programs work—in general terms—and what kinds of things they can accomplish. This chapter gives you a little background for the two following chapters, which cover two specific types of programs, operating systems and applications. Chapters 7 and 8 will show you what to do with those. If you are interested in how programs are made, Chapter 12 will answer the question, "what is a programming language?"

What Does a Program Do?

A computer program is a special kind of file stored on disk. Instead of holding your information, a program file holds information that your computer needs. It's like a musical score that lists each note in order, or a recipe that describes what steps to follow.

NEW WORD: A computer program is a special file that tells the computer, in its own words, how to work. Programs as a group are also called software. Your computer will have several different program files that tell it how to do different things.

When you use your computer to total a column of figures or draw a floor plan on the screen, your PC is following a detailed program. Your PC can't do these things "naturally;" it needs a program to tell it how to act and what to do. It has to follow a program to do even the most rudimentary functions. That's not because of any fault in your computer's hardware, but because it was designed that way. Computers aren't supposed to do anything on their own.

Ingredients don't cook themselves on their own, and notes don't spontaneously create music. They require someone to mix them

There's a big
difference
between using
a program
and creating
a program.

together in the proper proportions at the proper time. By following a precise recipe or score, the pieces make a pleasing whole. The creator of that "computer recipe" is the programmer, and your computer is the cook that follows the instructions. You get to enjoy the results.

A person who "composes" computer programs is a programmer or a software engineer. Writing a program is called programming. Computer programming is a difficult and complicated job, and professional programmers are well compensated for their skills. Using a computer program is another thing entirely. Using a program on your PC doesn't require any special math, typing, or programming skills. If a program is difficult to use, then the programmer probably hasn't done a good job.

When Do You Use a Program?

6

The short answer is: always. If your computer is turned on, it is running some program. There are very basic programs that come with your PC or Macintosh that make it just smart enough to turn itself on and make your screen glow when you flip the switch. Then there are other, slightly more exciting programs that teach your computer to pay attention to the keyboard when you press a key. Finally there are the "real" programs that let your computer work with you to calculate figures, draw architectural diagrams, plan landscape arrangements, create newsletters, check inventory, and on and on.

There are
many
different
programs
available for
many
different
uses.

The program that is running on your computer at any given moment determines what your computer will do. Each program controls the screen, keyboard, and mouse (if you have one) in its own way. Programs give your computer its "personality," if you can call it that.

For example, if you want to do word processing, you need to make your PC run a word processing program. The instructions in that program direct your computer in such a way that you can enter sentences, erase words, rearrange paragraphs, edit punctuation, and so on. You will see your words on the screen, and you will have certain keys you can press to erase words, or to enter a new paragraph, or move a sentence from here to there. These all depend on the particular program you use to do word processing. Different word processing programs do these things in different ways. Just as different cars have different dashboards, with the knobs and dials in different places, so will each computer program look and act differently.

Technical Stuff

The way programs work is based on simple principles, even though the actual workings are complicated. The idea of any program is to tell the computer what to do, in a tedious, step-by-step manner. Most personal computers can only understand about ten or twenty rudimentary instructions. This is the limit of their "vocabulary." Using these instructions, a programmer has to make the computer perform wonderful feats.

You may be more familiar with the basics of programming than you realize. Everybody has seen the instructions on a shampoo bottle:

```
Lather
Rinse
Repeat
```

That's an excellent example of a basic computer program. The numbered instructions on the back of a box of cake or biscuit mix are also like a computer program.

Computer instructions must be extremely explicit. No detail can be left out or assumed, no matter how minor. Computers are not endowed with common sense, nor can they make intuitive guesses. Each and every step must be spelled out for them to do their work. Otherwise, you can get unexpected results.

Changing Course

Computer programs can take shortcuts to be more efficient.

A lot of computer tasks are repetitious, like the "repeat" instruction on the shampoo bottle. To handle repetitious tasks efficiently, computer programs are able to execute in loops. That is, the same set of instructions might be followed 500 times. Instead of listing the same sequence of instructions 500 times over, wasting memory and taxing the programmer's patience, why not tell the computer to "repeat"? Figure 6-1 shows a sample of a loop in a program.

Another time- and space-saving feature that most programs use is the branch. When the same set of instructions needs to be executed at several different places in the program, those instructions don't need to

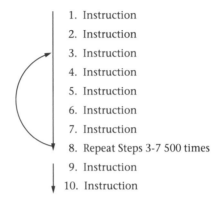

1. Instruction
2. Instruction
3. Instruction
4. Instruction
5. Instruction
6. Instruction
7. Instruction
8. Repeat Steps 3-7 500 times
9. Instruction
10. Instruction

Program loop
Figure 6-1.

6

be repeated every place that they're required. Instead, the computer is able to branch to that set of instructions (called a subroutine), and then return to the instruction from which it branched. Figure 6-2 illustrates a programmed branch.

Part of the programmer's job is to anticipate every possible mistake in advance.

Program Bugs

If the programmer isn't explicit about what course to follow in absolutely every case, the computer might run astray when something unexpected happens. For example, a program might be designed to ask you for the date. It wants you to enter the date like this, 1/9/62, for January 9, 1962. But one day, by accident, you enter all zeroes, 0/0/00. Hopefully, if the programmer has anticipated that bonehead move and instructed the computer to reject the date and ask you to enter a legitimate one, then there won't be a problem.

Otherwise, you have a programming bug. A bug is something that a program does that it's not supposed to do. Bugs are the fault of the programmer, not the computer, but that doesn't help anyone much. If

1. Instruction
2. Instruction
3. Branch to Step 10
4. Instruction
5. Instruction
6. Branch to Step 10
7. Instruction
8. Branch to Step 10
9. Instruction
10. Instruction
11. Instruction
12. Return

Using a branch
to a subroutine
Figure 6-2.

your bank makes a mistake on your statement, you probably don't care whose fault it is; you just want it fixed.

NEW WORD: A program bug is an error in the computer's instructions. Bugs usually pop up when somebody uses the computer in a way the programmer didn't expect.

Programming mistakes are called bugs because the early computers had real live bugs in them. When computers were big, expensive machines that took up an entire room, they were filled with mechanical relays that switched off and on, like an old switchboard. Each computer had thousands of these relays, clicking away. Every so often, a moth might fly into one of the relays and get caught, causing a failure. The computer was broken until all the bugs were found.

Different Kinds of Programs

Computers are designed to do many different tasks, so there are many different kinds of programs. There is software for controlling your computer's display screen, for reading from and writing to the disk drives, and for making the keyboard work, to name just a few. All of these programs work in concert to provide you with a working system. Because of the many and varied tasks that software must perform, programs are divided into the following major classes:

✦ Application programs

✦ Operating systems

✦ Device drivers

✦ Language compilers

✦ Overlays

These classes are described in the following sections.

6

Application Programs

Application programs let you do your work instead of telling the computer how to do its work.

Starting at the top of the software heap, with the programs that are most visible to you, you find the application program. This is the kind of software most computer users are familiar with. Some examples of application programs are databases, spreadsheets, word processing programs, games, filing programs, and communications programs. The application program is the software you interact with to get specific kinds of tasks done. Most application programs, like spreadsheets, are specific to one type of task. You can buy as many application programs as you like, and use each one whenever it suits you. You'll look at some specific programs in Chapter 8.

NEW WORD: Application program is the name given to the whole category of programs that people use every day. Programs for word processing, CAD (computer-aided design) drafting, financial analysis, inventory control, payroll management, and so on, are all examples of application programs. They're called applications because they let you "apply" your computer to your work.

Operating Systems

The second major class of software, right under the application, is the operating system. Grasping the concept of operating systems can be more difficult than understanding application programs. The operating system is the program that is running when you're not using an application program, but you need it to make your application program run. Most people use their operating system software all the time but are not aware of it.

 NEW WORD: The operating system is the software that takes care of the mundane chores of making a computer work. It is the software that allows the system to operate. Each computer has only one operating system.

The operating system is the go-between; between you and your computer hardware.

The operating system oversees all of the "housekeeping" chores of running a personal computer. This is the kind of stuff that many people assume computers do on their own. It finds files for you, lists disk contents, starts running application programs when you ask it to, and copies and renames files.

A computer usually has only one operating system. To some extent, the kind of computer hardware that you have determines what operating system you can use. Operating systems have names like MS-DOS, UNIX, Macintosh System, PC-DOS, CP/M, XENIX, Apple DOS, and OS/2. Recognize any one of these? Operating systems are discussed more extensively in Chapter 7.

Device Drivers

At the bottom of the software hierarchy are the device drivers. These are special programs that work in the dark recesses of your computer. They control the individual components (chips) in your computer's hardware. They look after the keyboard, disk drives, mouse, printer, and display. The job of the device driver is to handle the nuts and bolts of making the disk drive spin around, moving the read/write heads to the proper track, and so on. It "drives" the device. The average PC user does not work with device drivers, but you may come across them when you add new hardware to your PC or buy a new program.

 NEW WORD: A device driver is a special kind of small program that works on a very specific part of your computer. It does the lowest-level work of making your computer run smoothly.

Language Compilers

All computer programs have to be created by someone. But a computer's natural language of bits is too complicated for most people to master. It would be nearly impossible to write even a short program if each and every instruction had to be specified with only 0 and 1 digits.

To make programming quicker, easier, more reliable, and much more enjoyable, there are a number of computer programs that can translate other instructions into the necessary binary computer instructions. In this case, the "other instructions" aren't human language by any means, but a kind of halfway communication between the programmer and the programmed.

There are several different programming languages that programmers can use. Many programmers can "speak" a few different languages, although most have a favorite that they prefer to use. By learning one of these languages, the programmer can give instructions in a form that the computer can almost understand. Almost, but not completely.

Compilers translate between special programming languages and pure computer language.

The final step is to translate the programmer's halfway language into fully understandable computer instructions. That is the job of the language translation program. The translation program reads the programmer's instructions and converts them into the appropriate binary computer instructions. A different translation program is required for each programming language. There is no such thing as a universal translator, just as there is no person who can translate among all possible human languages. Depending on the particular language used, the translator may be called a compiler or an interpreter. The difference is mostly a technical one. Programming languages are discussed in more detail in Chapter 12.

6

Overlays

A disk may be able to store thousands of files and hundreds of megabytes of data. That's usually far more information than your computer can hold in its memory. However, a program must be loaded into memory before it can be executed, so it's possible that the program file is bigger than the available memory. What happens when the program file is too big to fit in memory? Normally, that means your computer won't be able to execute that program. You'll have to either add more memory to your computer or use a smaller program.

To overcome this problem, some application programs come divided into multiple files on disk, instead of in one big file. As Figure 6-3 shows, some of the program's instructions are in one file, some in another, and so on, much like the way a large book can be divided into volumes. Usually there will be one main file (Volume I) where execution starts. The remaining files are called overlays. When your computer comes to the end of the first file's instructions, it loads the next file into memory (Volume II), overlaying the instructions from the first file, and continues on.

Some large programs are divided into volumes so you don't see the entire program at once.

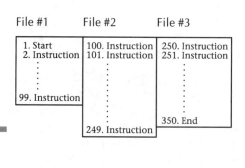

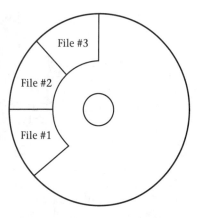

Program
overlay files
Figure 6-3.

Programs that use overlays do not run quite as quickly as programs that fit into memory all at once, because your computer must pause and load some of the instructions from disk from time to time. However, if you have limited memory, it's better than not being able to run the program at all.

Creating Your Own Programs

After you've become familiar with your computer, you might find that you would like to create new programs of your own. There are many good reasons for wanting to write new computer programs, but creating software is not for everybody. Programming is an acquired skill that you do not need to learn. You can use your computer efficiently and enjoyably without learning how to create your own programs.

Making your own programs isn't necessary, but it can be fun.

Some users do create their own programs to fill a specific need not available in "store-bought" software. Others write software for the enjoyment and challenge of it. For example, you might be using accounting software on your personal computer and need it to create a particular type of report that it was not designed to do. It would be convenient for you to write a small program that could produce such a report.

You might want your computer to perform some function for which there is simply no software available at all. Your needs may be so unique that creating a new program is the only solution. If, for example, you wanted to use your PC for picking the horses at the local track, it's unlikely that you'd find a program that used your own particular "system."

If you want to create custom software, there is another alternative to learning to write it yourself. Many professional programmers will, for a fee, advise you or do the actual programming.

6

In this chapter you have been introduced to what a program is and how it works, to programming, and to the major categories of programs. In the next chapter, you'll take a closer look at one of the most important classes of programs—operating systems—and see how they affect the "personality" of your personal computer.

CHAPTER

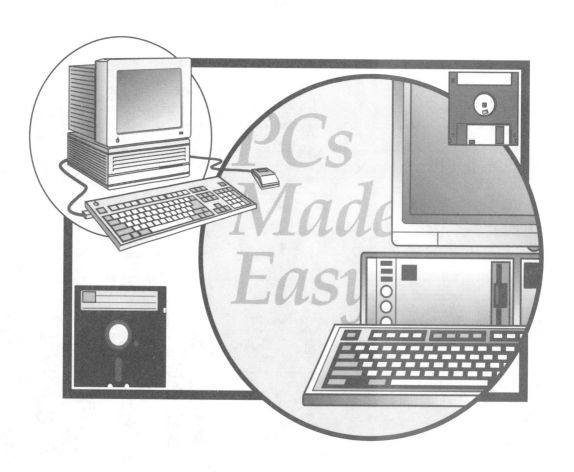

7

WHAT IS AN OPERATING SYSTEM?

More than any other single factor, the operating system determines the "personality" of a personal computer. Your PC's operating system determines whether you begin executing an application program by typing the program's filename or by pointing to a picture of it and clicking a mouse button. Two different computers that use the same operating system will operate the same way. If you know how to use one, you will know how to use the other, even if you've never seen that particular computer model before. In contrast, you may find it difficult to use a computer with a different operating system. All of the commands that you've become familiar with will not work, and the type of information displayed on the screen may be different. Just about any computer has a monitor, disk drives, and a keyboard—those parts are always more or less the same. The major differences lie in the computers' operating systems.

NEW WORD: An operating system is a collection of programs that keep your computer running smoothly. Most of the work that an operating system does is invisible to the user.

An operating system is a special kind of software that every computer must have. In fact, it is the only piece of software that everyone has. It is not an application program. Application programs (discussed in the next chapter) are used to do particular kinds of work, for example, financial analysis, word processing, or games.

Operating systems handle the mundane chores of keeping computers running efficiently. Most of the work an operating system does is behind the scenes, and you don't have to be familiar with it. However, your computer's operating system also has a number of commands that will be important to you and very helpful to understand. This chapter explores what an operating system is and what it does and describes the six most popular operating systems for personal computers and their features.

What Does an Operating System Do?

Your personal computer's operating system software takes care of the "housekeeping" chores inside the computer. It reads and writes files, maintains disk directories, allocates memory to application programs, and usually handles the mechanical chores of reading the keyboard when you press a key and of updating the screen when something needs to be displayed. All of these tasks require a surprising amount of software, and every computer requires some piece of software to do these jobs. This is the software that turns your computer hardware into an "operating system."

Why Have an Operating System?

Some of the things that an operating system gives you are

◆ Easier programming

◆ Smaller programs

◆ Control of the user interface

◆ Record of the time and date

◆ Reliable disk operation

Make Programming Easier

One important reason for having an operating system on a computer is so that all of the other programs can use parts of it. The operating system contains all of the sub-programs that make the disks, keyboard, and screen work. Since just about every program has to use the keyboard, screen, and disks, it makes sense to have one set of computer instructions that all can share. That way, every programmer doesn't have to rewrite those functions from scratch.

An operating system serves two purposes: It lets you operate your computer's basic fuctions and helps programmers build applications.

Granted, that's an advantage for the computer programmer, not for you. But you benefit too, because it makes the programmer's task much easier, and that means that it takes less time to create the latest, hottest new program that you're looking for.

Make Programs Smaller

Another advantage to having a pool of shared programs in the operating system is that application programs can be smaller. They don't each have to carry around the excess baggage required to work the screen, keyboard, mouse, and disks. That can save a lot of space in most programs. In fact, some applications would probably be twice as big—and use up twice as much of your disk storage—if they had to supply their own instructions for all these things.

Control the User Interface

Sharing computer instructions can make application programs smaller and more efficient, but there's a bigger benefit, too. It can also make your programs more reliable and more like each other.

7

Programs become more reliable because they can use and reuse pieces of the operating system to carry out standard chores; pieces that have been tested and had all the bugs taken out (*debugged* in computerese). Programs also become easier to use when they all use the same pieces of the operating system to work.

One of the biggest problems facing first-time computer users has been the fact that every application program worked a different way. That meant learning each one from scratch, like learning how to drive each different car all over again. The problem is slowly fading away because applications now can use the operating system to help make them look and act more alike. This means learning each new one isn't as much of a chore.

Some operating systems enforce their "look and feel" on application programs more than others do. When you're using Windows, for example, all your applications will look pretty similar. The MS-DOS operating system doesn't offer the same features as Windows, so DOS applications tend to look very different from one another. They look like whatever their creator wanted them to look like.

You'll normally use your computer's operating system to view disk directories and launch application programs.

Keep the Time and Date

Whether you use a Macintosh or an IBM PC, your computer always keeps track of the current date and time. Every time one of your files on disk is modified, the date and time of the modification is recorded, too. This can be a real boon when you have multiple copies of a file and can't remember which one is the latest version, or if you want to know if someone has been tampering with your information.

The operating system records this information for you automatically. Most PCs have a battery that runs the electronic clock and calendar even when your computer is turned off. Without that service, every application would have to ask you what day it is.

Provide Reliable Disk Operation

When you store your information on disk it's important that it stay there. You don't want to worry about whether or not it got stored properly and safely. Your computer's operating system makes sure that happens.

Running a disk drive is a tricky thing. There are a lot of things for a program (and a programmer) to keep track of: the speed of the disks, how much space is left, where the other files are stored, and a whole lot of other things besides. Your operating system is specially designed to take care of all these things and lend that service to any application programs that need it. That way, every application on your PC can use exactly the same method of adding, erasing, or moving files. There's no chance that somebody's program does things a little differently and puts your disk at risk.

Disk Functions

No matter which operating system you have, it will have commands that help you manage your files and disks. Each command is like a mini-application program, but they are included in the price of the operating system. They are also quite simple to use. Your operating system will have commands to perform at least the following tasks:

Your operating system offers a lot of functions, but you'll most likely use the same half-dozen over and over.

7

+ List the files on a disk

+ Change the name of a file

+ Copy files from one disk onto another

+ Copy an entire disk onto another

+ Format a new disk

These are the built-in commands that you normally use to do disk and file maintenance.

Supporting Application Programs

There is close cooperation between the operating system software on your PC and the applications software. Each and every application program is designed to work with one particular operating system. You can't take a program that runs on one type of operating system (DOS, for example) and run it on another (like the Macintosh System).

Even though all operating systems do essentially the same thing, they do them in different ways, so application programs won't transport from one operating system to another easily. Therefore you might be limited a bit in your choice of application programs. The applications you can run are determined by your operating system.

Fortunately, most software companies offer two or three different versions of the same application, tailored for different operating systems. If you really wanted to use a favorite spreadsheet program for a Macintosh, but you have a PC running Windows, you might be able to find a Windows version of the same program. There will still be some minor differences between the two, but chances are, they'll work very much the same.

User Interface

The most striking differences among operating systems are in the way they "look and feel." One computer can seem very different from another, when inside they're all pretty much the same. The difference is in their operating systems, and the difference in the operating systems is in the *user interface*.

NEW WORD: A user interface is an overly technical term that describes how a computer looks and acts. Some user interfaces use pictures and a mouse, others use words and a keyboard. The biggest difference between a PC running DOS and the same PC running Windows is the user interface.

The user interface is the way your computer communicates with you. It's how you enter commands. It's how the screen looks. It's the way the whole computer seems to work. Does your PC draw pictures on the screen, let you point to what you want, and move things around on an imaginary desktop? Or does it let you type commands at the keyboard, display information in neat rows, and offer a wealth of different commands? The difference is in the user interface.

Different people prefer different kinds of user interfaces. If you are an accomplished typist you might like the text-based user interface that comes with UNIX and MS-DOS. On the other hand, you might prefer the icon and mouse interface of the Macintosh System or Windows because of their intuitive approach to work and graphic displays. Each operating system offers a different way to work with the computer, and this might be something to consider when you're shopping for a new computer system. The six most popular operating systems for personal computers, including their user interfaces, are covered later in this chapter.

Multitasking

Normally, you use a personal computer to accomplish one specific task at a time—writing, calculating, or drawing, for example. You use a specific program for each task. With some operating systems, you must stop using one application before you start running another, sort of like turning off the television before you use the microwave. Some operating systems, however, will let you run more than one application program at the same time. This wonderful feature is called *multitasking*. With a multitasking operating system you can instantly switch from one application to another and back again, without ever stopping either program or interrupting your work.

NEW WORD: Multitasking means running more than one program at a time. It is like juggling work with your computer.

7

Operating systems that support multitasking do so in different ways. Some allow you to instantly switch between applications by pressing a certain key on your keyboard. The "outgoing" application is erased from the screen, and the "incoming" application takes its place. You see one application at a time. The other application (or applications) wait in the background.

In contrast, other multitasking operating systems let all your programs share the screen at once. Each application you are using will take up a part of the screen, called a *window*. This is a neat feature because it lets you see all your applications simultaneously.

NEW WORD: A window is a part of your screen in the shape of a rectangle. You can have multiple windows on the screen at the same time, overlapping if necessary. Each window displays different information, perhaps even from different programs all running at once.

Bootstrap

One of the more mundane chores of an operating system is to get your computer, well, operating. When you turn your PC on, it runs the operating system. In fact, until you tell it that you want to run an application program, that's the *only* program it will run. When you want to use an application, you tell the operating system to execute that program. But what tells the operating system to begin running?

What tells the operating system to begin running is the *bootstrap* program. Inside your computer's electronic circuitry is a small silicon chip that stores one very basic program. It's the only program in your computer that isn't stored on disk. The special chip is called a ROM chip (for read-only memory). It's special because the program can never be erased or altered, no matter how hard you try.

NEW WORD: A bootstrap program is a very small, simple program that gets your computer running. When your computer is running the bootstrap program, it is *booting*. Turning a computer on is also sometimes called *booting* a computer.

Your computer is designed so that the very first thing it does when you turn it on is to run the bootstrap program. That program starts running even before your finger is off the power switch. But the bootstrap program is so small that all it can do is tell your computer where to look for the next program. That program is your operating system and it's stored on the disk.

When an IBM-style PC is booting, it usually makes a few beeps and lights the lights on the keyboard to let you know that it's working. On a Macintosh, you'll see the "happy Mac" picture while it boots. When your computer is finished booting, you'll finally see your familiar operating system prompt or desktop.

Different Operating Systems

Now let's take a look at the choices you have in personal computer operating system software. Not all operating systems run on all kinds of personal computers. To a large extent, your choice of computer (hardware) dictates which operating system (software) you can use. And the operating system, in turn, may limit which application programs you can choose from.

The six operating systems covered here are

✦ MS-DOS or PC-DOS

✦ Windows

✦ Macintosh System

✦ UNIX or XENIX

✦ Apple DOS

✦ OS/2

The first three are the "big three" in the personal computer operating system arena, and they will be covered in a little more detail. The others are used by a lot of people, but for one reason or another, they have not gained the popularity of the first three. It's a near certainty that your personal computer will be using one of the most popular three listed here.

The operating system defines what your computer is and does more than the computer hardware itself.

MS-DOS and PC-DOS

7

DOS is the undisputed king of the IBM-style PC, XT, and AT world. There's hardly a single IBM-style PC that doesn't run DOS. Most IBM-style PCs even come with MS-DOS now for free, making DOS the most widely used operating system in the world.

First, the basics: The name MS-DOS stands for Microsoft Disk Operating System. Microsoft Corporation is the software company in Redmond, Washington that developed the software. When IBM started working on the original PC in 1980, they bought MS-DOS from Microsoft and modified it slightly, calling it PC-DOS. At one time, there was a real difference between IBM's PC-DOS and Microsoft's MS-DOS. That distinction has long since blurred. Now everybody uses the general term DOS to refer to either one. There's even a third contender from Digital Research in California called DR-DOS.

NEW WORD: DOS is the operating system of choice for IBM PCs and PC clones. Be sure to pronounce it so it rhymes with moss, not like the Spanish word for two.

MS-DOS was first available in 1981 as an alternative to the then-dominant operating system, CP/M. (Historical note: The first really popular personal computers used the CP/M operating system, upon which DOS is based. To this day they still work very much the same. The name CP/M stands for Control Program/Monitor.) When IBM first began selling the PC, MS-DOS was just one of three different operating systems you could get for it. Now DOS has become the *de facto* standard operating system for IBM PC-style machines.

Special MS-DOS Features

MS-DOS has a *text-based* user interface, which means you type commands using the keyboard, and the computer types its responses back on the screen. MS-DOS does not use graphics at all. That doesn't mean that the application programs for DOS don't use graphics. On the contrary, most of them do. It just means that DOS itself is not going to draw any pictures for you.

DOS relies on typed commands for its user interface. You don't need a mouse for this operating system.

This is the way most computers have worked in the past, and a good portion of the PC users prefer it. For one, your computer isn't "wasting" its time drawing pictures for you. For another, typing commands directly to the computer can give you more flexible control over your PC's operation.

MS-DOS does not support multitasking, so you can't run more than one application program at a time. Because of the hardware design of the original IBM PC, MS-DOS is not able to use more than 640K of memory to run application programs. (You may want to refer back to Chapter 3 here.) Normally, this is not a drawback, because most business and home application programs fit easily into this much memory. It can be a problem for larger and more advanced programs. However, there are add-on programs available for DOS that will overcome most of these shortcomings, allowing both multitasking and expanded memory usage.

MS-DOS Sampler

If you recall from Chapter 5, all your filenames must be no more than 11 characters long with MS-DOS. These must be separated into an 8-character primary filename and a 3-character file extension, with a period in between. Many times you don't get to pick the last three letters, so plan on using 8-character filenames. Filenames are always in capital letters. The MS-DOS commands are no longer than 8 letters, either.

MS-DOS provides a typical assortment of disk and file maintenance commands. Some examples are listed here.

DIR   This is short for *directory*. It lists the contents of a disk, including the size of each file. You saw an example of the DIR command in Chapter 5.

TREE   The TREE command displays a list of all of your disk's subdirectories (if any) and their subdirectories. This is helpful for locating a file. It's called TREE because the file hierarchy can look like an inverted tree.

TYPE   This command displays the contents of a file on the screen. TYPE does not allow you to edit a file, only to see it and read it.

REN   The REN command is used to rename a disk file.

You'll never need to remember a command that's more than eight letters long.

DEL   DEL is short for delete, and is used to erase files from a disk.

COPY   This is the command used to copy a file or files from one disk to another.

DISKCOPY   The DISKCOPY command will copy an entire diskette, making an exact duplicate of it.

FORMAT   The FORMAT command formats a new hard disk or a new floppy disk. You have to format a new disk before you can use it, but formatting a used disk will erase the data on it.

CHKDSK   This is an abbreviation for *check disk*. CHKDSK will tell you how much of your disk is being used and how much space is still free. It can also diagnose some disk problems.

SYS   This command permits you to copy MS-DOS operating system files to a newly formatted disk.

DATE   This command allows you to tell MS-DOS what today's date is. MS-DOS will record this date every time you create or modify a file. The DIR command shows the creation/modification date with every file.

7

TIME Like DATE, this command allows you to tell MS-DOS what the current time is. The time will be stored with every file.

VER This command displays the current version of the operating system.

Windows

Windows is changing the look of PCs. Before Windows, practically all IBM-style PCs used DOS and nothing else. Now people have a choice. Windows offers many of the advantages that people like so much about the Macintosh and other operating systems.

Windows also comes from Microsoft Corporation, the same people who brought you DOS. Perhaps that's not surprising when you consider how closely DOS and Windows work together. The first version of Windows, Windows 1, was a terrible failure. PCs at that time were just too slow to be able to draw all of the pictures on the screen that Windows requires, without losing people's attention. The next version, Windows 2, wasn't much better. Then Windows 3 came along, and everything changed.

Oddly, for many computers Windows isn't really an operating system at all. Technically, it's an application program that runs with DOS. Except for Windows NT, they all need DOS to run, including Windows versions 1, 2, and 3. That means that all of the same limitations of DOS like the 640K memory limit and the 8-character filenames are still there.

Technically, it's possible to run Windows without a mouse, but you wouldn't want to try it.

Special Windows Features

The outstanding feature of Windows is—guess what—its windows. Windows lets you view many different windows on the screen at once, like a collection of little computer screens. That in itself is fun and helpful for a lot of people.

Windows also imposes a certain amount of order on applications. That is, application programs must look and act a certain way. This is good news for you, because it means that one program will behave much like another, and learning one will give you a head start on any new programs.

Finally, Windows supports multitasking. If you can see multiple windows on the screen, that implies that you can run multiple programs at once, and with Windows, you can. There's no need to stop one program to start another one. Just use your mouse to point to the one you want to use.

Windows Sampler

Windows offers a "point and click" interface that's popular with beginners.

With a PC running Windows, you don't type commands at the keyboard anymore. Instead, you use a mouse to move the little arrow cursor around the screen and point to the things you want to do. There is a list of commands across the top of the screen at all times. When you run an application program under Windows, it will replace the Windows commands with the application's own commands.

Underneath it all, Windows offers the same kinds of functions as DOS; it just looks different. Figure 7-1 shows a sample of some of the Windows command menus on a Windows *desktop*.

The Windows desktop covers your entire screen. If you like, you can select a picture to use as your Windows "wallpaper," personalizing your desktop. In this case, it's the famous Schloss Neuschwanstein, near the

7

You can customize your Windows desktop

Figure 7-1.

Opening the
File Manager
window is like
typing the
DIR command
with DOS.

German-Austrian border. There are no windows on the desktop right now. Instead, there are some icons representing applications arranged across the bottom of the screen.

Figure 7-2 shows a window open. This is called the File Manager window (you can tell by the title across the top). The File Manager window lets you look at the list of files on a disk or in a particular subdirectory. Each file is listed by name with a small icon next to it representing the kind of file it is.

By selecting the View menu in the File Manager window, you can choose how the files in the windows will be sorted. You can sort them

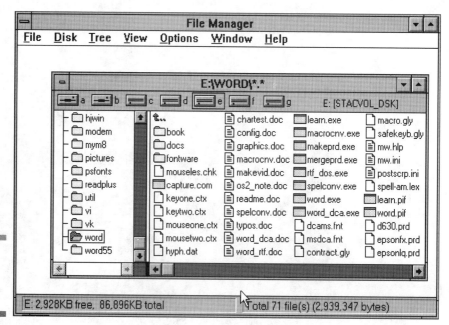

The Windows
File Manager
window
Figure 7-2.

by filename, by the type of file (that is, by the file extension), by size, or by the date last modified.

```
View
┌─────────────────────────┐
│ √ Tree and Directory     │
│   Tree Only              │
│   Directory Only         │
├─────────────────────────┤
│   Split                  │
├─────────────────────────┤
│ √ Name                   │
│   All File Details       │
│   Partial Details...     │
├─────────────────────────┤
│   Sort by Name           │
│ √ Sort by Type           │
│   Sort by Size           │
│   Sort by Date           │
├─────────────────────────┤
│   By File Type...        │
└─────────────────────────┘
```

With Windows, your options are limited only by the command menus shown on your screen.

The Close command will "shut" a window on your screen, making the window disappear. It may also stop an application program from running. If you are finished using your Windows word processor, for example, closing its windows will terminate the application. You access the Close command by pulling down the menu from the upper-left corner of the window.

7

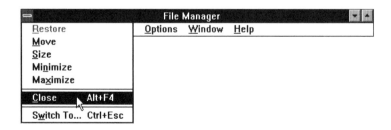

The Program Manager window shows your application programs. Each application is represented by an icon, usually a logo or picture that indicates what the program does. You can "launch" an application (start it running so you can use it) by pointing to it with the mouse and clicking the mouse button twice.

You can also create program groups to keep similar programs together. Program groups serve the same function as subdirectories for files. You can create them any way you like, to help you organize your applications and keep your work in order.

Instead of selecting an application or group by pointing with the mouse, you can select the Window menu from the Program Manager window and select the desired application or group from the menu.

Macintosh System

The Macintosh operating system is simply called System. The programmers at Apple Computer created it in the early 1980s, and it first appeared with the original Macintosh in 1984. It is probably the most well known example of a *graphical user interface* (GUI). The idea of a computer where commands are "pointed to" with a mouse instead of being typed with the keyboard was not originally Apple's. It was first developed by Xerox for the Star computer in the late 1970s.

NEW WORD: A computer that uses easy-to-understand pictures on the screen and a handy mouse is said to have a graphical user interface (GUI). Wits may like to call it a WIMP, "windows, icons, mouse, and pictures."

For most people, using a mouse and a graphical user interface is easier than using a computer that relies on typed commands and a screen that only prints text (writing, no pictures). That's a matter of taste, and there are many who prefer it the other way. Apple owes much of their success to the well-thought-out user interface on the Macintosh.

7

NOTE: Macintosh people make a distinction between the operating system, called System, and the user interface, which is called Finder. Technically, it is the Finder that many people find appealing.

Special Macintosh Features

Like Windows for the PC, System has windows. In fact, it had them first. The basic idea is the same, they only differ in some details. People who are familiar with one can usually start using the other after only a few minutes of orientation. The windowing ability of System lets you see your work from multiple applications at a time. For example, you can work on a financial spreadsheet, type on your word processor, and play a game all at once.

As you might guess, the Macintosh System supports multitasking, so you can have multiple applications executing, or "open," at once. Each application program appears in a window on the screen, and each window may be moved around, enlarged, or reduced, as desired. When a window is "closed," the application it displayed is stopped.

Mac Sampler

Basic Macintosh System commands are available as a list of choices found on five different menus of commands. The name of each menu is listed across the top of the Macintosh screen (except the "apple" menu, which appears as a picture of an apple), and individual commands are selected by first pointing to the menu, and then pointing to the command you want.

The first menu is the "apple" menu. It is always in the upper-left corner of your screen. It gives you access to some of the basic functions of your Macintosh, like the Control Panel, Calculator, and other desktop accessories.

The Macintosh and Windows operating systems both look very similar. This seems to be the wave of the future.

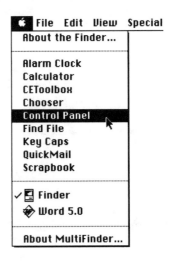

Underneath the File menu is a selection to create a new folder. This
command creates a new folder on the disk, or within the current folder.

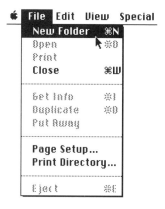

Select Open to open an application file and begin executing it. A new
window is displayed on the screen, and the application program's
output will fill it.

7

Use the Close command to close a particular window. The window that
the application was using will disappear.

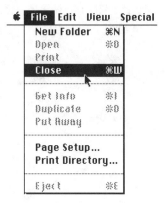

With the View menu, you can choose how the Macintosh System lists the contents of a disk. There are usually about seven choices:

✦ Small icon

✦ Large icon

✦ Name of the file

✦ Date of last modification

✦ Size of the file

✦ Kind of file

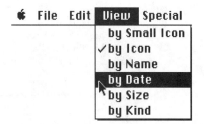

The Special menu includes choices to erase a disk, shut down your computer, or "empty the trash."

When files are erased by dragging them to the Trash icon, they are not erased permanently. If the trash has not been "emptied," you can still rescue a file you've erased. To permanently erase a file you must first empty the trash using this command.

The observant reader will have also noticed the "Clean Up Window" menu selection. This command tidies up a window so that all the icons line up.

UNIX

7

UNIX is recommended only for more experienced users, but it is not beyond the grasp of the beginner.

UNIX is probably the oldest operating system around for personal computers. UNIX was derived from an even older operating system called Multics that was used on the big mainframe computers in the 1960s. UNIX is still used on bigger computers, mostly in universities and businesses. Only recently has it been made available for smaller personal computers.

From the start, UNIX was designed to be an operating system for engineers and programmers. For the average nontechnical computer user, UNIX is extremely awkward and difficult to use. The user interface and the commands are cryptic at best, and can be very bewildering to the uninitiated. Technical users, on the other hand, find UNIX an unusually strong and powerful operating system to work with. UNIX was the first operating system to introduce the concept of subdirectories, widely used in most operating systems today. It also has advanced security features that allow only authorized users to modify data files or run certain programs. Each potential computer user is identified with a user ID and must correctly enter a password before UNIX will allow access to the computer.

UNIX was developed at the Bell Telephone research laboratories, which are now a part of AT&T Information Systems. AT&T owns the name UNIX, and any software that carries the UNIX trademark must come from AT&T. There are about a dozen UNIX-like operating systems, with names like Ultrix, XENIX, Solaris, and GNU ("GNU is Not Unix"). XENIX is a product of Microsoft Corporation (of MS-DOS/Windows fame), and is probably the most successful UNIX-like operating system for personal computers. There may well be more computers running XENIX than the original UNIX.

If you're tackling UNIX, make yourself a handy reference sheet, or better yet, find a good book on UNIX for beginners.

UNIX is a multitasking operating system. A UNIX computer will let you start one application program, and then start a second one while the first one is still running. If the first program needs information from you, it will pause until you answer it. You can run as many programs simultaneously as you wish. UNIX is also a multiuser operating system, meaning that it can handle more than one person at once, just like it handles multiple programs. Multiuser capabilities are superfluous for a personal computer, because you'd need an extra keyboard and screen for every additional person. On larger minicomputers and mainframes, however, this feature is extremely useful.

UNIX Sampler

Like other operating systems, UNIX offers an assortment of disk-related commands. It also offers more than 100 small "utility" programs that are usually only of interest to engineers or software developers. Filenames can be as long as you want them to be, with uppercase and lowercase characters freely mixed. Ironically, despite the flexibility in filenames, most UNIX commands are excruciatingly terse. In addition, all commands must be typed in lowercase letters.

ls   This command shows you a list of the files on a disk. Normally, the files are sorted alphabetically, with the size of the file, the date, and the time it was last modified also shown.

mv   The **mv** command is used to rename a disk file. It is an abbreviation for *move*.

rm   This command is used to remove (or erase) a file from disk.

cat   You use this command to display the contents of a data file on your screen. The **cat** command also can be used to combine two or more data files into one. The term "cat" is short for *concatenate,* meaning to combine.

grep   This command, short for *global regular expression processor,* can be used to search through data files for a particular word or phrase. This is a quick way to locate a particular file even if you have forgotten its name.

login   This command is used to log in to the computer, meaning to identify yourself to the operating system. After the computer identifies you, it may or may not restrict your access to certain sensitive data files or programs.

passwd   This command is used to give yourself a password. UNIX will ask you for a password when you log in. The **passwd** command can also be used to change your password whenever desired.

7

Apple DOS

Apple DOS is the operating system that all members of the Apple II family of computers use. It is a relatively simple operating system, ideal for home or small business use. It does not support multitasking, however, so only one application at a time can be run. Its user interface is text-based, although many Apple II application programs use graphics and a mouse to operate. It can handle small- to medium-sized programs, typically from 64K to 128K, which is as much memory as most Apple II machines are equipped with.

Apple DOS started the personal computer revolution but it's not as powerful, or as popular, as it used to be.

Apple DOS allows filenames to be up to 64 characters long, with both upper- and lowercase letters. Early versions of Apple DOS cannot create or manage subdirectories (folders), so you will have a so-called *flat* (undivided) file system.

Apple DOS Sampler

Apple DOS has a basic repertoire of commands. Because it is an older operating system intended for hobby users, some of the commands are a little technical. At the time, the Apple II and Apple DOS were very advanced.

CATALOG   This command shows you a list of files stored on a disk. CATALOG includes file size, date, and time information.

CAT   This is a short form of CATALOG, and displays only the names of the files.

BLOAD   This stands for *binary load,* and it is used to load binary files into memory.

BRUN   This command, which stands for *binary run,* begins execution of a program after it has been loaded with BLOAD.

BSAVE   This is the opposite of BLOAD, saving binary information onto disk.

RUN   This command is used to begin execution of programs that you may have written yourself, using the BASIC computer language. (BASIC and other programming languages will be discussed in Chapter 12.)

PREFIX   The PREFIX command appears in later versions of Apple DOS. It is used to tell the computer which subdirectory you want it to search to locate files.

OS/2

OS/2 also has a graphical user interface, like Windows, called Presentation Manager.

OS/2 is one of the later entries into the personal computer operating system arena. OS/2 is closely related to the PS/2 family of personal computers from IBM. Announced in 1987 along with the PS/2 lines, OS/2 was intended to be the successor to PC-DOS.

OS/2 was codeveloped by IBM and Microsoft Corporation for the IBM PS/2 line of computers. OS/2 was designed to address some of the limitations of MS-DOS and become the "second generation operating system" (hence the name) for computers previously using MS-DOS. OS/2 supports multitasking—multiple applications may be run simultaneously, each one appearing in its own window on the screen. It has an optional graphics/mouse user interface, called Presentation Manager, in addition to the traditional text interface. OS/2 also supports enormous amounts of memory for large application programs (or several application programs running at once). In fact, OS/2 requires about 2 megabytes (that's 2048 kilobytes!) of memory in the computer just to bootstrap itself.

OS/2 Sampler

The heritage of OS/2 is clear after a brief look at its commands. The majority of OS/2 commands bear a strong resemblance to MS-DOS commands and, in some cases, are identical. All of the basic MS-DOS commands are here, and some new ones have been added, mostly to support multitasking. As before, all filenames must be 11 characters or less, all uppercase. Subdirectories are, of course, supported.

DIR   Short for *directory*, DIR lists the files contained on a disk along with their size, date, and time of last modification.

TYPE   This command is used to display the contents of a data file. Unlike MS-DOS, OS/2 can display multiple files, one after the other.

OS/2 runs only on IBM PCs and PC compatibles. It's very similar to both DOS and Windows.

FORMAT   This is used to format a new disk.

CHKDSK   The check disk command shows you how much of your disk is being used and how much space is still free. It can also diagnose some possible disk problems.

7

TREE   The TREE command displays a list of all of your disk's subdirectories (if any) and their subdirectories. This can be helpful for locating a file.

DATE   This command allows you to set today's date. OS/2 will record this date whenever you create or modify a file.

TIME   Like DATE, this command allows you to set the correct time. The time will also be stored with every file.

REN   The REN command is used to change (rename) the name of a file.

DEL   DEL is short for delete, and is used to erase one or more files.

COPY   This is the command to use for copying one or more files from one disk to another.

DISKCOPY   The DISKCOPY command will copy all the files on a floppy disk, making an exact duplicate of it.

VER   This command displays the current version of OS/2 that you are running.

The commands given for the six operating systems are just a sample of some of the most frequently used commands. For a more complete listing and in-depth descriptions, refer to the manual for your operating system. In the next chapter, we will look at various kinds of application programs, what they can do, and some of their specific features.

Bibliography

You can find out more about operating systems by reading the following books, all published by Osborne/McGraw-Hill in Berkeley, California.

Coffin, Stephen. *UNIX: The Complete Reference*. 1991

Jamsa, Kris. *DOS: The Pocket Reference*. 1991

LURNIX. *UNIX Made Easy*. 1990

Matthews, Martin S. *The Mac Made Easy*. 1992

Schildt, Herbert. *DOS Made Easy, Fourth Edition*. 1993

Sheldon, Tom. *Windows 3.1 Made Easy*. 1992

Sheldon, Tom. *Windows 3.1: The Complete Reference*. 1992

Wyatt, Allen L. *Windows 3.1: The Pocket Reference*. 1992

CHAPTER

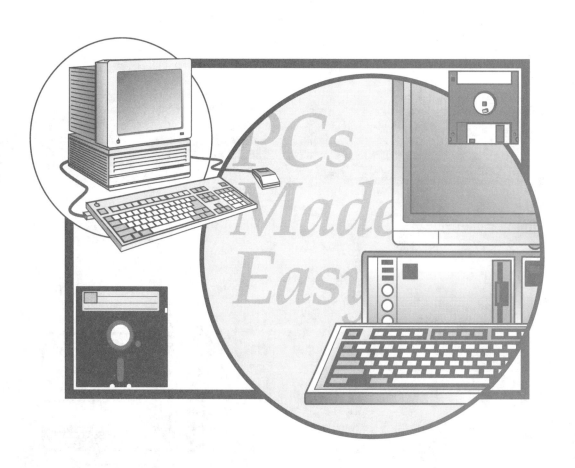

8

WHAT IS AN APPLICATION PROGRAM?

An application program is the software that you use to perform a certain job. The term application *indicates that you apply the software to the task at hand. Except for operating system software, application software covers almost every kind of program that you are likely to encounter with your computer.*

Applications are available for all kinds of work and play. There are applications for writing (word processors), calculating finances (spreadsheets), drawing (graphics), designing or drafting (CAD), bookkeeping (accounting), filing and organizing (databases), and games of skill and simulation, to name just a few. There are many competitive programs available in all of these categories, so you have a wide selection from which to choose.

As a computer user, you might have only one application program that you use regularly, or several that you switch between as the need arises. You can select just the applications that meet your current needs, and upgrade or add applications in the future as your requirements change.

This chapter covers just what an application program is and what kinds are available for personal computers. It will also describe how some popular applications work, how you use them, and what kinds of features they have.

Business Applications

More people buy computers for business use than for home use, so it follows that there is a wide variety of business-oriented application software. More and more businesses, large and small, are finding that personal computers can be an invaluable aid. New business programs show up all the time, and existing programs are updated and revised every few years. Prices range from under $30 to more than $5000. As a rule of thumb, most business applications are priced around $350.

Business programs are generally very reliable and error-free, especially if they are in a second or third release. If you think you've found a program bug, most software companies will try to fix it promptly, and will either fix yours or send you the next release of the program.

The majority of business applications fall into three categories: word processing, spreadsheet, and database. Although there are certainly other popular kinds of application programs, nearly all businesses use at least one of these programs.

Word Processing

Word processing software is the computer-age equivalent of the typewriter. You can use a word processing program to type legal briefs, letters, memos, invoices, reports, theses, or anything else that you might want written down. Where a word processor excels over a typewriter is in its easy remedy for typing errors and the creative freedom it allows you. Word processing programs also allow you to manage documents in ways that were never possible before.

This is a good place to explain the difference between a personal computer running word processing software and a *dedicated* word processor made by companies such as Magnavox, Wang, and Brother. A personal computer is a general-purpose machine capable of performing many different tasks, including, but not limited to, word processing. Dedicated word processors, on the other hand, are single-purpose devices, like highly advanced typewriters. They are not capable of performing any other tasks, but they are generally smaller and less expensive than personal computers.

NEW WORD: A dedicated machine is built for one purpose only and is not flexible and general-purpose like a personal computer is. Examples are a dedicated word processor or a dedicated fax machine.

8

There are many competitive word processing programs for personal computers. Each one has its own particular mix of features, options, and user interface. A good example is Microsoft's Word for Windows, shown in Figure 8-1. Keep in mind that learning to use one word processor won't necessarily prepare you to use a different one. Each program has its own way of doing things, and people often choose a program because of what the user interface is like as much as for the features that the program offers.

Entering and Editing Text

When you type a document using a word processing application, the computer screen becomes your rough draft. You can type whatever you want, spelling errors and all, and then edit what you've typed until it's just the way you want it to be. Editing can be as simple as changing a

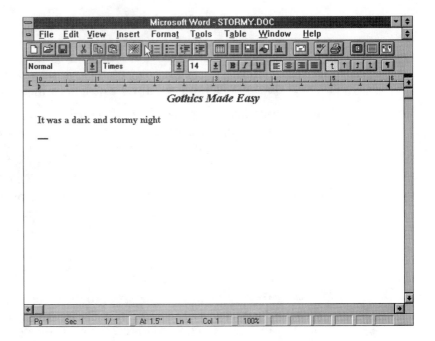

Typical word
processor
Figure 8-1.

few words or as substantial as deleting, adding, or relocating entire paragraphs. You can edit, reedit, and review your work as often as you like without wasting paper. When the final draft is just right, you can print as many perfect, identical copies as you want.

If by some chance you should make a mistake in your document, it is much easier to clean up than if you were using a typewriter. First, there's no paper to erase and no correcting fluid to shake up and then dry off. Second, you don't have to correct mistakes as you make them. Feel free to blithely type away at breakneck speed, misspelling every other word, if you like. You can always go back and correct them later.

For example, if you accidentally typed a word twice and don't really want both of them there, simply highlight the offending word and press the Del key.

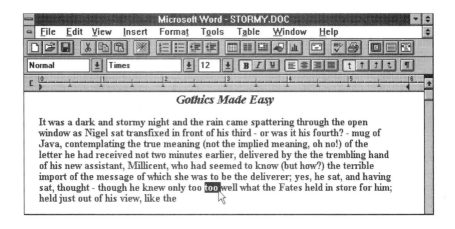

(On the key, Del stands for delete, or erase.) You can highlight the word you want using your keyboard or mouse. Correcting simple stray letters is just as easy.

What if you want a whole paragraph excised? No problem, just highlight the paragraph and press Del.

So much for erasing unwanted text. How about adding a little something? That's even easier and at least as much fun. If, after reading over your writing you decide there's still something missing, simply highlight the place where you want the new text added and start typing. All the words after that point will automatically move down to make room for your additions. You can add as much as you want this way, even doubling the size of your document.

Special Effects

Nearly any word processor will let you jazz up your writing by letting you use some special effects. You can <u>underline</u> words, print them in **bold face**, or *italics*, or even other combinations. If you're having

8

Special effects look great on your screen; make sure your printer can print them.

trouble typing foreign language characters, like Ñ, Ü, or Ʒ, your word processor can probably help you do that, too.

Your computer can help you with other common but tedious chores. To center a heading in the middle of the page, you don't have to count spaces anymore. Instead, just type in what you want, and then tell the word processor that you want it centered. As shown in the WordPerfect screen in Figure 8-2, the heading will automatically be moved to the middle for you. You can also edit the centered text and it will stay centered, even if you make it longer or shorter.

Helpful Tools

Perhaps best of all, there are lots of tasks that your computer can do with a word processor that you couldn't do with a typewriter at all. Let's say that you've typed a long business letter, but then you learn that you've misspelled the addressee's name all 17 times. You could go back and find the name every time, but wouldn't it be easier to let the computer do it? This is a feature called search and replace.

Using search and replace, you tell your PC what word (or words) to look for and then what word (or words) you want to replace it with.

Replace	
Fi**n**d What:	dark	**Find Next**
		Replace
Re**p**lace With:	dismal	Replace **A**ll
		Cancel
☐ Match **W**hole Word Only ☐ Match **C**ase		
─ Replace with Formatting ─		
Cl**e**ar	C**h**aracter... **P**aragraph...	**S**tyles...

Now your computer will scan the entire document and highlight each place where the pattern you specified appears. A dialog box will ask you if you want to change it or leave it alone.

On some word processors you can be very specific about what you are searching for. Maybe you only want to replace a word if it appears at

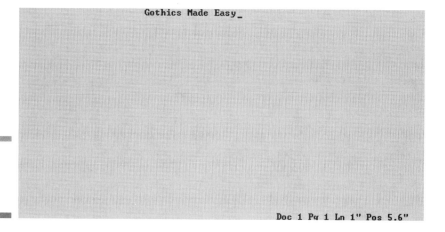

Gothics Made Easy_

Doc 1 Pg 1 Ln 1" Pos 5.6"

Centering a
head is a
breeze
Figure 8-2.

the beginning of a sentence, or if it's capitalized a certain way. Most word processors are even smart enough to copy the capitalization of the word they're replacing, so that if you are searching for "smith" and replacing it with "lean" you will get "lean" in the middle of a sentence, but "Lean" at the beginning or when it is being used as a name.

8

NEW WORD: A dialog box is something that both the Macintosh and Windows use. It's a small window that pops up after certain commands to ask you a specific question. You often have to type your answer. That's the "dialog" part.

Page Layout

Most word processors will let you manage how your typing looks on the printed page. You can control the left and right margins and the top and bottom margins, too. If you like, you can have a constant header or footer running across the top and bottom of each page, respectively.

One very tedious chore that nearly any word processor can do for you is to number the pages automatically just before it's ready to print. You don't need to worry about the page numbers changing when you add or remove paragraphs from your document, either. It will be renumbered every time.

You will probably also have a feature called widow and orphan control. That means that the first line of a paragraph won't be separated from the others at the end of a page (a *widow*). That looks funny, but it's hard to avoid when you're using a typewriter. An *orphan* is the last line of a paragraph all by itself at the top of a page.

Finally, just before you get ready to print out your work on paper, your word processor may allow you a print preview. That means that it will draw an entire page on the screen (normally only about one-third of a page will fit when you're writing), complete with all of the headers, footers, page numbers, and other layout items drawn in for you to review. You know you'll get it just right before you ever print the first page.

Added Features

There are more features, too; things that even the best typewriter could never do for you. If your word processor comes with a dictionary on disk, you can have it check your spelling for you. After your writing is done, but before you print it out, have the PC check your spelling to make sure that nothing was overlooked. Most PC spell checkers have electronic dictionaries with tens of thousands of words. You can even buy supplementary dictionaries with medical, technical, or legal terms. If your spell checker comes across a word it doesn't know, you can either tell it to correct the word, ignore it, or add it to the dictionary.

Going one step beyond simple spelling checkers, some word processing programs also offer grammar checking and a thesaurus. With a thesaurus, simply highlight the word you want to look up, and your computer will offer you a selection of synonyms.

Database Management

Database management is the sort of task that many people assume computers do "automatically." By now you've learned that there's nothing your computer can do by itself; even the most rudimentary tasks require some kind of software. A database is a lot like an electronic card file with imaginary 3 x 5 cards. You put your information in, and your computer helps you to get it back out.

A database management program is the electronic equivalent of the perfect, tireless file clerk and research assistant. It allows you to retrieve information from an assortment of facts and figures (a database) that you've collected in a file. You use a database management system (DBMS) program to enter information in an orderly manner, and later on, to retrieve it without searching for it manually. You can use a database program to maintain records of all kinds. Then you can file, sort, combine, or retrieve that information based upon different criteria. For example, if you have a database of customer information, you could extract the data for all those whose last name begins with "K," or who live within a certain radius, or who have purchased a particular product between March 16 and June 21.

Entering Data

The most important part of using a database is collecting the data you want to file. This usually involves plenty of typing. If you are collecting customer information for your shop, you might enter the information every time you make a sale. With a more advanced computer system, your PC might be tied in with your cash register, so that the information is entered automatically, without typing it.

A database is a perfect way to sort through all kinds of information. Enter it once and sort in myriad different ways.

Information for a mailing list might also be typed in from a list of church members, registered voters, donors, or other groups. There are also ready-made lists for sale. You can buy lists of names of people in a particular geographical area, or who meet other criteria.

Many database programs can accept input from files that already exist. That is, you don't necessarily have to type in all of the information that you want filed. Your database program might be able to "extract" names and addresses from the business letters you've created on your PC with a word processing program, for example. Or it might be able to glean the numbers you want from a spreadsheet.

Retrieving Data

Once you've got your information in—one way or the other—the most important step is getting it out again. This is where the power of the computer really shines. Database management programs are better than card files primarily because the computer can search your database for

8

you and extract the information in ways that you couldn't necessarily do yourself. Theoretically, you can search your electronic card file for any word, phrase, or number anywhere in the database. In practical terms, some databases are better than others at finding the information you want.

The average database assumes that you want to arrange your data just like cards in a card file. The collection of all the data is still called a file, just as you saw in Chapter 5. Each individual "card" is a *record* in the file. You can usually have an unlimited number of records in a database file (or at least some enormous number, like four billion). Each record would hold the information for one customer, household, recipe, inventory item, or other subject. Figure 8-3 illustrates this concept.

NEW WORD: A record is a part of the database where all the information on one particular subject is stored. It might represent one item in an inventory list, one customer, or one card in a card file.

A standard index card usually has more than one bit of information written on it before it goes into the file box. You might have somebody's

Each card represents a record; information is separated into fields
Figure 8-3.

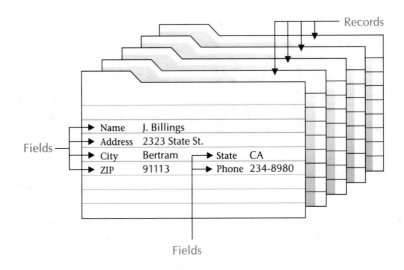

name and phone number, for instance. Each of these items on a card (or record) is called a *field*. One field holds one particular bit of information, and each record will usually have the same fields. A mailing list would have records for each person, and each person's record would have the same fields for name, address, and telephone number.

NEW WORD: A field is a part of a database record that holds one particular item of information about the subject like weight, price, color, address, or part number.

Sorting

Rather than extract specific information from your database, you might want to see the entire list. Your computer will allow you to sort and arrange the list by just about any criteria you choose. Coming back to the mailing list example, you could sort the list alphabetically by last name, by address, or by telephone number.

In the case of the address or telephone number, each record should have a unique value in the appropriate field. You wouldn't normally have two families with the same phone number, for example. But what if you are sorting by last name? It's entirely possible that you might have two or more records with the same value (the name) in that field.

In the database world, you sort by keys. A *key* is a value in a particular field that you tell the database management program to look for. The computer reports on all the records that have the requested value in the key field. This is called the primary sort criterion, or the *primary* key.

NEW WORD: A key is an item in the database that you want to search for or use for sorting.

If you know ahead of time that one field isn't enough to uniquely identify a record, you can specify two key values for two different fields.

8

This is called a *secondary* key. Most programs will let you sort your data with two keys, and many will allow more than that.

Spreadsheets

A spreadsheet is a little like a word processor for numbers. You can enter numbers instead of words, and move them around. But a spreadsheet goes much further than that. It will add your numbers up for you automatically and calculate percentages, amortization, gross margin, standard deviation, rate of return, or any number of other financial, statistical, and mathematical values that could possibly be generated from those numbers. So instead of being just a number processor, a spreadsheet is more like an automatic analyst, accountant, and statistician all in one.

Like the latest word processing programs, spreadsheets have become very, very advanced. Most people don't use all of the things that the program can do. Even people who use a spreadsheet everyday don't always need—or even understand—every advanced feature. That's okay; nobody's being graded here. All spreadsheets have the same basic functions, and those are the ones we'll look at now.

A spreadsheet program is a computerized accountant's ledger—and much more.

The spreadsheet program used in the following examples is Excel for Windows. If you remember from the previous chapter, Windows is an operating system (or an operating system add-on) for IBM-style PCs. Since the advent of Windows 3.0 in 1991, many programs have been modified to work with Windows. Excel is a top-notch program from Microsoft. There are other spreadsheet programs for Windows that are every bit as good. Quattro Pro is one example, from Borland. Another is Lotus 1-2-3, an early spreadsheet program that has grown gracefully and kept up with the best of them.

The Empty Spreadsheet

The first stop on our spreadsheet tour is to look at the basic screen or window. Figure 8-4 shows an empty spreadsheet, ready for you to start working. Notice all the Windows accouterments around the outside of the window. Across the top are various menu selection choices. Down

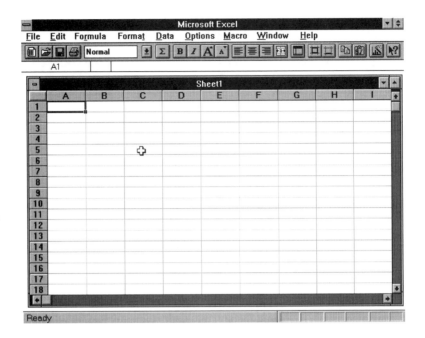

An empty
spreadsheet
Figure 8-4.

the right side and across the bottom are *scroll bars* that let you move up
and down, back and forth over the spreadsheet. These are basic
Windows features, and not specific to Excel, or even to spreadsheets.

8

NEW WORD: A scroll bar is something you see on many application
programs, particularly with Windows or the Macintosh. It is a
narrow stripe along the edge of a window. You use your mouse on the
scroll bar to rearrange the picture inside the window so that you can see
different parts of the file.

The main part of the spreadsheet is the "sheet." It looks like a ruled
accountant's ledger. There are lines drawn both horizontally and
vertically, making rectangular boxes. Each of these boxes is called a *cell*.
Each cell can hold a number, like this:

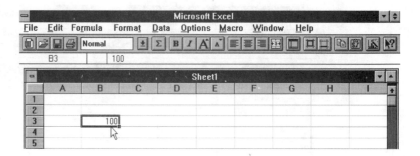

You can fill in any cell by pointing to it with your mouse and clicking in it. If you prefer, you can use the arrow keys on your keyboard, too.

Most spreadsheet programs identify each cell by the row and column it is in, like numbering seats in a stadium. The upper-left cell is A1. The one just beneath it is A2, and so on. Look near the upper-left corner of the window to see where Excel tells you which cell you are writing in.

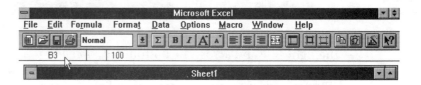

Entering Numbers

Now you're ready to enter a number. After pointing to cell B2, you can type in a number, say, 1234.56.

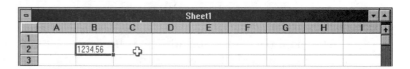

Press the ⬇ key to move down to cell B3, where you can enter another number. Repeat this a few times until you have a column of numbers.

	A	B	C	D	E	F	G	H	I
1									
2		1234.56							
3		99.21							
4		145.01							
5		406.94							
6		55.77							
7									

This might not look like such a big deal, yet. Now, for one tiny bit of magic, you can have the spreadsheet tally up the entire column. For this particular spreadsheet program, select the sum button from the menu bar, and it will automatically place the total in the selected cell.

	A	B	C	D	E	F	G	H	I
1									
2		1234.56							
3		99.21							
4		145.01							
5		406.94							
6		55.77							
7									
8		1941.49							
9									

8

Let the Spreadsheet Do the Work

So far, so good. But the spreadsheet's ability to sum a column of numbers is more valuable when you know that it will automatically update that figure all the time, any time you change one of the numbers in the column. In the example, if the number in cell B4 changes, the total in cell B8 will change too.

	A	B	C	D	E	F	G	H	I
1									
2		1234.56							
3		99.21							
4		24.99							
5		406.94							
6		55.77							
7									
8		1821.47							
9									

Your figures will be kept up-to-date no matter how much things change. If you have several columns of numbers, and the total at the bottom of each column is used in the next column, then changing one number in the first column will change every single total in the entire set of numbers—automatically!

More Than Just a Calculator

The power of a spreadsheet lies in its complex calculations. You can let it pull information from different parts of the page and even different files.

Adding numbers is all very well, but that's a simple parlor trick compared to other things your computer can do. It's not limited to simple add-subtract-multiply-divide functions. As stated previously, your spreadsheet can calculate rates of return, averages, means, standard deviations, and other values. If a number can be calculated precisely from a dozen or so other numbers, your spreadsheet can probably do it.

As an example, let's say you want to calculate the amount of a loan payment for a new car. As anyone who's tried this knows, this is not as easy to calculate as it sounds. With a properly designed spreadsheet, like the one shown in Figure 8-5, it's simply a matter of entering the pertinent numbers.

You need to enter the amount of the loan, the term of the loan (the number of monthly payments), and the interest rate. All the rest is automatic! Your PC can even calculate what the final partial payment will be.

Making Charts and Graphs

One of the greatest features of all of the better spreadsheet programs is the ability to make charts and graphs from your numbers. If you're

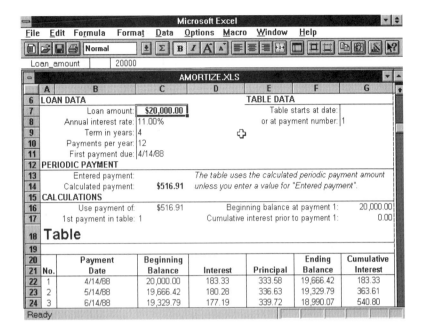

A more complex spreadsheet demonstration

Figure 8-5.

storing your company's monthly sales figures with a spreadsheet, wouldn't it be nice to be able to produce bar charts showing growth over time? Or a pie chart that divides sales by region? Or how about a line graph that plots each salesperson's activity against forecast?

This can all be as simple as selecting the data you want to graph with the mouse,

	A	B	C	D	E	F	G	H
14			Fixed	Variable	Total	Profit		
15		Revenue	Expenses	Expenses	Expenses	or Loss		
16		$138,892	$150,000	$51,682	$201,682	($62,790)		
17		$148,892	$150,000	$55,403	$205,403	($56,511)		
18		$158,892	$150,000	$59,124	$209,124	($50,232)		
19		$168,892	$150,000	$62,845	$212,845	($43,953)		
20		$178,892	$150,000	$66,566	$216,566	($37,674)		
21		$188,892	$150,000	$70,287	$220,287	($31,395)		

and then selecting the graphing option from the menu. If more than one type of graph or chart is available, you can select the kind you like best. Choose whatever suits your purposes or best displays the data you want highlighted, and *voila!*

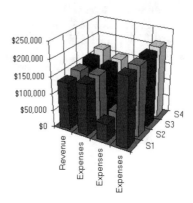

You've produced an impressive chart. You can save your chart or graph onto disk and retrieve it later, if you like. Or, with the appropriate added equipment, you can make a colorful overhead slide for a company presentation.

Other Business Applications

Only some of the most common and popular types of business applications have been discussed so far. There are many other kinds of application software used in business. Desktop publishing, for instance, is a growing field for people who want to produce professional-looking brochures, manuals, reports, and other documents using their personal computers. There are also graphics programs and full-featured accounting packages, including general ledger, accounts receivable, accounts payable, inventory, payroll, and so on.

Desktop Publishing

Desktop publishing (or DTP) is like a deluxe version of word processing. With DTP software you can take your written documents one step farther and turn them into professional-looking brochures, newsletters, flyers, advertising copy, or anything else you can imagine.

What DTP programs offer above and beyond basic word processing is the ability to merge graphics into your documents, and access to more varied types of print. The graphics can be hand-drawn figures or sketches, professionally acquired graphic arts, photographs, or nearly anything else. You can also lay out your work in newspaper-style columns, with headlines and different typefaces. Desktop publishing applications also give you many new tools for controlling page layout, color, borders, and other stylistic elements that are normally the realm of professional typesetters and graphic artists.

Desktop publishing is like word processing, but adds graphics, art, page layout, and many other advanced features.

Paint or Draw

If you want to use your PC to draw, there are dozens of programs available. You might want to use one of these in conjunction with your word processing or desktop publishing software, or just by itself. A paint or draw program, like the one in Figure 8-6, allows you to use your computer screen as a palette and easel. You can draw freehand figures, or regular shapes like rectangles and ovals, with mathematical precision.

Some programs let you draw in color, others in black and white. Almost all can shade areas of your drawing or fill them with a pattern. You can use a paint/draw program to draw a map to a party or to design a new company logo. Many talented graphic artists draw useful figures and sell them to other computer users as *clip art*.

8

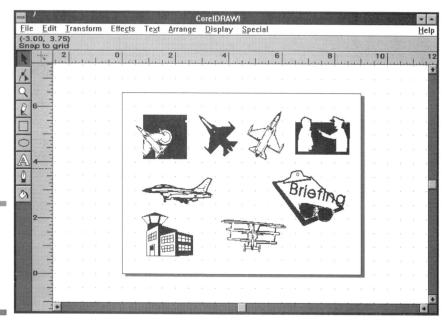

With drawing programs you can create useful and fun graphics
Figure 8-6.

NEW WORD: Clip art is a casual name given to pictures that have been drawn by an artist to be "clipped" and used in your desktop publishing documents. Many companies sell disks filled with hundreds of clip art figures. Using somebody else's clip art can relieve you of the task of drawing your own pictures.

Accounting

Thousands and thousands of small businesses trust their books to personal computers. Business accounting is a complex task, and many have found their PC to be of invaluable help. There are many general accounting programs tailored specifically for small businesses.

Tax Preparation

An application that is popular both at home and in the office is tax preparation software. There are many different tax preparation packages to choose from, each with its own advantages. Most can help you fill out a federal income tax return and many of the more common schedules and supplementary forms. Some will even print the actual return for you. As of 1990, California will accept returns filed electronically right from your computer—you don't even have to mail it in!

Typing Instruction

Since many people can't type well, and since all computers have keyboards, doesn't it make sense to have the computer teach typing? Of course it does, and you can pick the typing tutor program of your choice.

There are typing instruction programs available for all skill levels, even for children. Obviously, you aren't expected to be able to type before you run the program, so using it is simple. Many include practice drills to improve your skills and can guide you at exactly the pace you choose.

Games

As personal computers steadily become less expensive, more and more of them are appearing in homes. Just as in businesses, people are finding uses for them in varied and unexpected ways. Personal computers can be used for personal records and bookkeeping, entertainment, education, research, and just about anything else. All of the same programs you use at work may also be useful at home. One big market for at-home software is games.

There are so many different kinds of games it's nearly certain you'll find one you love to play.

There are strategy games, sports games, fast-action arcade games, and just about anything else you can imagine. The average computer software store sells many times more games than it does "serious" software.

Simulations

Simulation games are usually less fast-paced or action-packed than arcade-style games. They might create the world of a red ant colony, and you have to forage for food, fight off attackers, and generally try to take over the entire backyard.

Flight simulators are especially popular. Microsoft's Flight Simulator 4 lets you fly most types of aircraft, from a little Cessna 152 to a Boeing 747-400 or an F-117A Stealth fighter. You can even design your own airplane and fly it. Air flight programs run the whole gamut, from glorified arcade games to meticulous re-creations of flight conditions, weather, instrument failures, and air traffic. Figure 8-7 shows a typical flight simulator.

8

Strategy

Computers have been playing chess for years, but it wasn't until recently that they attained Grand Master status. Today, there are purpose-built computers that can beat virtually any human opponent; playing by international rules, including time limits. Even chess programs for a run-of-the-mill personal computer can challenge most people. In fact, most chess programs allow you to control the level of play so that your PC doesn't beat you *every* time.

Besides chess, there are programs for playing cards (poker, bridge, solitaire), checkers, Mah Jongg, even three-dimensional tic-tac-toe. And, there are strategy games on another level.

How would you like to control an entire army, re-creating a famous battle of years gone by? Complete with historical weather conditions, manpower, weapons, and terrain, you can be in charge of historical situations like never before. The scenario is from the history books, but the strategy is yours.

Sports

You can find sports games for every level of armchair athlete. Football, baseball, golf, tennis, and basketball are all available. Some let you manage teams of real-life players and create your own championship series. Others pit you one-on-one against a computer-controlled opponent.

Obviously, the skills you need for a computer simulation are much different from those needed for the real sport. But the realism of the graphics, the fluid motion, and the actual sounds of a ball game—or the quacking of ducks in the water hazard—can all contribute to an exciting game.

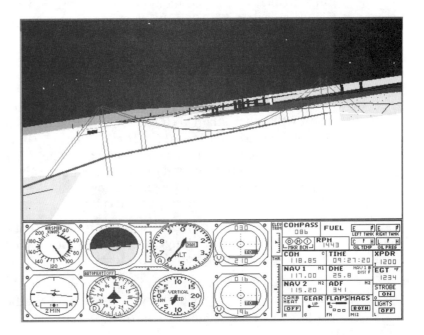

At the controls of a flight simulator **Figure 8-7.**

Educational Software

A personal computer can make an attentive and patient instructor. You can find software to teach children spelling, math, reading, or counting skills, or to teach yourself auto repair, cooking, or another language. You can find programs for numerous subjects and for varying audiences.

Bibliography

You can find more information about application programs in the following books, all published by Osborne/McGraw-Hill in Berkeley, California.

Biow, Lisa. *Quattro Pro 4 Made Easy.* 1992

Campbell, Mary. *Harvard Graphics for Windows Made Easy.* 1992

Campbell, Mary. *1-2-3 Release 2.4 Made Easy.* 1992

Ettlin, Walter A. *WordStar for DOS Made Easy.* 1992

Fingerman, Daniel J. *Ami Pro Made Easy.* 1992

Hoffman, Paul. *Microsoft Word 6 Made Easy.* 1993

Ihrig, Emil, Sybil Ihrig, Martin S. Matthews, and Carole Boggs Matthews. *CorelDRAW! 3 Made Easy.* 1993

Johnson, Yvonne and Bruce C. Smith. *TurboTax Made Easy.* 1993

Jones, Edward. *Paradox 4 Made Easy.* 1993

Jones, Edward. *FoxPro 2.5 Made Easy.* 1993

Liskin, Miriam. *dBASE III Plus Made Easy.* 1988

Matthews, Martin S. *Excel 4 for Windows Made Easy.* 1992

Mincberg, Mella. *WordPerfect 5.1 Made Easy.* 1990

Nadler, James. *Microsoft Publisher Made Easy.* 1992

O'Brien, Stephen K., John V. Hedtke, and Arnold Berman. *Peachtree Accounting Made Easy.* 1990

8

CHAPTER

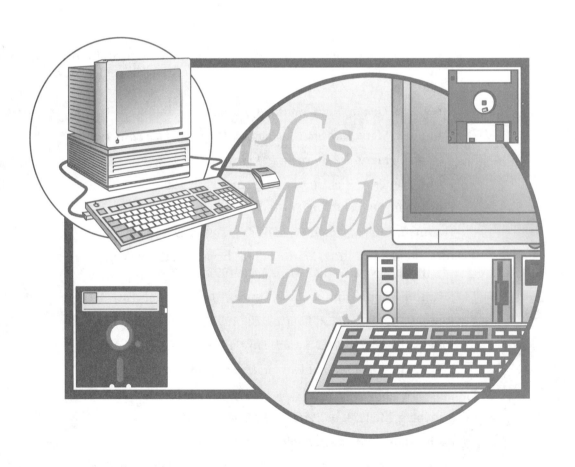

HOW DO I PRINT?

Word processing lets you print letter-perfect documents, desktop publishing lets you go one step further and make terrific presentation materials, and with a spreadsheet you can make a detailed and automatic ledger. But how does all of this stuff actually find its way onto paper? Your computer can't print automatically and it can't operate a typewriter by remote control. If you want to print something and not just admire it on the screen, you have to have an additional piece of equipment called—you guessed it—a printer.

Printers come in all shapes, sizes, and prices. If you don't already have a printer, you'll have a lot of choices when you pick one out. Some printers offer better print quality than others, some are faster, and some can print in color. Nothing says you must have a printer to go with your personal computer, by the way. You and your PC can have a full and rewarding life together without the benefit of a printer. But if you're looking forward to seeing your name (and your other work) in print, this chapter will spell it out for you.

Printers

Before getting into the details of printers and printing, let's take a moment to look over the whole concept of printing.

Figure 9-1 shows a typical arrangement of a PC and printer. Your PC sits on your desk or table, wherever is most comfortable and convenient for you. Your printer normally sits somewhere nearby, say within about ten feet. The two are connected by a cable.

When you're ready to print something, your computer sends the appropriate electrical signals to your printer through the cable. It tells the printer what to print and where and how. Printers normally print

A typical PC
and printer
arrangement
Figure 9-1.

from left to right across the page, and from top to bottom, just like a typewriter.

When it gets to the end of a page, and needs to start a second page, you can have your printer stop and wait until you manually feed another sheet of paper into the printer—again, just like a typewriter.

A printer is not a necessary accessory, but it sure is a useful one.

You can also have your printer go from one page to the next automatically. One way to do this is to use the infamous "computer paper" with the holes along the edges, fan-folded into one continuous sheet. Banks and other companies that print many long reports like to use this kind of paper. There are also printers that can simply feed a new sheet of regular 81/2-by-11-inch bond, though. You supply the printer with a stack of paper like a photocopier, and it automatically pulls the next sheet off the stack.

It used to be that computer printers required special paper to print on. We've all seen the fan-fold paper, with the row of holes along both edges, or the "green bar" paper, with its alternate pale green and white stripes. Fortunately, that's not true anymore. With just a couple of exceptions, any printer you pick to use with your PC should be able to print on any paper you give it. That means you can print business letters directly on your company letterhead. You can even print overhead "slides" directly onto clear transparencies.

Laser Printers

9

If you're only going to get one printer, and you've got the money, a laser printer is the way to go. Laser printers are still relatively expensive compared to other kinds of printers, but they produce terrific results and can handle text and graphics with equal ability.

Some printers can print only basic letters and numbers; others can print pictures as well.

Laser printers are a medium-sized piece of equipment, probably about the size of your personal computer. They are boxy looking, with a paper feed tray sticking out from one end. Figure 9-2 shows what the typical laser printer looks like. They are not too heavy to place on a desk or small table, and they are very quiet when they are running.

As the name implies, laser printers use a laser beam to "draw" the words you want printed onto paper. The finished result looks almost like it came off a printing press. Technically, laser printers operate on the same principle as photocopiers, but since most people don't understand

Laser printers
are about the
size of your
personal
computer
Figure 9-2.

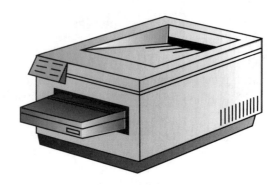

photocopiers either, that's not a very helpful comparison. Suffice it to say that laser printers produce the best, cleanest, most professional-looking documents of any printer you can buy.

This is an example of text printed with a laser printer.

One of the reasons that laser printers are so popular with small businesses is that they can print on nearly any kind of paper. They don't need the ugly fan-fold paper that some other printers do. Instead, laser printers can print right onto your company's letterhead or on colored stock, for example. Many laser printers can even print directly onto clear plastic transparencies so you can make overhead presentations. About the only kind of paper that a laser printer can't use is heavy card stock or oversize sheets.

Laser
printers are
the top of the
line for PC
printing, and
priced to
match.

Basic laser printers will set you back about $1000. Newer ones are introduced all the time, and a top-of-the-line printer may be $3000 or more. What the added cost buys you is faster printing, more and varied fonts (covered later), multiple paper hoppers, and better *resolution*. Some of the medium- to high-priced laser printers also offer something called PostScript. For a quick description of this feature, look ahead to the section on PostScript.

NEW WORD: Resolution is the measure of how smooth or grainy the output of your printer is. The higher the resolution, the smoother and more attractive the print will be.

All laser printers are reasonably fast. They can typically produce four to six complete pages every minute. More expensive printers can run even faster. Also, laser printers have a paper hopper, where you place blank paper for them to print on. The hopper holds about 100 standard sheets of paper. Some printers have more than one hopper so you could, for example, load one with letterhead and the other with typing bond.

Laser printers are very versatile and can print on many kinds of paper.

Because laser printers work very much like small photocopiers, you maintain your laser printer in much the same way. Every so often, you have to replace the *toner* (the black powder that acts as the ink) and maybe clean out some of the inside of the printer. Changing the toner turns out to be very easy. Nearly all laser printers keep their toner inside a sealed cartridge that also holds the printing drum. Whenever the toner runs out, you simply replace the entire cartridge, drum and all. New toner/drum cartridges cost about $75 to $120, but you'll only have to replace it after thousands of pages have been printed. For the average small office, that's four months or more between changes.

All laser printers can print graphics as well as text. If you want to be able to print charts, graphs, pictures, or other figures on paper, you'll have to select a graphics printer, and laser printers offer graphics printing capability without sacrificing the quality of text. You can print a business letter one minute and a map to your weekend party the next.

9

LED Printers

LED printers offer you all the same features and benefits of laser printers, but for a little bit less money. An LED (light-emitting diode) takes the place of the laser, making the average LED printer a little bit smaller than a laser printer.

Dot Matrix Printers

By far the most popular kind of printer for the average personal
computer user is the dot matrix printer. These are capable, low-cost
printers that can be used for nearly anything. They're fast and
inexpensive, they produce good quality printing, and they're available
from any number of manufacturers. There are probably five times more
dot matrix printers in use than all the other kinds of printers put
together.

Dot matrix printers get their name from the way they make impressions
on the paper. The printer looks more or less like an electric typewriter
(see Figure 9-3), but without the keyboard. (Who needs a keyboard?
Your computer will do the "typing.") The paper rolls from the back of
the printer, around a hard rubber platen, and up between the ribbon
and the print head. On a typewriter, there would be a bunch of keys or
a print ball in front of the ribbon, but a dot-matrix printer has a bunch
of fine pins instead.

Zippy Pinhead

The pins on a dot matrix printer are arranged in a vertical column, the
ends pointing toward the ribbon and paper like a firing squad. To make
a letter, the pins extend forward just enough to strike the paper and
then pull back into place. That makes a vertical column of dots.

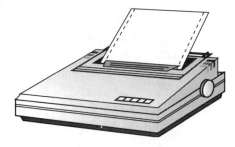

Dot matrix
printers look
like an electric
typewriter
without the
keyboard
Figure 9-3.

Then the print head, with the pins, moves a little bit to the right and makes another column of dots.

If you repeat this procedure about eight times, you've got one letter printed. As tedious as this sounds, a good dot matrix printer can print an entire line across the page in less than a second!

Most dot matrix printers have more than one speed: fast or high quality.

The price you pay for this speed is that the printed output looks, well, like it was printed by a computer. If you look at the example in the following illustration, you can see the individual dots that make up each character. On the whole, the printing is very legible, though. You just wouldn't want to send an important business letter that way.

This is an example of dot matrix ouptut.

To solve the grainy dot matrix "computer look" problem, many dot matrix printers have two or even three print modes. The fastest, but worst-looking mode is sometimes called *draft* mode. This is great for printing things for yourself or when the quality of the print is not important. They'll have another, better looking *letter-quality* mode. In this mode the printer will print more slowly, moving left to right at about half the speed of draft mode. This allows the printer to place the dots more precisely so they line up better. It may even allow your printer enough time to put twice as many dots in the same space, so they "fill in" a little bit and look more solid.

9

NEW WORD: To judge how good a printer's print is, use this rule of thumb: Does it look good enough to use for a business letter? If so, it's letter-quality, or LQ printing. If it's almost good enough, it could be NLQ, or near letter-quality.

Rather than call it letter-quality printing, some printer manufacturers are humble enough to recognize the limitations of their printers. They use the term *near letter-quality* printing; better than draft, but not quite good enough for your best letters.

This is an example of dot matrix "NLQ" output.

Pins and Needles

Most of the least expensive dot matrix printers have a print head with 9 pins it. A 9-pin dot matrix printer printed the examples shown previously. You can also find printers with more than 9 pins, and they produce better quality output. Naturally, they cost more, too.

The more pins the dot matrix printer uses, the closer it comes to laser printer quality.

While 9-pin printers produce decidedly grainy characters, dot matrix printers with 16 or even 24 pins can produce some very nice printing, indeed. Coupled with the lower speed, letter-quality printing mode, 24-pin printers can produce very professional looking results. You may want to compare the print quality of a 24-pin dot matrix printer with that of a laser printer.

Paperwork

Unlike a laser printer, some dot matrix printers compel you to use special computer paper. Depending on your particular printer, you may have to use continuous, fan-fold paper from a box. This is the stuff with the rows of little holes down each side of the paper. The holes match up with a sprocket or tractor feed mechanism on your printer. Your computer or stationery store will have plenty of this on hand, and it's not particularly expensive, but you won't be able to use just any old paper.

The fan-fold paper is handy because you only have to feed in the first sheet; after that, the printer pulls the rest of the paper out of the box. Some people don't like this paper because you have to tear the little perforations off at the edge of each sheet. If these bother you, you can get *laser-perforated* fan-fold paper. Whether they have anything to do with lasers or not, the perforations are much smaller and are nearly invisible after you separate the pages.

Other Features

Nearly all dot matrix printers can produce graphics as well as text. Because they make everything out of dots anyway, there's nothing technical preventing them from printing any arbitrary pattern. The only requirement is that your PC and, more importantly, the software you have running on it, be able to control the printer and make it produce graphics. Look carefully at what printers your PC software can use and select your printer accordingly.

If you look around, you can also find dot matrix printers that print in color. These are about the only kind of printer within the average person's price range that can make color printouts. A color dot matrix printer uses a special ribbon with four colors of ink on it (black, yellow, red, and blue) and some tricky machinery to move the ribbon up and down while it's printing.

Daisy Wheel Printers

Before the advent of laser printers, daisy wheel printers were the printer of choice for most business users. With the alternatives of dot matrix printers or typewriters, daisy wheel printers were the only choice for truly professional-looking printing at an affordable price.

While a daisy wheel printer will produce top quality type, it doesn't do pictures at all.

Daisy wheel (or thimble) printers get their silly name from the little metal or plastic disk that they use to print. In principle, it operates very much like a typewriter. The disk has 40 or so little fingers surrounding it, like the petals on a daisy. Each plastic "petal" has a letter or number embossed on it. The disk spins around its center so that each petal on the daisy wheel can be aimed straight up. Behind the topmost position is a small hammer. To print a character, the printer spins the daisy wheel to the correct position, strikes it from behind with the hammer, and moves to the next position to the right. As the printer moves to the right, it rotates the daisy wheel again in preparation for printing the next character.

The quality of the printing is very good, since it uses a standard typewriter ribbon and fully formed characters from an embossed wheel, not unlike a typewriter's keys.

```
This is an example of text printed with a daisy wheel
printer.
```

9

On the down side, daisy wheel printers are very noisy, like an electric typewriter operated by a very fast typist. Also, daisy wheel printers cannot print graphics, since they have only the standard numbers, letters, and symbols at their disposal.

Ink Jet Printers

Ink jet quality is comparable to dot matrix, with the added advantages of light weight and quiet operation.

Ink jet printers work on much the same principle as dot matrix printers. Each character is formed by a group of dots spaced closely together. But where dot matrix printers use pins and an inked ribbon to make a mark, ink jet printers actually spray the ink directly onto the paper!

Ink jet printers are not nearly as common as dot matrix printers, and it's hard to be certain why. They produce printed pages every bit as good as a comparable dot matrix printer. Ink jet printers are also a lot quieter. Because they use no pins, there's no contact with the paper, making these "non-impact" printers quiet enough to use in a library.

Perhaps ink jet printers aren't more common because of the special paper they require. In order for the tiny ink droplets to form nice even spots, the paper must be of very good quality, without being porous. Otherwise, the ink smudges and spreads like coffee on a paper towel. Most any computer store that sells ink jet printers will also stock the proper paper, but many people would rather use whatever is at hand.

Thermal Printers

The final classification of printers covered here is thermal printers. As you might have guessed from the name, these printers use heat to print. They have no ink of any kind and they are very quiet. But how do you print without ink? The answer lies in the special paper.

Thermal printers require you to use special heat-sensitive thermal paper. The paper comes in rolls, like paper towels, and looks slightly shiny. To make a mark on the paper, a thermal printer places the end of a hot wire against the paper for just a fraction of a second. In that sense, thermal printers are much like dot matrix printers, but without the ink. The hot wire makes the paper darken automatically, without using a ribbon or spraying ink.

Thermal printers are normally used where portability is an issue, because they are very small. You would never want to use one to send professional correspondence because the silvery thermal paper doesn't look good. The quality of the print is about on par with an inexpensive dot matrix printer. Be forewarned: the thermal paper is very sensitive to heat, and placing a printout in the sun for a few moments can erase the entire page. Even holding it in your hands for a few minutes will leave "fingerprints."

Plotters

There is a whole different family of printing devices other than printers. They are not as common as printers and not as flexible. They are used primarily in engineering laboratories or by architecture, engineering, or drafting professionals. If you have a particular need, these devices may fit the bill.

A plotter prints, but it is not a printer. Plotters are used for drawing lines, particularly the lines on an architectural or engineering drawing. Where printers are used primarily for text, with perhaps a little bit of graphics, plotters are used primarily for graphics. An example of plotter output is shown in Figure 9-4.

A plotter is different from a printer because it holds the paper still and moves a pen around to draw. In fact, plotters can be fascinating to watch, as a little mechanical hand clasps a colored pen or pencil and draws figures across a sheet of paper. Where plotters excel is at drawing on large sheets, like building plans, rather than standard letter-sized paper. Nearly all plotters can plot in color, too.

9

What Is an Interface?

Before you can print, your computer needs to be able to "talk" to your printer so the printer knows what to print. Usually, it does this through the cable that runs between the two machines. You attach one end of the cable to your computer and the other end to the printer. Seems simple, right?

Naturally, it can never be that simple. Different computers and different printers have been developed by different engineers at different companies with different ideas about how this should all

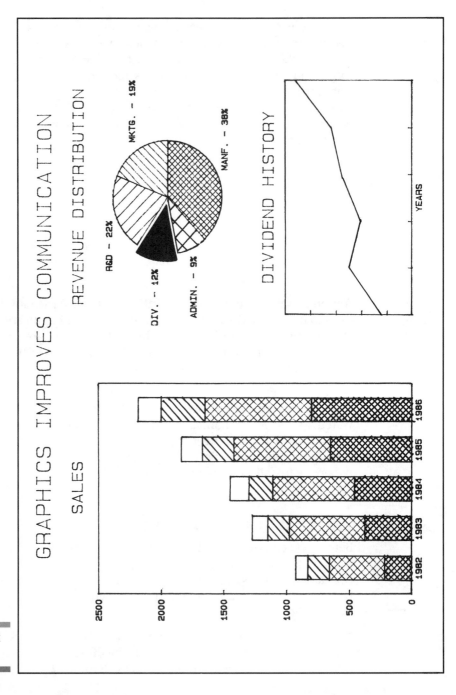

Plotter output
Figure 9-4.

work. It's not surprising then, that there are a few different ways to make your computer and your printer communicate. All of these issues fall under the heading of printer interfacing.

Interface is one of these horrible technical words that should have been left in the laboratory. Briefly, it describes the way that two different things (in this case, your computer and your printer) can work together. An interface defines what kind of cable you need, how you connect the cable, and how the two machines will "talk" to each other once the cable is connected. The whole subject is fairly technical, but there are a few things that you need to know.

NEW WORD: An interface is a method of communicating between two different pieces of equipment. It originally comes from mathematics or geology, and describes that flat surface where two different surfaces touch.

There are three basic kinds of interfaces: serial, parallel, and network. Of these three, the first two are the most common. There are no real advantages or disadvantages to any of them, except where noted in the following descriptions. Where you need to pay attention is when you want to buy or attach a printer to your computer. You must have the same kind of interface on each one.

9

Parallel Interface

Probably the most popular way (by a whisker) to connect a printer to a PC is through a *parallel* interface. There are two reasons for this. First, a parallel interface is easier to set up and configure than a serial interface. The other reason is that parallel interfaces aren't good for anything else. If you don't use your PC's parallel interface for a printer, it's wasted.

A parallel interface sends data between your PC and your printer through a cable with a bundle of a dozen or more wires. The first eight wires each carry one bit of data (remember eight data bits to a byte?). The other wires are used to control the flow of information. Theoretically, a parallel interface should be able to move information to your printer eight times faster than a serial interface, but that's not the case. Don't let speed sway you. The two interfaces operate at comparable speeds, and either one will be faster than your printer anyway.

A parallel interface is also sometimes called a *Centronics* interface, after the printer company that popularized it. If you have an IBM-compatible PC, your parallel interfaces will be called LPT1, LPT2, and so on. You may have up to three of them. We can only assume that LPT is an abbreviation for line printer, an indication of just how old the roots of PC-DOS are.

If your PC does, in fact, have one or more parallel interface ports, they probably won't be labeled as such on the back of your computer. Instead, you'll have to learn to recognize the connector. Virtually all PCs use the same 25-pin female D-shaped connector for their parallel interfaces. It looks something like this:

Your PC will dictate which type of interface you use. The difference is all on the inside.

The irregular D shape is to keep you from plugging in the cable from your printer backwards. As such, it works, so don't force it. Pay particular attention to the 25 little holes in the connector. Is it really a female connector? If it's not, you may be looking at a serial interface port, which, by a very unhappy coincidence, looks almost identical.

Serial Interface

A *serial* interface uses a cable that only has a few wires in it. All of the data is transferred from your computer to your printer down one wire, one bit of information after another, in a series; hence, the name.

If you have an IBM-compatible PC, your serial interfaces (you may have up to four) are called *COM ports*. *Port* comes from the fact that your PC imports and exports data from the serial interface, like ships from a port; *COM* is short for *communication*. The PC manual calls them COM1, COM2, and so on.

When you have time, look on the back of your PC for the serial interface connectors. They are usually not labeled, so you have to learn to recognize them. Some are small 9-pin male D-shaped connectors, like this:

Other PCs use the larger 25-pin male D-shaped connector. Your computer may very well have both kinds. There's absolutely no difference between the two connector styles. Neither one is better or worse than the other, they're just different.

Either way, the connector will always have pins sticking out at you. If you find something that looks close but is a female connector, it may be a parallel interface port instead.

Setting up a printer with a serial interface can be somewhat more complicated than setting up a parallel interface. There are just more things that need to be attended to. On the other hand, serial ports are, in general, more useful than parallel ports, which are only used for printers. Serial interfaces are also good for a modem, a mouse, or many other add-on devices.

9

Baud Rate

Your PC and printer must be in sync to transmit data. The baud rates must match.

If you're setting up a printer with a serial interface, you should get some help from the printer manual. One of the things it will tell you to do is to configure the serial interface on your PC the same way as the serial interface on the printer. Here's what some of those terms mean.

The most important thing about a serial interface is the speed that it transmits data. Your PC and your printer have to agree on how fast the data will be transmitted. If they're not exactly the same, your printer won't print. The speed of a serial interface is measured in bits per second. Oddly, nobody abbreviates this as BPS; instead it's called *baud rate*. Regardless of what it's called, it always runs in multiples of 300. A speed of 300 baud is a snail's crawl, 1200 baud is tolerable, 2400 is fair,

4800 is good, 9600 is better, and 19,200 is great. If you can get it to run faster than that, write and tell me.

NEW WORD: Baud rate is the measure of speed for a serial communications interface. It is almost, but not exactly, the same as bits per second. The word *baud* is a corruption of the French name Baudot.

Data Bits

You may have to select the number of *data bits* you want to transmit. This doesn't mean the total number; nobody could be expected to know that in advance. It means the number of data bits in each "packet" sent to your printer. The value isn't important, as long as you pick something that both your computer and your printer agree on. Normally, this would be eight data bits.

Start Bits and Stop Bits

On interface details: after the first time, you should be able to set 'em and forget 'em.

After setting the correct baud rate, you will need to make sure that the number of *start* and *stop bits* is compatible. Don't worry about the technical meaning of all this, just pick a value that both your PC and your printer can support. When in doubt, pick 1.

Parity

Occasionally you will be called upon to select the parity of the communications interface. *Parity* is something that checks that the data you sent from the computer got to the printer okay. It sounds like a terrific idea, but it's next to worthless because data never gets lost along the way and even if it did, the parity would only detect it half of the time. Your choices are usually odd parity, even parity, or none. Select none unless you have a compelling need to do otherwise.

Using the MODE Command

If you are running a PC with DOS, you can set all of these serial communications values (or *parameters,* in the parlance) with one command. That command is MODE. The MODE command will set data bits, stop bits, parity, and baud rate all at once. (The number of start bits is always 1.)

The general format is to type **MODE** and all of the values you want set, one after the other, with commas in between. Your DOS manual will spell this out for you in detail, but an example should help:

```
C:\>MODE com1:9600,N,8,1

COM1: 9600,n,8,1,-

C:\>
```

This example sets serial port COM1 to 9600 baud (the speed), no parity, 8 data bits, and 1 stop bit.

After you type in this command and press ⌈Enter⌉, your PC will report back what the port was set to. The port will be set until you turn your PC off or reset it. After that, you'll have to set it again.

Using the Windows Control Panel

If you're running Windows, there's a simpler way to set your serial port. From the Program Manager window, select the Control Panel application.

From the Control Panel window, select the Ports icon.

From the Ports window, select the serial port (COM1, COM2, and so forth) that you want to configure. Click the Settings... button with your mouse.

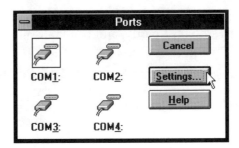

Now you will see the current setting for that serial port. You are given the opportunity to change as many values (parameters) as you want. When you've got them set the right way, select the OK button.

TIP: If you want to set up more than one serial port the same way, you can drag the icon of one serial port (COM1) over the icon of another (COM2). This works from the Control Panel/Ports window.

Network Interface

If your personal computer is attached to a network, you may be able to connect your printer to the network as well. (For a description of computer networks, turn to Chapter 10.)

Apple LaserWriter printers are good examples of printers that are available with network connections. A good laser printer like the LaserWriter is a significant investment, and it can be easier to justify if more than one person can share it easily.

Apart from Apple printers, most PC printers do not offer network connections. If you do have a network, this is worth exploring with your printer salesperson.

Printer Buffer

When you are printing something, it can often take all of your computer's attention. Unless you have a very fast computer you might not be able to use your PC again until all of the printing is finished.

That's because there's a lot of data that has to be transferred from your computer to your printer, and most printers can't accept very much at once. Consequently, your PC has to "spoon feed" your printer at the printer's preferred rate.

A buffer can store a file to be printed, freeing your PC for the next task.

There are a couple of different solutions to this problem. First, some printers have more memory than others, and a printer with a lot of memory will be able to accept and store more printing commands before it forces your PC to slow down. Printers can always accept printing commands from the PC faster than they can actually print, like filling a bucket with a small leak. Printing commands pour in and printed copy dribbles out. You might be able to increase the size of your printer's bucket by adding more memory.

Another, less-expensive approach is also more automatic. Many application programs now allow you to do something called "background printing." When you give the print command, your application program (a word processor is a typical example) will divide its attention between the printer and its normal function, so that you can keep working. This works better on faster PCs, with more CPU horsepower to spare. Any application running with Windows does this automatically.

If you do a lot of printing and "printer slow down" becomes a problem, you might want to investigate something called a printer buffer. A printer *buffer* is nothing more than a little box with some memory. You plug your printer cable into the box and then use a second cable to connect the box to your computer. That puts the box in between your PC and printer.

9

NEW WORD: In general, a buffer is an amount of memory that's used for temporary data storage. A printer buffer collects data to be printed, thus freeing the PC.

The printer buffer acts as a big sponge, soaking up all of the printing commands as fast as your computer can send them. Then, when it gets full, it forwards the information to your printer, perhaps at a slower rate.

Sharing a Printer

If you don't have a network and you want to share one printer with different people, each with his or her own PC, you can use a combination printer buffer and multiplexer. Where a standard printer buffer has just one input for your computer and one output for your printer, a printer-sharing buffer will have five, six, or more inputs for multiple computers. Some even have more than one printer output. Such a box allows any computer to use any printer at any time.

As this illustration shows, the printer-sharing buffer sits at the middle of a big "octopus" of cables, computers, and printers.

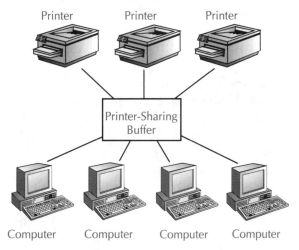

Each computer is connected to the box via a cable, and each printer, too. When you buy the printer-sharing buffer, you should also receive some software and instructions. The instructions will explain how to install the software on each PC that will be using the buffer box. When you are ready to print, you may be required to type a special command, so that the printer-sharing buffer knows which printer you want to use.

If more than one person tries to use the same printer, the buffer box can often store one person's entire print job in its memory until the other person is done using the printer. This gives the appearance of both computers printing at once.

What Is a Font?

Many, many, many times when you're dealing with printers you'll hear or see the word *font*. You see it in word processing manuals, in printer manuals, in advertisements for desktop publishing programs, and even throughout this book. If you don't understand what a font is, you'll find a lot of the information that follows confusing.

Any printer that can print graphics can print unusual fonts too.

A font is a particular style of print. No two people write their names exactly the same way. Different newspapers use different styles of print. A book is not printed in the same style as a newspaper or an advertising brochure. These are all examples of different fonts. It used to be that computer printers could only print in one particular, fixed font, so the issue of fonts never came up for most PC users. But now, as printers and printing programs become ever more capable, you are faced with a lot of happy decisions.

Type Style

A font consists of two related things: type style and type size. Let's look at the style first because it's the most interesting, and because it has more of an effect on how your printed material will look.

There are literally thousands of different type styles available in the printing industry. Newspapers, books, magazines, brochures, typewriters—they all use different type styles. A *type style* is like a person's handwriting; it gives personality to printing. Some type styles look very elegant, others are bold and attract attention. Type styles can be silly, elaborate, futuristic, or old-fashioned.

9

If you look at the two samples of type in the following illustration, you can see how different they look. Everybody who can read has been exposed to hundreds of different type styles; you just may not have known what they were called.

Each particular type style has a name. Helvetica, Times Roman, and Courier are all popular type styles. Of the thousands of type styles that have been developed, many look similar, but each one is a little bit different from the rest.

NOTE: Many people don't know that type styles are copyrighted. Each type style is created by a font artist, whose job it is to create a particular type style or "face." Each individual letter and number must be made just so, and upper- and lowercase versions created. They must all look like part of the same set and line up attractively next to each other on the page. Font artists treat each letter as a tiny piece of art, and they are granted a copyright on the design. That means that font styles may not be copied without the permission of the font designer.

Generally speaking, the more type styles your printer can print, the better off you are. Having an assortment of type styles at your disposal gives you more creativity in your printed output. You may never use them all, but it's nice to know they're there.

Some printers can print in more than one type style, but can only use a limited number of them on a page. For example, a dot-matrix printer may be capable of printing in seven different styles, but only allow you to use two of them on the same page. Another model of printer might print with an unlimited number of type styles, but only a few at a time. Still other models can print with any number of type styles in any combination at all. If you're still shopping, check each model for its capabilities.

Type Size

The other part of a font is type size. The type size is just that, the size of the print. Headlines in the newspaper are printed in a large size, while the captions under the pictures are printed in a much smaller size.

Type size is measured in *points*. One point is 1/72 of an inch high, so 1-point type would be extremely small. The proverbial "small print" at the bottom of a contract is typically about 6- or 8-point type. Another measure is the *pica*. Twelve points make a pica, so there are 6 picas to the inch. (The reasons for this are historical, dating back almost to Gutenberg's time, and aren't important here.)

 NEW WORD: A point is a measure of how big a printed character is. Most of the print in this book is 10 points high, or about 1/7 of an inch tall. A pica is 12 points, like a foot is 12 inches.

The combination of a type style (Helvetica or Courier, for example) and a type size (8-point, 12-point, and so on) makes a font. Courier 10 is one font, while Courier 12 is another, slightly larger, font.

Downloaded Fonts

If your printer can print more than one font, it might have the fonts "built in" or you might be able to "download" fonts to it. Most printers fall into the first category. When you buy the printer, it comes with anywhere from one to a dozen fonts built in. Your PC can use any one of these by sending the proper commands to the printer when it comes time to print. But you may be able to expand on those built-in fonts.

Dot matrix and laser printers can change fonts automatically. You must change a daisy wheel yourself.

Other printers come with font cartridges. These are plug-in packages, about the size of a deck of cards, that you can plug into a special socket in your printer. Each font cartridge will let your printer create additional fonts. These are in addition to whatever built-in fonts you already have. Most printers that use font cartridges have sockets for one or two of them at a time.

The third alternative is to download fonts. Most printers can do this, but some can't. Downloading fonts works just like font cartridges, except the font information comes from your PC instead of from a cartridge that you plug in. Just before you print, your PC will send a lot of special information to your printer to "teach" it how to print in a particular font. That's called downloading. The whole process only takes about 30 seconds.

If your printer will accept downloaded fonts, you can buy font software at your computer store and build a library of different fonts to keep on disk. TrueType and Bitstream are two examples. They may cost a few dollars each, or they may cost several hundred. Remember, most fonts

9

are copyrighted, and many people are surprised at how much it costs to license a copyrighted font.

When the font is downloaded, it is stored in the memory inside the printer. Some printers have more memory than others. A printer with a lot of memory (say, 1MB or more) can hold more than one downloaded font at a time.

Proportional and Fixed Spacing

In font spacing, there are two broad categories of fonts: proportional fonts and fixed-width fonts. You probably already know what the difference is between them, but just don't realize it.

Proportional spacing has a more natural look than fixed-width fonts.

Let's start with proportional fonts. Apart from how tall a printed character is, there is also the width to deal with. Every character in the font set (letter, number, symbol, and so on) has a particular width. A capital letter *W* is wider than a small letter *i* for example. To make the page look as nice as possible, you want to space the characters side-to-side based upon the width of each individual character. That is, the spacing is *proportional* to the width of the characters.

Nearly everything you read is proportionally spaced. This book is printed with proportionally spaced characters. So are newspapers, magazines, and professional advertising. About the only thing that's not normally proportionally spaced is typewritten text.

If you don't use proportional spacing, you get *fixed* spacing between characters (also known as *monospacing*). Each letter, number, and punctuation mark gets the same amount of room (side-to-side) as every other character. This is how typewriters work. You can always tell fixed-space (or fixed-pitch) printing because the letters line up into neat little columns down the page.

```
This is an example of a fixed-space typeface.
Notice how the characters are vertically aligned.
```

These days, fixed-space printing is considered unprofessional and there's no real reason to use it. Nearly any new printer that you can buy today will include at least one proportional font. Use it, and you'll find that your output looks much better.

Choosing a Printer

There are many things to consider when choosing a printer. Do you want one that can print graphics as well as text? Do you want one that's fast, or one that's quiet? How much are you willing to spend? A good dot matrix printer can be had for just a few hundred dollars. For that price, you can have both text and good quality graphics, use standard paper, and have a reliable machine that won't need a lot of maintenance. This section explores some of the features of today's personal computer printers and defines some new terms.

Pages per Minute

One measure of a printer's speed and performance is the page-per-minute, or *PPM,* rating. This measures just what it sounds like it measures—the number of complete pages that a printer can print in one minute. The higher this number, the better.

 NEW WORD: The abbreviation PPM stands for pages per minute. The PPM rating measures how many pages full of text a printer can print in one minute.

The PPM rating is used more often with laser printers than with dot matrix or daisy wheel printers. That's because they really do print entire pages at once, not line-by-line as the other kinds do. A speed of 4 to 8 PPM is about average for a low-cost laser printer. The more expensive laser printers can go faster, and they usually have other more exotic features, too. While 4 pages per minute may seem awfully fast now, you'd be surprised how quickly you'll become impatient with it and wish you'd bought a faster one.

Be careful when comparing different printers' PPM ratings. All may not be as it appears. Any laser printer can print pictures as well as text, but the pictures normally take longer to print. The PPM rating is usually only valid for printing text. The printer will slow way down when it comes time to print a picture (even a small one) in the middle of a page. Pay attention to the fine print when comparing speeds.

9

Characters per Second

If you're looking at dot matrix or daisy wheel printers, their speed is measured in characters per second, or *CPS*. The more characters per second a printer can print, the faster it will finish your page.

 NEW WORD: The abbreviation CPS stands for characters per second and it measures how fast some printers can print. The higher the number, the faster the printer.

There are usually two trade-offs you have to make for a higher CPS speed. First, the printer will be noisier, because it's trying to move more paper through and it's moving its print head faster. Second, the quality of the print will go way down. It's not possible to print characters as accurately at 180 CPS as it is at 40 CPS.

Laser printers and LED printers don't have a CPS rating because they don't print individual characters, as dot matrix and daisy wheel printers do.

Printing Graphics

Everyone expects a printer to print words, letters, and numbers. But some printers can print pictures, too. Graphics can be a picture of a car, a house, or a horse, or it can be a pie chart created with your spreadsheet. Graphics aren't necessarily pictures in the common sense. Graphics are anything that's not text. If you can create it with a standard manual typewriter, it's not graphics.

It used to be that most printers couldn't print graphics; now it's unusual to find a new printer that *can't* print graphics. Carefully evaluate your needs and decide if graphics is something that you'll ever need to print. It sure doesn't hurt to have that capability on hand, even if you don't anticipate a need for it right away.

Dot matrix printers can print graphics because everything they print is made up of little dots anyway. As long as your PC can send the right commands to it, the printer is capable and willing. Laser printers can also print graphics, for much the same reason. Even though their dots are much closer together, they still make every character out of a matrix of dots. Consequently, they make much sharper graphics than a dot matrix printer can.

About the only kind of printers that can't print graphics are the daisy wheel and thimble printers. They use fully formed letters stamped from a plastic or metal mold, so they can't make the shape of anything that's not on their wheel or thimble. On the other hand, the quality of their letters is top-notch. Until laser printers became popular, they were the printers of choice for most businesses.

Dots per Inch

For laser and LED printers you'll hear about something called resolution and *DPI* (dots per inch). These two terms describe the quality of the printed output, or how smooth or grainy it looks. Obviously, the smoother (less grainy) the printing is, the better.

NEW WORD: The abbreviation DPI stands for dots per inch. It measures how many tiny dots of ink a laser printer uses for every square inch of paper. The more dots, the better the printing looks.

9

Since laser and LED printers create the final page with dots of laser light, it makes sense that the closer together the dots are, the better the output will look. If the dots are too far apart, you'll be able to see them, and the words, letters, and numbers will appear grainy, as they do from a dot matrix printer. If the dots are too close together they will touch and seem to run together, and you will have a much harder time seeing the individual dots.

The smoothness or graininess of laser printer output is measured in DPI. The more dots per square inch, the better, kind of like the threads in an Oriental carpet. The rating of 300 DPI has been the standard for many years. If you look very closely (perhaps with a magnifying glass), you can see the individual dots, but other than that, the output looks very good.

For truly professional work, though, 300 DPI is not enough. You will want a printer that can produce 600 or even 1000 DPI. These are considerably more expensive than "standard" 300 DPI printers, though, and out of reach for the average personal computer user.

Software Support

There's sometimes a lot more involved in getting your new printer to work than just picking it out and plugging it in. Unfortunately, this part can be a little bit tricky, and it is necessarily a bit technical, so hang on tight.

When you get your PC and your printer connected via a cable they should be "talking." That is, your computer should be able to send electronic signals to your printer to make it do things. But what is your computer going to say? Attaching the cable and configuring the interface is only the beginning. That takes care of the hardware. The rest involves software.

Make sure your application program will work with your printer.

No two printers are alike. Manufacturers build their printers differently, and different models from the same manufacturer have different features, too. Some are wider than others, some are faster. Some can print graphics, and some can print in multiple fonts. You'll want your computer to take advantage of all the neat features that attracted you to your printer, but it may not know how.

Is there anything that all printers do the same way? Fortunately, all printers agree on how to print the alphabet. As ridiculous as that sounds, that's about all that they all agree upon. They don't all agree on how to print graphics, or how to switch fonts (if at all), or how to underline a word. But they can all print the alphabet, so let's start there.

For the last several years, there has been a standard that computer and printer manufacturers adhere to called the *ASCII* standard. (ASCII is pronounced like *ASK-ee*, not *ASK-ee-too*.) The ASCII code defines what the electronic computer codes are for all the letters of the alphabet (both upper- and lowercase), the numbers (0 through 9), and the dozen or so most common punctuation marks; in short, the stuff on a typewriter keyboard.

NEW WORD: The American Standard Code for Information Interchange (ASCII) defines how computers and printers store and transmit letters and numbers. It does not define how to store or transmit special effects, like underlining, bold face, or italics, nor is it good for pictures. ASCII is universally pronounced *ASK-ee.*

What the ASCII code is not good at is describing how to make your printer do anything other than print the alphabet. That's where the printer manufacturers have taken things into their own hands, and everyone has come up with a different scheme. What makes one printer underline a word may make another one change colors or stop printing altogether.

That means your application programs (word processing, spreadsheet, and so on) each have to know how to "talk" to your particular brand and model of printer. If an application program doesn't support your particular printer, you may not be able to print from that application. For example, if your word processor supports your printer but your spreadsheet doesn't, you'll be able to print written documents with no problem, but you may have trouble when printing spreadsheets.

Each application program normally comes with the ability to talk with many different kinds of printers. The printers that are supported may be listed on the outside of the package. Each different printer supported requires a little piece of software called a printer *driver*. If your application doesn't support your chosen printer, you may be able to request a driver from the printer maker, or from the software company.

9

 NEW WORD: A device driver is a special kind of software that lets your computer work with a new device, peripheral, or printer.

If you have a PC running Windows, some of the problem goes away. Windows applications don't need to know what kind of printer you have. Instead, Windows takes care of it for them. Consequently, Windows does need to know what kind of printer you have. If not, none of your applications will be able to print.

PostScript

To help remedy the compatibility problem, a company in California called Adobe (as in mud bricks) developed a "printer description language" and called it PostScript. The plan was to use PostScript as a universally accepted middle ground between computers and printers. If all computers would print to an imaginary PostScript printer, and all printers accepted PostScript commands, then the whole printer compatibility problem would go away.

A PC and a printer that both use PostScript are automatically compatible.

The problem was, PostScript was very expensive and printer makers were not motivated to change over from their old ways. Today, PostScript has some support, but it is by no means universal. Several printers support PostScript, typically the more expensive ones (PostScript compatibility adds nearly $1000 to the price of a printer). There are also many applications that will "talk" to a PostScript printer.

Hopefully, in this chapter you've seen the many options available to you for printing. There are certainly a lot of choices and if you're evaluating what printer might be best for you or your workgroup, you'll find the time well-spent.

CHAPTER

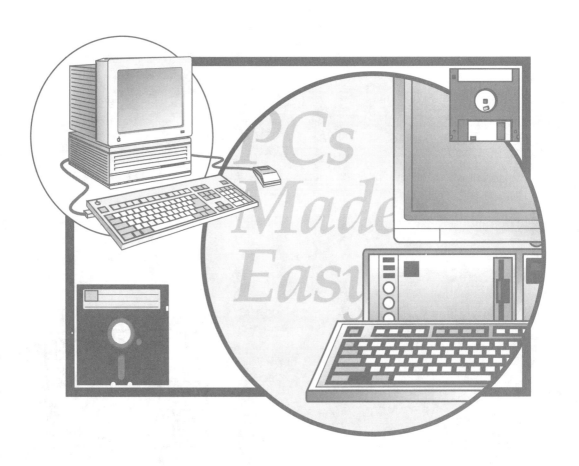

10

WHAT IS A NETWORK?

A new, exciting, and fast-growing part of the personal computer world is networking. Networking allows you and the people you work with to share information easily. Networking also makes it easier for a group of computer users to work together. You can exchange files between computers instantly. You can exchange messages with electronic mail. And you can share the workload during group projects. Networking turns each person's computer island into part of a computer community.

How Does a Net Work?

A computer network is a new idea for most people, and it takes a little bit of explaining to understand. First of all, a network, like a telephone, only makes sense if you have two or more computers to connect. Secondly, those computers should be relatively close together—in the same office, or at least on the same floor. Most people using a computer network use it to connect about half a dozen computers within the same office.

A network (also called a *local area network,* or *LAN*) is an electronic highway connecting personal computers. Adding a network to your computer group involves connecting them all to each other with wires, like stringing Christmas tree lights, but not as pretty. There are different ways to connect a computer network, so let's take a look at those now.

NEW WORD: A local area network, or LAN, is simply a network that works over a limited, local area. It might cover a few PCs or the entire floor of an office building. A wide area network (WAN) is one that spans several buildings, cities, or even countries.

Daisy Chain

The first network layout is illustrated in Figure 10-1. Each computer in the network has a wire running to its nearest neighbor. It doesn't really matter which computer connects to which. Everybody winds up making this decision based upon the easiest way to string the wires.

This type of network connection is called a *daisy chain,* for obvious reasons. The network cable itself is small and flexible. Some networks use telephone cord, which makes it easy to slip the cable behind desks and under carpeting. Other networks use somewhat heavier wires, like

Typical daisy chain network layout
Figure 10-1.

cable TV. These are a little tougher to hide in the average office environment.

Ring

A very popular kind of network is the *ring* network. A ring operates very much like a daisy chain network, except that the first and last computers on the net are linked, closing the circle, as in Figure 10-2.

Some of the more advanced ring networks are actually two rings in one. Each computer has two connections to each of its neighbors. Then, if one computer in the ring fails, the network can continue to operate as though it were connected daisy chain-style.

There are many different ways to connect to a network. Some are more sophisticated than others.

Star

Another way to connect computers in a network is to connect them all at a central point. Figure 10-3 shows an example of this kind of *star* arrangement. One disadvantage of this sort of network is that you must have an extra computer in the center of the star, called the network *server*. In most networks of this type, the server is not used as an individual PC by someone on the network. It works on keeping the network running smoothly.

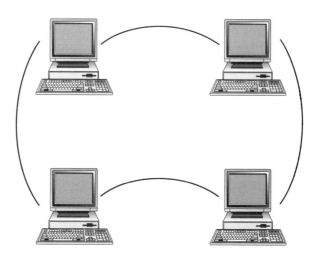

Ring network
Figure 10-2.

10

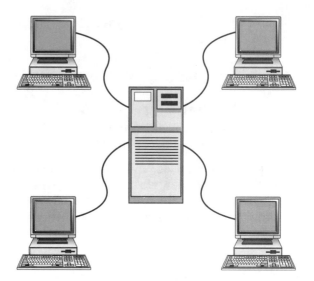

Star network
Figure 10-3.

 NEW WORD: A server is a special computer included as part of a network. It "serves" the other computers in the network with files and other services. Some networks require a server, others don't. The server can be just like the other PCs or it might be a special kind of computer.

On the other hand, having a network server in the center of the network has advantages, too. These are covered a little bit later, under "Network Resources."

Backbone

The third style of network connection (or *topology*, in the vernacular) is called the *backbone* network connection. For this type, you run one big cable through the whole area and every computer "taps" onto this main, backbone cable. See Figure 10-4 for an idea of how it works.

The backbone cable will often run right through the walls of your building, meaning that it has to be installed professionally, ahead of time. The advantage is that it is fairly easy for everyone to reach the

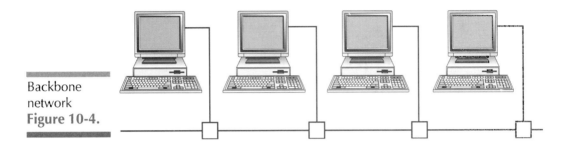

Backbone network Figure 10-4.

backbone cable at some point, without needing to reach all the way to the next computer or network server. This is especially useful in large organizations with many computers on the network, or where computers are spaced far apart.

NEW WORD: Network topology is nothing more than the way you connect computers to each other with cables or wires. Different topologies are star, daisy chain, ring, and backbone.

Network Functions

Now that you know how a network works, you might be wondering what a network is good for. Well, truth be told, a network is not for everybody. Just because you have a dozen computers in your work place doesn't necessarily mean that you need to network them. But there are some real advantages to adding a network. Some of them are discussed here.

10

File Sharing

When you have multiple computers communicating with each other across a network, it's much easier to share information and files. You can send data files to a coworker's computer almost instantly rather than making a copy of the file and delivering it on diskette. Making multiple copies of a file on diskette can sometimes lead to problems. If you and your coworker are each working on a different copy of the file, how do you keep abreast of each other's modifications? With a network, that problem goes away.

NOTE: If you're currently running back and forth from PC to PC swapping disks with your coworkers, you're using the oldest and most popular computer network of all, the *sneaker* net.

Most networks allow you to do some limited file sharing. That means that your coworkers can access files on your hard disk drive just as though they were stored on their own disks. In return, you can access their files, too. If all of you are working on a large shared database, like an inventory list, that feature alone may be worth the price of the network.

This kind of *peer-to-peer* file sharing works by making everybody's disk available to everyone else. That can eliminate the need to keep multiple copies of data on everybody's disks. It also means that when you all share one file, the file will be updated every time somebody makes a change. Nobody ever has to have outdated information.

NEW WORD: A peer-to-peer network means that all the PCs are equal on the network. No one PC is burdened with the task of managing the network traffic.

Your network may use a central file server instead of allowing peer-to-peer file sharing. With a central file server you store all of the files you want to share on the server's disks. To keep files private, you store them on your own disks. If you want to share a file, simply copy it to the server's disk.

Some networks allow you to share application programs as well as data files. You can share just one copy of a word processor or database management program stored on a disk that everybody can use. Not all programs work this way, though. You'll have to check at your computer or software store to find applications that can run across the network.

File Security

The other side of the file sharing coin is file security. While there are certainly advantages to being able to access each other's information, there are some things that are best kept private. Fortunately, most networks that let you share files also let you *not* share files.

A network lets you share your work. But you can also keep things private.

When a group file is shared across a network of computer users, some of those people might be authorized to make changes (for example, order-entry personnel modifying an inventory file) while others are not. Some users might only be allowed to read or view the data, but not make any changes to it. There may be other files that are not shared at all, like an executive's personal planner or financial information. Keeping these separate is easily done. Depending upon your particular network, keeping a file private may simply be a matter of storing it on a different disk, or in a special subdirectory. For many networks, a file is assumed to be private unless you explicitly share it with other users on the network.

Electronic Mail

Another big advantage to networking is the ability to send electronic mail. *Electronic mail,* or *e-mail,* is simply a means of sending instant messages to anybody who has a computer on the network. It's just like picking up the phone and dialing an extension, but with some advantages.

NEW WORD: Most computer networks allow you to send electronic mail messages, or e-mail, to other computer users on the network.

10

One advantage of e-mail is that you can attach a file to your typed message. If you want a coworker to examine a report you're writing (using your word processor, naturally) you can e-mail it to her. She can send her comments and suggestions back via return e-mail.

Another advantage is that your coworkers don't have to be at their desks when you send e-mail. Typically, when you send e-mail, a tone will sound at the receiving computer, or a brief message will appear on the screen to let the recipient know that mail is waiting. If they are inclined to read your e-mail right away, they can. Otherwise, the message waits, like a letter in a mailbox, until the recipient retrieves it.

You can also "broadcast" e-mail to many people across the network at once. This is a great tool for calling meetings or soliciting input on a new idea. Again, some people may answer your e-mail directly while others may not read it until later.

Groupware

A new generation of application programs designed especially for people who work together with personal computers on a network is called *groupware*.

NEW WORD: Groupware is a special kind of application program that helps people collaborate on a project over a network.

Often the people working in an office are working on some project together. Each person has his or her part, but they may all be contributing to the whole. As an example, let's take the case of a small company working on a magazine advertisement. There may be one or two graphic artists designing elements of the ad, a copy writer who writes the text, and a lead designer who creates the overall look of the presentation and places each of the other elements. Normally, each one creates his or her piece, and they exchange them with each other. Then, after several iterations of creating, reviewing, changing, and reviewing again, the final ad might take shape. With groupware, the whole process can be streamlined.

The elements that each member of the group creates become instantly accessible to each of the others in the collaborative effort. What one member designs or writes appears on the screen of the other members, ready for inclusion in their work. Even with a member of the group out of the office, the project can move ahead because everything is shared across the network.

Network Resources

When you attach your computer to a network, it becomes a part of a larger system. Your disks and files might be shared with other computers on the network, and their disks and files may be shared with you.

One thing that's not shared, though, is the processing "brains" of each computer. Connecting ten computers on a network doesn't make the whole system run ten times faster, any more than gathering ten people in a room doesn't seem to make them any smarter. You can't create a "super computer" this way. That's strictly for the science-fiction movies. Each computer will still run just as quickly (or just as slowly) as it did before.

Network Printers

A printer placed within the network allows all the PCs within the net access.

If your work group is typical of the thousands of others that are out there, you probably spend a lot of time waiting to print something on a printer. In most groups of five or more personal computers, printers have to be shared. Usually, one or two computers will have printers attached to them, and the others have to do without. If you're one of the unlucky ones, you probably have to take your files over to somebody else to have them printed.

There are a couple of ways around this. First of all, you could use a printer-sharing buffer (see Chapter 9), which lets you and your coworkers all connect to one or two shared printers. The other, better way is to use a network printer.

A network printer connects to your network cabling the same way that another computer would. If you have a daisy chain network topology like this:

10

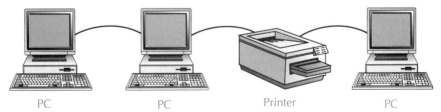

| PC | PC | Printer | PC |

then the network printer would just be another connection along the line. There are a couple of advantages to this arrangement. First, your printer can be placed wherever it is most convenient, as long as you can run the network cables to it. Second, you don't have to attach separate cables between every printer and every PC that wants to share it. Finally, you don't need to buy and install the printer buffer box at all.

A network printer isn't really a different kind of *printer*; it's just a printer with a different kind of interface. It can be a top-quality laser printer, a dot matrix printer, a daisy wheel printer, or even a plotter. The difference is in the printer's computer interface, not the printer itself. Instead of having a serial or parallel interface, your network printer will have a special connection for your kind of network.

Not all printers are available with network interfaces, so pay special attention to compatibility when selecting a printer. Your choice of network may affect your choice of printers, and vice versa. Most Apple laser printers come with Apple Talk connections, so attaching them to a network of Macintoshes is simple.

Network File Server

A file server can sometimes be little more than a giant disk drive, supplying extra storage space for all the PCs on the net.

You can also add shared disk storage to your network. A shared, centralized disk allows everyone on the network access to additional disk storage, above and beyond what is on the individual PCs. As your work group grows, you may find yourself running out of space. A shared, networked disk is the ideal solution to this problem.

Disk drives don't come with their own network connections. They're installed as part of a network file server. Your file server may be like the other PCs on the network, or it may be a bigger, much different kind of box. Generally, you can't use the file server as your only PC because it is too busy taking care of the network, running special network software. Its purpose is to fetch and store files for the other PCs on the net. Your file server may not even have a keyboard or a monitor. Normally, it will have much more disk storage than the other computers, plus enhanced expansion capabilities for additional memory, tape backups, and more disks.

Network Administrator

A small network is easy to manage and maintain. If you have just a few PCs and a shared printer or two, you shouldn't encounter any complications. But if you have a large and growing network, keeping track of all of the computers, printers, and users can take up more and more of your time.

If your network grows large enough, you may need a full-time person to manage it. Your *network administrator* will oversee the addition and removal of disks, the connection of new PCs to the network, the assignment of passwords and other security issues, and the maintenance of the network itself.

The network administrator will also be charged with the task of making regular and periodic backups of the network disks. As your network grows, so will your disk storage requirements, and with it, the opportunity for loss if a disk crashes. Making regular backups to tape or floppy disk is important anytime, but it becomes even more important as the number of users increases.

Network Security

A password can keep somebody else from seeing your work or altering your files.

For large or medium-sized networks, you may find yourself needing some form of network security. There may be some sensitive information stored on network disks that should be carefully controlled. Users probably have some files on their disks that they don't necessarily want to share with the rest of the group. Any network that allows file sharing also supports file hiding. But without extra security measures, this might not be enough.

For many networks, each user must be given a password. The password identifies who is using the computer, rather than just which computer that person is using. In a network of computers, it is sometimes important to differentiate between the person and the person's computer. You wouldn't want to divulge important financial data to just anyone who had access to the financial controller's computer. On the other hand, wouldn't it be convenient for financial personnel to access records from someone else's PC? A password guarantees security in the former case, and freedom in the latter.

10

Networking Different Kinds of Computers

So far the discussion assumed that your network includes all the same kind of computer. It's fairly easy to network computers that are all compatible with one another. But can you network different kinds of computers? The answer is a cautious yes. You can do it, but it's a lot more work than connecting compatible computers, and the results are sometimes not entirely what you expect.

The basic idea of a network is to allow lots of people to exchange files with one another, and maybe a little e-mail. You may even be able to run the same application programs. That works very nicely as long as all of the people use computers that store files the same way, treat mail the same way, and execute programs the same way. If your network includes just IBM-compatible PCs, or just Macintoshes, everything will work out just fine.

It is possible to bridge the gap between two different networks.

But when you mix IBM- and Apple-style computers, you're mixing oil and water. It's difficult at best to get these two warring computer factions to communicate. It can be done—if you're willing to give up some features. The situation deteriorates further if you try to include more computers, like engineering workstations running UNIX, or the company mainframe that runs VMS, for example.

Network Bridges

A number of companies offer network-to-network "bridges." A bridge is usually a small box that has two connections, one for each network. The purpose of the bridge is to translate what one network is doing into something that the other network can understand. Ideally, this translation runs in both directions simultaneously.

NEW WORD: A network bridge is a special device that connects two networks together. Sometimes this is easier than expanding a single network. Network bridges are also called gateways.

There are a certain number of things that a network bridge can translate, and some that it can't. Simple things, like e-mail messages, can almost always be passed from one network to another. Text is text, for the most part, and translates easily. Some nice features of your message may be lost, though, like underlining, bold face, or other special effects. Plan on just the basic message getting through.

File sharing is a bit more difficult. PCs and Macs don't store files the same way, and there's no well-defined way to translate a file from one type of computer to the other. It really depends on what kind of file it is and what you'll be using it for. These are decisions that the network bridge can't make for you, so once you've brought a file "over to your side," you may have to do some additional massaging of the data before you can use it.

As for application programs, there's no way that your PC can run a Macintosh program, network or no. Likewise, you won't be able to access the company mainframe in any but the most rudimentary sense. Again, networking does not turn a collection of computers into one super computer, any more than telephones can help a group of foreigners to speak one language.

Different Networks

There are many different networks to choose from, just as there are competing computer makers. If you want to add a network to your computer group, you'll have many options to consider. Some networks are more expensive to connect than others, and some offer better features. Look carefully, spend a lot of time asking questions, and read up on the subject, if you can, before making any decisions.

10

Apple Talk

The network that most Apple Macintosh computers use is called Apple Talk. With Apple Talk you can connect dozens of Macintosh computers, along with Apple printers and other network resources. Apple Computer sells Apple Talk hardware, naturally, but other companies, like Farallon, offer a selection of Apple Talk devices as well.

Nearly all Macintoshes are already equipped with network connections. All you need to do is plug the computers together. Look for the printer port icon on the back of your Mac to find where to connect your Apple Talk interface:

The interface box is small enough to fit in your hand and has three connections: one for the Mac and two for the Apple Talk network cable. One cable goes in, the other comes out. This makes the network daisy chain. If your Mac happens to be at the end of the daisy chain you won't have a network cable to plug into one end.

PC Networks

Adding a network interface is as easy as installing a card and loading some new software.

The PC networking world is very fragmented. There is really no single major network standard. There are a handful of different companies who compete for the IBM-style PC network market. Microsoft has Network Manager, Novell offers NetWare, and ArtiSoft supplies LANtastic, to name just a few.

To add a network to your computer (or to add your computer to a network) you will have to add some special hardware to your PC. Hardly any IBM-style PCs come with network connections already installed. Instead, you get to open up your PC and add a network adapter card to it. This is just like adding a memory card or a different video card. It's nothing to worry about. Your network card will come with installation instructions.

Ethernet

Some networks use something you may have heard of called Ethernet. Ethernet is a very popular kind of network, but it's used mostly on big computers, engineering workstations, minicomputers, scientific installations; that kind of thing. Ethernet cards are also available for PCs. Ethernet was invented by Xerox at the Palo Alto Research Center (PARC) in California, and has probably become the most popular type of computer network in the world.

There is not just a single Ethernet. In the same way that there is more than one Apple Talk network, there are many thousands of computers all linked via Ethernet networks. Because it is so popular, especially among bigger computer installations, many Ethernet networks have since linked up with other Ethernet networks, forming huge "extended" networks.

Internet

By far the largest of the extended networks in the whole world is called the Internet. The Internet has been around for years and is mostly publicly funded. In the past, it was used primarily by DARPA (Defense Advanced Research Projects Association), the National Science Foundation, and various universities for basic research. As such, the Internet has always been a source of nearly limitless amounts of scientific news and reference material. The Internet stretches around the globe, reaching every continent and more than 100 countries. It includes big computers, bigger computers, and huge super computers.

The Internet is a big-league network for advanced players.

With an Internet connection, you have at your fingertips the ability to exchange e-mail with someone in Japan, send a file to your drama group, see if a Macintosh sitting in a lab in Canada is turned on, and find out if someone happens to be sitting in front of a computer in Australia, all within half an hour. (As you will see in Chapter 11, many of these feats are also available from other networks and services.)

Today, the Internet is being used less and less for government and defense work and more by universities and the general public. That's us. Membership has shot up at a fantastic rate since 1990. Still, the Internet retains its research-oriented flavor as a vast repository for information and access to cutting-edge research.

10

Usenet

The Internet is so large and sprawled out that even the boldest computer adventurer can get lost navigating the seas of information available. Considering the sheer number of computers that are an active part of the Internet, megabytes and megabytes of new information are made available every day from sources all over the world. There must be some means to filter out all the data that isn't of any appreciable value and "zero in" on just the new items that interest the overwhelmed computer user.

Enter Usenet. Usenet has been around since 1979, the computer industry's early Pleistocene era. It is not another network, per se, but a very loose collection of network users, mostly Internet users. Their computers monitor the traffic on the Internet and other networks, pulling off information and news items that might be of interest to the group of people they serve. Then they forward the information to those people's computers. The groups are called *newsgroups,* and they act like electronic mailing lists. You can "join" as many newsgroups as you like, and your local Usenet connection will forward the selected data to you.

Some Usenet locations charge money for this service. Others are operated free of charge on the general principle that spreading news and knowledge is a worthwhile endeavor in itself.

Connecting to either one of the mega-networks, the Internet or Usenet, is not a particularly good place to start your networking. Unless you are interested in research, or general hacking, Usenet and the Internet are probably not for you. What you very well might want to consider, though, is a subscription to an online service. These, and other topics, will be explored in the next chapter.

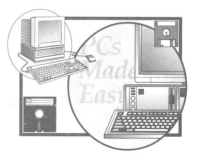

CHAPTER

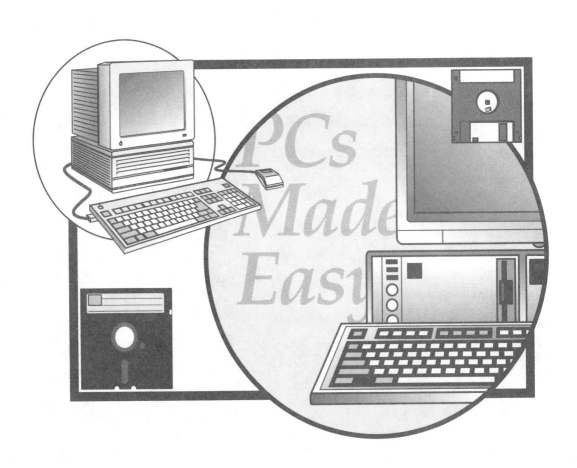

11

WHAT ELSE CAN I DO?

This chapter tells you about all kinds of other neat things you can do with your PC. Some are serious, business-related tasks and others are a little more frivolous. As you will see, there are many different things you can do with a personal computer besides just compute numbers and process words.

These applications require special hardware or software, or both, before you can get started. Each section tells you what you need to start using the application on your basic PC or Macintosh.

Modems and Telecommunications

In the previous chapter, you saw how personal computers can be networked to allow a work group to share information. Networking assumes that the computers are physically grouped together and that everyone on the network is working more or less toward a common goal. There is another way to connect to other personal computers; a way that is more common than networking.

Almost everybody in the modern world uses the telephone to communicate with other people. Your computer can use the same telephone system to communicate with other computers. With just a small investment in extra hardware and software, your computer can have access to hundreds of thousands of other personal computers all over the world. The world of telecommunications is yours, almost for the asking.

Telecommunications allows you to access other personal computers that have the necessary hardware, as well as a wealth of public and private data networks available from all over the world. Your PC can communicate with another PC from across town or from across the continent, as shown in Figure 11-1. Anywhere that the telephone can reach, your personal computer can connect.

NEW WORD: When you're communicating with a telephone you're using telecommunications. Your PC can also take advantage of telecommunications.

The only extra equipment you need is a modem and some telecommunications software. A typical *modem* is just a small box about the size of a paperback book. You can also choose a modem that plugs directly into one of your PC's expansion slots. What a modem does is allow your PC to talk on the telephone, just as you would use the telephone yourself to talk to someone else. It works by converting the digital electronic signals inside your computer to sounds, which can then be sent over the telephone wires. You don't need to have a special telephone hookup or pay special rates. There's also no danger to the

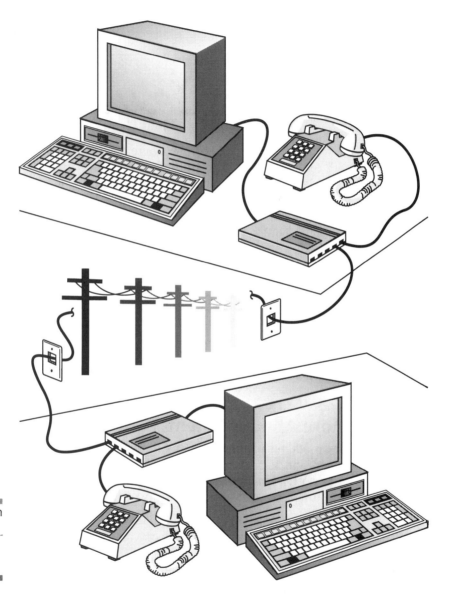

Using a modem
to link
computers
Figure 11-1.

telephone system or risk to your normal service. Modems are simple
and completely safe.

NEW WORD: A modem is a device that lets your PC talk to other PCs by converting electronic digital signals to tones that are sent over the telephone line.

Of course, just like a telephone, there must be a modem at the other end, too. If there is, then your two computers can communicate and share data as though they were connected via a network. You can *upload* data to other computers or *download* data from other computers to yours. You may even be able to operate the other computer remotely! Your keyboard and screen will act as though they were attached to another computer, miles away.

NEW WORD: When you upload, you are sending data from your PC to another computer somewhere else. Downloading is just the opposite: you receive a data transmission from another computer.

More About Modems

Any modem can work over any normal public telephone line, local or long distance. Fortunately, virtually all modems are compatible with one another, even if they are connected to different kinds of computers, so you can "talk" to any other computer, anywhere. About the only thing that distinguishes one modem from another is speed.

A modem converts your PC's electrical impulses into sound so that it can work like a telephone. The digital "on/off" signals from your computer become audible "high/low" tones on the phone. The speed at which the modem can do this is measured in bits per second (BPS), or baud rate. If you recall, a bit is the smallest amount of computer information. It takes about ten bits of data to transmit one letter of the alphabet across the phone lines. If you want to transmit a lot of information, this speed can be important. It can become especially important when you're transmitting via an expensive, long distance call.

The faster the modem converts data to sounds (and back) the better. The slowest modems work at 300 baud. A new 300 baud modem is difficult to find anymore. The minimum speed you're likely to see for a new modem is 1200 baud, or four times that fast. Better still is a 2400 or even a 9600 baud modem. Even though a faster modem will cost you more in the beginning, you can often make up that difference in just a few hours of modem use. Of course, the modem at the other end must be able to keep up with you to achieve the higher data rates.

Like the weakest link in a chain, a PC-to-PC transmission is only as fast as the slower of the two modems being used.

If you consider that it takes about ten data bits to send one character, and that a full page of text has about 4000 letters, numbers, or punctuation marks in it, then Table 11-1 will give you some idea of how long it takes to transmit or receive text at a given baud rate.

Data Compression

Some modems can also compress data before they send it. The receiving modem then decompresses the data. By "squeezing" the data, you can save significant amounts of time in transmitting and receiving large files. Naturally, data-compression modems cost more than their non-compressing counterparts, but that cost, too, can be made up over a short period of time. More importantly, not all data-compression modems compress data the same way. There are, in fact, several competing data-compression methods in use. Be careful to select a data-compression modem that is compatible with the modem you plan to call on the receiving end. Better yet, buy both modems at the same time.

Two popular compression schemes used by modems are called MNP 5 and V.42bis. The actual meaning of these cryptic monikers isn't important, and you'll be happier not learning them. The important part to remember is that they aren't compatible. If you use one kind of

11

Speed	1 Page	25 pages
300 baud	2 1/4 minutes	55 minutes
1200 baud	30 seconds	14 minutes
2400 baud	15 seconds	7 minutes
4800 baud	8 seconds	3 1/2 minutes
9600 baud	4 seconds	2 minutes

Modem
Transmission
Rates
Table 11-1.

data-compression system to send, you'll have to use the same one to receive. There are several modems that support each of these.

Another alternative is to compress the files yourself before you send them. You can find public domain (i.e. free) and shareware data-compression and decompression programs like PKZIP or LHA on most any public bulletin board system. Of course, the person at the other end must have a copy of the program too.

Error Correction

Apart from data compression, there are also a lot of modems that can automatically check that the data you are sending is received properly at the other end. If there's an error, the modem will automatically send the data again. These are called error-correcting modems. They are also identified with mysterious mnemonics, like MNP 2, MNP 3, and MNP 4. An alternate error-correcting scheme is called V.42, not to be confused with the V.42bis data-compression system.

Although you do need special hardware and software to telecommunicate, you don't need to alter your phone lines.

Modem Software

Before you can operate your modem, you'll need to have a special telecommunications application program. There are many programs to choose from. Some are even available free from other PCs, via modem! If you're buying a new modem, it may already come with the necessary software.

Basically, what any telecommunications program lets you do is control your modem so that it can dial the phone and upload or download files. Beyond those basic functions, your program may also help you manage a "directory" of telephone numbers, or provide an attractive windowed user interface on your screen. Some telecommunications programs are definitely more full-featured than others.

Public Bulletin Board Systems

The simplest way to use a modem is to "talk" to another personal computer. This might be a PC at your office that you communicate with while you're on the road, or a neighbor's computer around the corner. There are also thousands of people who leave their PCs running 24 hours a day, 7 days a week, just to encourage people to call. Chances are that your city or community has several of these "public" PCs that you can call without incurring long distance charges. They don't cost anything to call, and they can be very interesting.

So, what do you get when you call another PC? That depends on the PC. File sharing is one of the main features. Another is access to online bulletin boards. A computer bulletin board system, or *BBS*, is simply a PC with a modem that acts as a repository for callers' files, information, and miscellaneous messages. It is, in a sense, a public bulletin board, open to all who care to call and leave messages.

 NEW WORD: A BBS is an electronic bulletin board system, or a PC with a modem attached to it that you can call. There are BBSs in nearly every town, specializing in all kinds of things, from skiing to computers, travel to weaving.

You can find all kinds of information on BBSs. Some are general purpose, accepting all files and messages. Many others are more specialized. For example, you can call a BBS that specializes in astronomy, one that specializes in soap operas, computer programming, games, sports, or almost any other field of interest that you can name. These specialized bulletin boards have many files to download, plus hundreds of messages left by other PC users with similar interests.

Some bulletin boards do charge for access to their files and messages. They do this by offering subscriptions. Normally, you would call the BBS one time for free and leave your name and address. Within a few days you should receive a password in the mail from the manager of the BBS (usually called the *sysop,* or system operator). With a password and a paid-up subscription you can now call the BBS as much as you like. Rather than charge subscriptions to everybody, some bulletin board systems also allow you to read and leave messages and upload files for free, but not download without paying a fee. You can give, but not take. Subscription fees usually go right back into buying and upgrading the equipment (bigger hard disk, faster modem, and so on).

11

Online Services

With the increasing popularity of PCs, modems, and public bulletin board systems, it was inevitable that some businesses would take notice. Now, in addition to the public BBS, you can access several private, commercially run systems. These new online services are vastly more professional and exciting than most amateur BBS systems. They are also available to hundreds or even thousands of PC users at once.

With a subscription to one of the large commercial online services, you can still upload and download files, but you can also gain access to a wealth of other services. Some allow you to make your own airline reservations, trade stocks, check the weather, read the international news wires, or just chat with other PC users on the system. The options are truly amazing and far beyond what a single PC with a modem can offer.

You have your choice of several major online services throughout the country, including Prodigy, CompuServe, America Online, GEnie, the Source, and Dow Jones News Retrieval. Each one has its own special mix of features and they appeal to different people. You may find that you like one over the others, too. But first, let's see how they work.

Using an Online Service

To use an online service, you first need to pay for a subscription. Like cable TV, an online service subscription is usually billed monthly. For your monthly fee, you get a password and a telephone number to call in your area. You usually also get some nice brochures and a handbook describing how the system works. Some services charge a one-time sign-up fee, which may be from $5 to $25. Monthly fees are usually in the $5 to $10 range. For that price, you may get unlimited access to the service, or it may be limited to a certain number of "online hours" per month.

Because the online services offer so many services to so many subscribers, one little PC couldn't hope to handle all the traffic. Instead, these services use large rooms full of mainframe computers, like a university or large corporation might have. These computers are connected to hundreds of modems as well as being networked to other computers. To call the service, you simply dial a local telephone number. That connects you with a "gateway" computer networked with the main computers, which may be located across the country. There

are thousands of these small gateway computers all over America so that you never have to make a long distance call to reach the service.

Most of the popular online services are easy to use. They are designed for novice or occasional computers users, and so they avoid technical details and difficult-to-remember commands. America Online, shown in Figure 11-2, uses friendly graphics and windows.

After calling the service, you select the feature you want by pointing with your mouse or pressing a key. One selection may give you access to the upload/download section, where you can browse through nearly endless file directories. The files will usually be sorted and indexed, so you can quickly zero in on whatever looks most interesting. Then, with a few commands, you can have the online service transmit the file to your PC.

Another part of the service may let you participate in a live "chat" with other online subscribers. At any given time, there may be as many as 100 other users on the system. You can type messages back and forth to

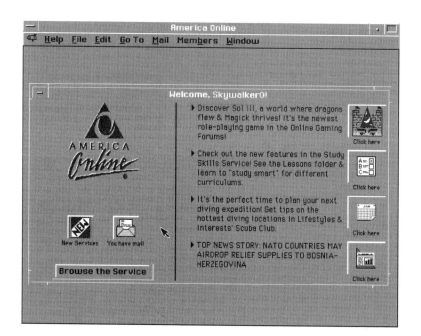

America Online is a popular online service with easy to use windows
Figure 11-2.

11

each other, like talking on the telephone. On some systems, users are identified by a "screen name" or "handle" rather than their real names, so you can be as secretive or as forthcoming as you like.

You can scan the latest news and weather reports as they come in from reporting bureaus around the world. These are the very same news wires that newspapers, magazines, and television news crews use for their information, so you'll always be up-to-date on the latest events in sports, news, and business.

There are even more features available to you when you become an online subscriber. The best way to find out what's available is to try it. Many of the services offer free trial offers for a month, or a limited number of calls. Check your local newspaper or your favorite computer magazine for offers.

FAX/Modems

Many offices today use electronic facsimile (fax) machines to send documents back and forth. Now, you can also use your PC to send and receive fax transmissions.

A *fax* machine sends a copy of a printed document to another fax machine over the telephone. It works like a photocopier, but the copy comes out at someone else's location. They are extremely useful for sending letters, contracts, drawings, or handwritten notes at the fastest possible speed. Sending a one-page fax typically takes about 30 seconds.

The fax process works so well because most printed material is only two colors: a white page and black ink. By sending a high-pitched tone for each white spot on the page, and a low-pitched tone for each dark spot, the fax can "whistle" the entire page to another fax machine. As you can see, the "high/low" tones work just like those for a modem, described previously. So why not send faxes via modem?

Unfortunately, the developers of the fax machine never consulted the developers of personal computer modems. What should have been a wonderfully simple and elegant collaboration of computer, telephone, and printing became a woeful mess. You see, fax machines don't use the same "high/low" tones that modems do, and the way they compress data is also different. In short, everything that could have been done differently, was.

But there is hope. For a little extra money, you can buy a combination fax/modem for your PC. Fax/modems merge the two capabilities into one unit, so that you have only one telephone connection and one hookup to your computer. Inside, though, are basically two different devices working together in the same box.

A fax/modem lets you communicate not only with other PCs, but with fax machines as well. You can send a fax directly from your PC without ever printing it.

Combination fax/modem boards can usually send fax transmissions faster then they can send "normal" computer data. That's because all fax documents are compressed, whereas most modem transmissions aren't. With a fax/modem, you can send a file directly from your PC to a remote fax machine, where it will come out on paper. Using the modem portion, you can also send files directly from your PC to a remote computer, where it will become another disk file. In neither case do you ever need to actually print the file before sending it.

Some fax/modems can also receive fax transmissions. You'll have to leave your PC on, of course, and set up the fax/modem to answer the phone when it rings but this is usually quite simple to set up, using the supplied instructions. Now somebody else can send documents to you from their fax machine, and they will become disk files on your computer.

Tricky Data Conversion Questions

With a modem, you can send computer-to-computer. With a fax machine, you can send fax-to-fax. With a combination fax/modem, you can send computer-to-fax, fax-to-computer, or computer-to-computer. What's the difference?

The difference is a tricky one to understand, but important if you don't want to be disappointed in the results. When you use a modem (or fax/modem combination) to send files from one PC to another, both computers are exchanging data directly. It is as though you had made a copy of the file on disk and mailed it to your recipient. That also means that the recipient should have the same application program to use that file, or at least a compatible one.

11

For example, say you transmit a word processing file to your sister via modem. She will get the file, and she can use her word processing program to make edits, changes, or just look at the contents of the file. She could even make changes to it and then send it back to you. Nothing is lost in the translation, and eventually, one of you could print the document on a printer.

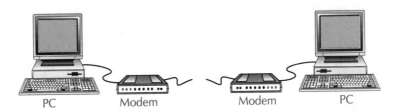

PC   Modem   Modem   PC

Now let's say you take that printed document and send it via a fax machine to your brother. Your brother now has a printed copy of the document. His copy will be somewhat lower quality than yours, because the output from a fax machine is typically a little grainy; about as good as a cheap dot matrix printer. Your brother will not be able to make any changes to the document, because he doesn't have the file and no PC to edit it with.

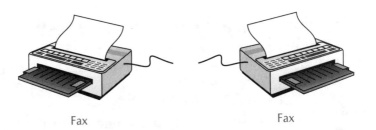

Fax   Fax

In your third experiment, you use your fax/modem to send a copy of the word processing file to your uncle, who has a fax machine. You don't have to print the file because you have a fax/modem and can send it directly from disk without ever printing a copy. He gets a printed copy that looks just like your brother's.

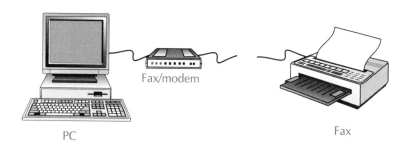

Finally, you take the printed document again and send it via fax to your aunt, who has a PC with a fax/modem. She will receive a fax transmission from you, and the file will be stored on disk in her PC. The question is, can she edit that file with her word processor? The surprise answer is no.

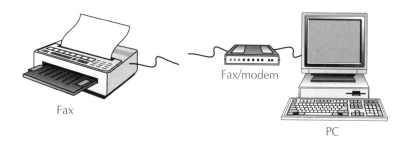

Fax machines were developed to send and receive just about anything, including pictures, typing, handwriting, or whatever. Therefore, it treats everything as a picture. Even a neatly typewritten page is treated as a picture. The fax machine doesn't "know" what writing is—it just whistles in time with the light and dark areas of the page. When you send a file via a fax/modem to another fax/modem or a fax machine, your file is converted into a picture, too. That means that your aunt's PC can't tell whether the page it is receiving is coming from another PC or from a real fax machine that is scanning a piece of paper. In the

11

latter case, her PC obviously can't re-create a word processing file when there never was one. The incoming fax will be stored as a picture file, not a word processing file.

Receiving a fax is like getting a picture of a letter instead of the real letter.

Consider the difference between receiving a letter in the mail and a photograph of that letter. Either way, you can read what's written in the letter. But you can put the actual letter into your own typewriter and make small changes (a few extra words here, a little correction fluid there). You can't put the photo in your typewriter, though.

The bottom line is, when you send a file from a fax or to a fax, it is not useful for word processing anymore. It loses all the information that a PC needs to make it back into a word processing file. Even though you and your aunt both have a PC, she cannot edit or use the word processing file you sent to her because it was converted into a fax during the transmission, and there's no way to convert it back.

Well, almost no way. The next section covers scanners, a kind of specialized fax machine.

Scanners

A scanner is an extra piece of equipment that you can attach to your PC. It will let you enter pictures, figures, illustrations, and printed pages into your PC without drawing or typing them again. In short, it lets you take what somebody else has already printed and put it back into PC form.

You can think of a scanner as a reverse printer. A printer lets you take files in your PC and turn them into printed documents. You can print written pages, figures, or charts. Depending on your printer you may even be able to print in color. A scanner works the same way, but in reverse. If you want to include your company's logo in all of your business letters but don't want to try to draw it with a graphics program, you can scan it into your PC instead.

Most scanners work equally well with printed material or with pictures. That's because all scanners treat printed words as pictures. That may or may not be what you want. For example, you can scan in a newspaper article just as easily as the company logo, but you won't be able to edit that article or include it in a word processing document because the scanner doesn't turn it back into words. It's just a picture that has words in it.

That's a difficult concept for many first-time users to understand. It creeps in when you are using a fax/modem, too, as you saw before. To your PC, a picture of a printed page and the words on the page are two very different things. Your PC can't read any of the words on the page, even though you can. Your PC makes a definite distinction between pictures and words, and it's hard to convert one to the other.

A scanner can create a copy of anything— picture, letter, or photo—on your PC. You can then edit, translate, or modify the copy with special software.

If you're scanning in pictures, no conversion is required. Once you scan in the logo, a hand-drawn picture, or a photograph you can move it and shape it with your favorite graphics application program. A scanner is a wonderful tool for jazzing up the company newsletter or any other kind of desktop publishing task. In fact, that's the major difference between word processing and desktop publishing: the latter lets you manage pictures as well as words.

Optical Character Recognition (OCR)

If you want your PC to "read" what's printed on a page and be able to edit and otherwise word process it, you need some additional software. It's called an optical character recognition program, and it's expensive.

Optical character recognition, or *OCR*, software teaches your computer to read. After you scan in a page from a magazine article, you've got nothing more than a picture of that page. You could print it out again if you want, but a photocopier could do that job a lot easier. What you want is to be able to convert that picture back into the words the magazine writer wrote so that you can edit them with your own word processor. What you want is the writer's word processing file.

11

NEW WORD: OCR stands for optical character recognition. It is a kind of application program that helps your computer read printed text and convert it back into a text file for word processing.

With an OCR program, your computer will slowly analyze the page that you've scanned looking for patterns that it recognizes. It has been designed to recognize all the letters of the alphabet, plus digits, punctuation marks, and common symbols. As long as the scanned document is mechanically typed or printed, your PC should recognize about 95 percent of the writing. That percentage goes down if the copy is blurry or printed in a font that the OCR program doesn't recognize. It goes down to nearly 0 percent for handwritten pages.

It is surprisingly difficult for a computer to recognize printed characters. Even small imperfections in the printing will confuse it. Your PC can also only recognize a limited number of fonts. Although we have no trouble reading text printed in a number of type styles, your PC isn't so flexible. Each letter of each new font has to be learned individually.

At no time will your computer attempt to try to make sense of what it is reading. It does not read whole words at a time, just the individual letters. That means, for example, that it will read misspelled words or even different languages with no problem.

When your OCR program is finished, you will have a word processing file ready for editing. Most OCR programs can store the scanned file in a number of different word processing formats, or as generic ASCII text.

With OCR software, you can take a scanned or faxed copy of a document and turn it back into a word processing file.

Multimedia

Multimedia is one of the newest things that has the personal computer industry buzzing. It's the long-awaited fusion of television, computers, high-fidelity stereo audio, and new software. A multimedia PC can blow the roof off normal computer applications. With the combination of sound, light, and data you can do almost anything you can imagine. Finally, personal computers are beginning to live up to their grandest expectations.

Multimedia is not *one* particular thing, it's several things all rolled into one. It's a catchall term that means different things to different people. It's part computer, with high-capacity CD-ROM drives, lots of RAM, and a super-fast 32-bit microprocessor. It's part stereo, with multi-channel digital audio effects and CD-quality sound. It's TV, too, with crisp, sharp resolution, bright colors, and access to hundreds of channels of broadcast and cable programming. Take every high-tech electronic device in the average household and put them all together, and you begin to see the possibilities of multimedia.

NEW WORD: Multimedia is uniting the technologies of television, computers, and stereo audio. It multiplies the capabilities of each individual medium (hence, the name). A PC equipped with multimedia hardware and software has the potential for far more than the average computer.

Multimedia Components

To be "multimedia ready," you need all of the right components in your personal computer system, as seen in Figure 11-3. Even with all of the added hardware, the computer is still the heart of any multimedia system. Start with a top-of-the-line PC. Anything less than a 486DX system won't do. You need to have the fastest speed and the highest performance if you really want to enjoy all the benefits of multimedia. Make sure that you have at least 8 to 10MB of RAM as well, and a big (200MB+) hard disk. Clearly, this isn't going to come cheap.

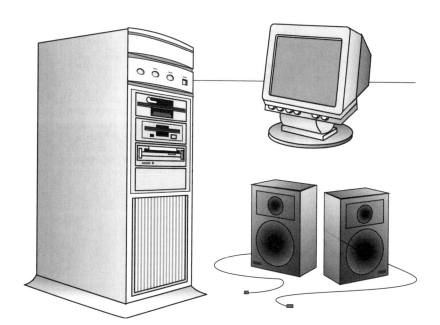

A multimedia system includes a top-notch computer, audio, and video components **Figure 11-3.**

11

Sound

After the PC comes the sound board. There are many sound boards available, with prices beginning at about $25. The less-expensive sound boards have been a favorite for years, and their popularity with game players has shown the computer companies that this is a market worth pursuing. Creative Labs, with their Sound Blaster Pro series of boards, and Microsoft's Windows Sound Source are just two examples of the next-generation sound boards.

There's no set of features in particular that make a sound board multimedia-compatible. Buy the best that you can afford. Like a stereo system, the better sound boards offer better sound quality, but they also offer more powerful sound generation effects. Any good board can play two channels at a time (stereo), but some also have more "voices" than others. The more voices, the more different sounds your computer can play at once. It's like having a whole orchestra playing inside your PC instead of just a quartet.

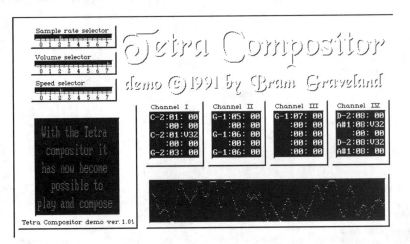

Video

The third component in the multimedia system is video. Computer monitors have improved to the point where they look nearly as good as a photograph, and the resolution is actually better than on a television. A Super VGA card and a monitor with 1024 x 768 resolution can display pictures that rival color photographs, as seen in Figure 11-4. You can also get 24-bit video boards and monitors that can display 16,777,216 colors simultaneously. They aren't called "true-color" monitors for nothing. There are also *accelerated* video boards that have their own processor on them, just to do the video. That lets your main processor do what it's best at—processing.

Multimedia Applications

All of the extra hardware may be fun, but what do you do with it? Where the promise of multimedia comes through is in the software—the synergy of applications that make the best use of audio, video, and computer.

Fantastic resolution is possible with a Super VGA card
Figure 11-4.

11

Imagine having an entire encyclopedia within your computer. All the research, descriptions, cross-references, even the color illustrations. Imagine all of that available at your fingertips, in full color right on your screen. Your PC can look up, index, and cross-reference an entire encyclopedia stored on CD-ROM. Better still, imagine that the pictures move. Apollo rockets blast off, giraffes gallop through the veldt, and drawbridges crash down across the moat. But wait, imagine that you can even *hear* the Berlin Philharmonic performing Beethoven or the sounds of a bumblebee in flight. It's all true, courtesy of your PC and multimedia.

With the addition of some adapter cards and software, you can use microphones, video recorders, CDs, even your television to create and manipulate on your PC.

Let's take another example. Since most computer CD-ROM drives will accept prerecorded music CDs, just as well as pure data CDs, it should be possible to read in an entire song or track and store it in memory. Then maybe you could draw the musical staff on your screen and edit the music, note by note with your mouse. If you had a MIDI interface board, couldn't you also sample the sounds played on a keyboard instrument and perhaps mix those in as well? Finally, why not play the whole thing back on your attached stereo speakers and then record it all on tape? The answer to all of these imaginative inquiries is yes, you could.

A multimedia-equipped PC with the right software can take moving video images, like short movies, and tie them in with recorded audio tracks. Because it's a computer, it can play and replay these snips under software control; for example, tying in the images of the Apollo moon lander with the encyclopedia entry for space flight. Your images can be cross-referenced like so many cards in a file.

A whole new world of database applications opens up with multimedia. A mail order company can maintain its order entry database by storing and retrieving images of the real catalog. The bill of materials for a complex machine can include photographs of each part, in color. Your personal telephone directory can feature portraits of all your friends and contacts; even maps to their home or office. And, with a modem, your PC can dial for you.

You can even watch television right on your PC screen! Optional plug-in expansion boards are available that pipe television broadcasts directly onto your monitor. You can switch channels with a keystroke or with your mouse. The TV broadcast can take up your entire screen, or fit into a window alongside your other applications. Add a cable TV or satellite hookup, and you have access to over 100 different channels.

Educational Software

As PCs are becoming more popular in the home, so are children's programs for PCs. It's only natural that children are curious about the PC in the living room or den, especially if a parent is staying up all night to "play" with it. To help more people rationalize the purchase of a personal home computer, there is a growing number of software titles aimed at children.

Of course, there are many, many games for PCs. Some are fast action arcade games, others are more complex strategy games, with thousands more somewhere in between. These appeal to children of all ages. But over the last few years, there has been a great increase in the number—and the quality—of educational software for small children. You can find educational programs for children from preschool age on up. There are programs to teach reading, or spelling, or math to youngsters. Most are colorful and fun, with simple goals and lots of encouragement. If you have a sound board in your PC, you can take advantage of educational programs that talk, sing, or play music, too.

There are also many training and continuing-education programs aimed at adults. You can teach yourself another language or better typing skills. You can even get a program that teaches you how to use your PC. Once you insert the disk and turn your computer on, it will guide you through step-by-step lessons at your own pace.

Home Control

Your PC can act as the heart of a home security system or as the central control for lights, heating, and appliances. If you are willing to leave your PC on all the time and invest in some additional hardware and software, you can make it do almost anything you want. There are window and door security sensors that can connect to your PC or to a control unit that your PC commands. There are also special appliance modules that your PC can use to turn your household devices on and off; for example, you can control the washing machine or start the coffee maker in the morning.

11

After you get your morning coffee, you might be ready to try your hand at creating your own cutting-edge multimedia applications. The next chapter will give you an introduction to computer programming. A programming language can be your ticket to a new and interesting hobby.

CHAPTER

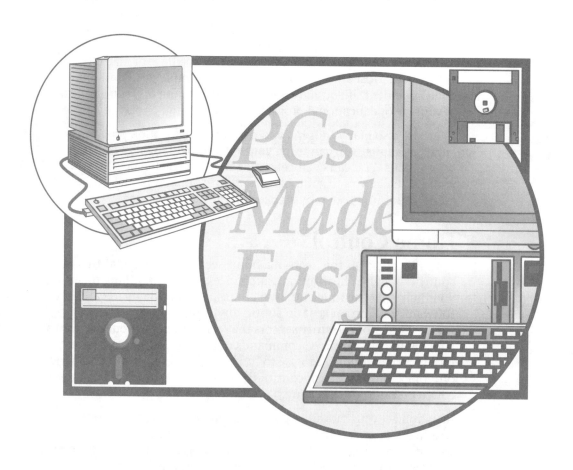

12

WHAT IS A PROGRAMMING LANGUAGE?

In previous chapters you've read that all computers must have software to run or they're useless. Software, or programs, are composed of a sequence of carefully arranged instructions that the computer can understand. The computer hardware reads and executes each individual instruction of the software program from memory, one by one, until the entire task is completed. Each instruction is a very basic one. But like single notes of music, these instructions combine to form a complete work. Several hundred or several thousand instructions, properly sequenced, allow your personal computer to do amazing things. In Chapter 6 you saw that there are programs that instruct the computer in how to perform all kinds of complex tasks and procedures, from chess games to spreadsheets.

How are these programs created? How do you teach a computer to do a new kind of task? This chapter examines programming and various computer programming languages. Remember, you don't have to understand computer programming to use your computer effectively. Many PC users (in fact, most users) have no need to learn about programming, nor have they any interest in the subject. If you are one of these, skip over this chapter. But if you're one of those people who wonders what makes a computer work and how programs are created, or if you have a desire to create programs of your own one day, then read on.

Languages to Create New Software

Teaching a person how to perform a new task can be relatively easy if you both speak the same language. If not, then one of you must learn the other's language, or you must make use of an interpreter. The interpreter can then translate your directions into a language that the student can understand. This interpretation is the basic concept behind all computer programming languages.

Programming a computer is a lot tougher than teaching another person, though. First of all, the language barrier is greater. No matter what their origins, all human languages have at least some things in common. It's doubtful that you and your computer have much common experience to share.

Second, you and your student share common experiences, so there are certain things that you both can take for granted. For example, you don't have to teach which end of a pencil to write with. The student is also equipped with some common sense. If your directions aren't clear, he or she can probably figure out what to do, or guess. Failing that, your student can ask for clearer instructions. Finally, no matter how poor your instructions may be, the student is not likely to do anything self-destructive.

Unfortunately, computers don't share a single one of these traits with us—they have no biological needs or common sense, and they certainly can't make guesses, not even to the smallest degree. They are absolutely literal machines, obedient to a fault; willing to obey any directions, no matter how irrational, even to the point of self-destruction. Their vocabularies are so limited that describing a task in their terms is extremely tedious and frustrating. Nonetheless, many people enjoy computer programming, either as a profession or as a pastime. Its very rewarding and exciting to see a program that you've written running for the first time.

Charting the Program

When programming a computer, you must be absolutely clear in stating your directions. Every step of the program must be explicit and unambiguous. This forces you to think the task through very carefully and to plan each step. If you can't explain the necessary steps to yourself, how can you teach them to a computer that hasn't got any common sense and can't ask questions if it gets stuck? One of the best ways to do this is to draw a flow chart.

You outline each step of the task you want the computer to accomplish in the form of a *flow chart* like the one shown in Figure 12-1. This might be something as simple as teaching it to add a series of numbers that you enter at the keyboard or as elaborate as a spreadsheet application. The more complex the task, the more steps it will probably require.

NEW WORD: A flow chart is a schematic diagram or representation of how a program will work. It is not part of the program, just a model of how it will work.

12

The flow chart shown in Figure 12-1 outlines the steps required for a pretty simple program. The program displays the numbers from 1 to 10 on the screen. Remember, this is not the actual program yet; it is just a chart of how the program will flow when it is written. Notice that the flow chart has definite starting and ending points, represented by ovals. The flow chart also specifies steps that will always be followed,

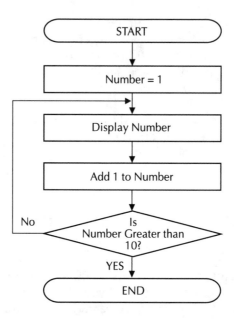

Flow charts
outline the
steps for a
simple program
Figure 12-1.

represented by rectangles. There is one decision point, represented by the diamond, where the computer may take one of two paths. Even though this flow chart is a simple one, it does show you all of the elements that make up a finished program: a starting point, an ending point, a series of statements, and a decision, or *conditional branching,* point.

Even a mindless task like counting to ten needs multiple program steps and at least one decision point on the computer's part. Without that decision block, the computer would run forever, displaying all the integers one after another, until you unplugged it or otherwise forced it to stop what it was programmed to do. This illustrates a very important principle basic to all computer programming: computers do what they're *told* to do, not necessarily what you *want* them to do.

The flow chart also illustrates how limited the vocabulary of your PC really is. For a student, the instructions "print the integers from 1 to 10" would be adequate. If your student got confused or needed more instructions ("Where do I print them?"), he or she could always ask you for clarification. A computer, on the other hand, has to be led through each individual step of counting, displaying, and stopping.

The Language of Computers

As you know, the only "language" that your computer really understands is the combination of binary 1's and 0's that make up its instruction set. The microprocessor chip in your computer can understand about 150 different instructions. Actually, that's a misleading statistic because there are really only about 12 different instructions, but they come in many variations. Everything your computer does is described by means of these instructions.

Arranging and entering these binary patterns of 1 and 0 would be unbelievably tedious and error-prone work for any programmer. People really did this only during the earliest days of digital computers. Today nobody actually programs directly in binary, also called *machine code*. Instead, more convenient shorthand ways of programming computers have come about. They let the programmer concentrate more on how the program should work rather than on the actual binary instructions for each step. The result is a little more like drawing a flow chart than arranging a sequence of binary bits.

NEW WORD: Machine code is the binary or digital patterns of 1 and 0 that your computer "understands" as its instructions. These electrical on and off signals make up its native "language."

These shorthand notations are known as *programming languages*. The purpose of a programming language is to make the programmer's task less toilsome. It lets the programmer describe a task in more general, high-level terms, and thus make better use of his or her time and talents. Each programming language has its own particular vocabulary of instructions, with its own particular grammar and syntax. Although by human language standards these programming languages are far from complete, they are a giant leap forward from binary machine code.

12

NEW WORD: A programming language is an invented language used as a halfway point between binary computer language and human languages.

There are several different programming languages in common use today. Different ones are used for different programming tasks. For instance, some languages have a vocabulary better suited for mathematical problems, while others are ideal for graphics programs or for database management. Some programming languages are also much easier to learn than others. Most professional programmers are familiar with one or two languages, which they use extensively.

Translating Text into Binary Instructions

As a rule of thumb, the easier it is for a programmer to understand a programming language, or the more it is like human language, the further removed it is from the actual binary machine code that eventually must be created. Although the programmer is able to write the program using instructions like "print," "multiply," or "add," the computer, of course, understands only "01000010," "00110111," and "01101001." It is the job of the programmer's "translator" to convert the directions in the program into the instructions for the computer. This translator is called a *compiler* or an *interpreter*.

NEW WORD: Compilers and interpreters are two kinds of programs that act as translators for your PC. They translate the programming language to the pure binary language that your computer understands.

The compiler or interpreter takes the programmers' written instructions and converts them into binary machine code that the computer understands. Because each programming language has a different vocabulary with different rules about word order and so forth, there are different compilers for each language. Depending on the programming language, each instruction that the programmer writes may be translated into a dozen machine instructions, or a hundred. When all of the instructions have been translated into their binary equivalents, the program is ready to run. Figure 12-2 illustrates the role of the compiler.

A programmer only needs two things to write a program: a word processor and a compiler or interpreter. To write the program, the programmer simply uses a favorite word processing application to create a file that contains the instructions of the program. It's like writing a letter, but the words and the grammar look funny. This file is called the *source code* file. After the source code file is completed, the programmer uses the compiler or interpreter to translate the source code file into a form that the computer can understand.

As the compiler does its translation, it reads each line in the source code file carefully. It checks that each word in the source file is a valid word in the vocabulary of this particular programming language. It also checks that all punctuation marks are in the proper place and correctly used. These matters are important because computer programs must be very explicit and complete. Assuming that it finds no errors, the compiler will then convert that line of instructions into their equivalent binary instructions and store these in another file called the *object code* file. The entire translation process may take anywhere from 15 seconds for a very short program, to 30 minutes for a very large one.

NEW WORD: An untranslated computer program is called source code. After it has been translated by a compiler or interpreter it is called object code.

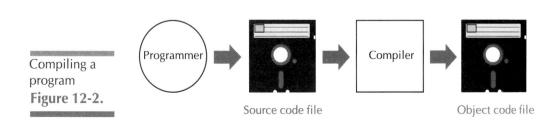

Compiling a
program
Figure 12-2.

Source code file   Object code file

The object code file becomes a translated version of the original source code file. Like foreign language translations of a book, these two files say the same thing, but in two different languages. One is in the binary system of 1 and 0 that your computer understands, and the other is in language that a person (or at least a person familiar with the programming language) can understand.

Compiler Versus Interpreter

There is a subtle difference between a compiler and an interpreter. On the surface they both do the same thing, convert human-readable instructions into machine-readable instructions. The difference is mostly a technical one. It lies in the way they work. A *compiler* translates an entire source code file all at once, producing a complete object code file that is ready to run. After the source code file has been compiled once, it doesn't ever need to be compiled again unless the programmer wants to change it. You can even delete the source code file from your disk, because the computer will never refer to it again.

Except for the BASIC programming language, the choice of compiler or interpreter depends on the language itself.

An *interpreter,* on the other hand, translates source code instructions into object code on the fly, as the program runs. Instead of translating the entire source code file all at once, and then having two copies of the program (one executable and one not), there will always be only one copy of the program—the source file. Every time you run that program, it is translated (interpreted) again.

Interpreted programs generally don't run as fast as compiled programs because they have to be translated each time they are run. Compiled programs are translated ahead of time. On the other hand, if you need to make a lot of changes to a program (a common enough event when it is first being written), you will see your changes sooner with an interpreted program. You can run the revised version immediately, without waiting through the entire compilation process.

The choice of compiler versus interpreter is really no choice at all, because most programming languages only come one way. You will rarely find both an interpreter and a compiler for the same programming language. The biggest exception here is the popular BASIC language, which is available in both compiled and interpreted forms. Compiled languages are more popular with professional programmers because they produce quicker, more efficient programs.

Interpreters are popular with the simpler languages favored by beginning programmers or hobbyists because they give more immediate results.

Programming Languages

In this section, you can take a look at all of the most popular programming languages for personal computers. Some languages lend themselves to certain types of programming chores better than others. Some languages are easier to learn. Each one has something unique in its favor, and all of them are used regularly by thousands of programmers worldwide. Most community colleges and universities now offer computer programming courses, and they will certainly use one of the languages discussed here. There are also many excellent books that can help you sharpen your skills at programming. Some are geared toward beginning programmers; others are more advanced, teaching subtle tricks and procedures for getting the maximum amount of power and performance out of your own programs.

It's possible to learn any programming language as your "first" language but it's a good idea to start with BASIC. It teaches the "logic" of programming without many of the headaches.

In each of the discussions that follows, the programming language is introduced with a brief description. You'll see each language's strong and weak points listed along with a somewhat subjective rating of its difficulty for a beginning programmer. If you intend to start writing programs soon, you'll want to begin by learning the language rated *Easy*.

For a side-by-side comparison, there's a sample program included for many of the languages. The programs all accomplish exactly the same thing. You can compare the various steps in each language to get a better idea of how an actual program might look. The programs all display the numbers from 1 to 10 on the display screen, print the message "Hello, world!", and then display the sum of 46 plus 72.

BASIC Programming

As the name implies, BASIC is a, well, very basic programming language. That makes it the ideal first language for a beginning programmer. Among home computer users and hobbyists, BASIC is by far the most popular programming language used today. BASIC is normally an interpreted language, meaning that BASIC programs are converted into machine code as they run. However, BASIC is also one

12

of the few interpreted languages for which there are also compilers available.

Developed at Dartmouth College in 1963, BASIC is a somewhat strained acronym for Beginner's Allpurpose Symbolic Instruction Code. It is available for practically every computer, from home computers and PCs to large business machines and super computers. Although BASIC is not a particularly strong language for any one special type of programming task, it does not have any major weaknesses, either. Overall, it is a very capable language, and for those learning programming it rates an *Easy*.

The following listing shows how the sample program might be put together using the BASIC language.

```
10   LET X=1
20   PRINT X
30   LET X=X+1
40   IF X < 11 GOTO 20
50   PRINT "Hello, world!"
60   LET A=46
70   LET B=72
80   LET C=A+B
90   PRINT C
100  END
```

First of all, you may notice that each line of instructions in the BASIC program is numbered. Your computer executes the instructions in numerical order, not necessarily from top to bottom. It is customary for BASIC programmers to number the lines of their programs in increments of 10. That makes it easy to insert a new instruction between two other instructions by giving it a line number like 42.

The first instruction (Line 10) creates a variable called X. If you're not familiar with algebra, it is common to represent an unknown number by a letter of the alphabet. The value of X is set to 1. The program then progresses to the next line. Line 20 displays the value of the number assigned to the variable X. Note that it will not display the letter "X" but the number 1. If you want it to display the letter "X," you must put quotation marks around it. Without the quotation marks, BASIC assumes that you are referring to a variable called X.

After displaying the value of X, the program proceeds to Line 30, which adds 1 to X, so X now equals 2. Note how the actual BASIC language instructions closely parallel the flow chart from Figure 12-1. Line 40 is the conditional branch instruction. It checks to see if the current value of *X* is still less than 11. If so, the program will branch back to Line 20.

Eventually, after the program displays the number 10 it will add 1 to *X*, making *X* equal to 11. When it repeats line 40, the computer will find that *X* is, in fact, no longer less than 11. Now, instead of branching to Line 20, it will "fall through" to Line 50. Line 50 simply displays the message, "Hello, world!"

The final step in the program is to add two numbers and display the total. Three new variables are created, *A*, *B*, and *C*, with *C* defined as *A* + *B*. Line 90 displays the value of *C*. Finally, Line 100 tells the computer that this program has come to an end, and to stop executing instructions.

C Programming

For professional programming, the language of choice is identified by the single letter C. This is a very powerful, flexible language and was developed, obviously enough, as the successor to the languages called A and B. Programming in C is more difficult for the beginning programmer to learn, earning an *Intermediate* rating.

C is a compiled language used for all kinds of programming tasks. It was originally developed by Brian W. Kernighan and Dennis L. Ritchie, who also had a hand in the development of the UNIX operating system. UNIX itself was written completely with C. It's a safe bet that at least half, if not more, of the commercial application programs for personal computers have been written with the aid of a C compiler.

The following listing shows how a C programmer might accomplish the same task as the BASIC program shown in the previous listing.

```
main()
{    int x,a,b;

    for (x=1; x<11; x++)
        printf("%d", x);

    printf("Hello, world!");

    a=46;
```

12

```
    b=72;
    printf("%d", a+b);
}
```

What a difference! Although the BASIC program and the C program produce exactly the same output, the source code files are not at all alike. To begin with, C language files do not have their lines numbered, and almost every line ends with a semicolon. The differences only begin there. Let's examine this C program to see how it works.

First, the program starts with the line "main( )." This tells the computer that this is the beginning, or main part, of the program. The next line contains a single curly brace character, {. This marks the beginning of the program "main." The final curly brace at the end of the program listing marks the end of the program.

Next, the program defines three variables, *x, a,* and *b*. The word "int" tells the computer that these three variables are all integers. This is known as *declaring variables*. In C programs, all variables must be declared before they can be used, so these kinds of instructions appear often at the beginning of most C programs. These next two lines display the numbers from 1 to 10. The line beginning with "for" accomplishes three things simultaneously. It gives *x* an initial value of 1, it specifies that the program should repeat while *x* is less than 11, and it specifies that *x* should be *incremented* after every repetition. In a C program, the statement "x++" means to increment the value of the variable *x*.

NEW WORD: Increment is a verb that means to add 1 to a number. Incrementing 43 gives 44. You can also decrement a number, which means to subtract 1 from it.

The next line, starting with "printf..." is the one that will be repeated ten times. It displays the current value of the variable *x*. The two characters in quotation marks specify that the variable should be printed as a decimal (base 10) number. After the comma, *x* is specified as the variable to print. Oddly enough, the characters in quotation marks will not appear on the screen, unlike the BASIC program.

After the first ten integers are displayed, the program will print "Hello, world!" using another "printf" instruction. This one is a little more traditional, displaying the message that appears without the quotation marks. Finally, the two variables *a* and *b* are assigned values. Then the "printf" statement that follows adds them together and displays the result at the same time.

Pascal Programming

The Pascal programming language is very popular, especially with students and first-time programmers. It was never actually intended to become a real programming language. It was invented as a hypothetical language meant to teach programming principles at the University of California at San Diego, and was named for the famous French mathematician, Blaise Pascal. So many students learned the Pascal "language," however, that it eventually became a bona fide programming language, supported on many different computers.

Pascal is quite similar to C, for they share many underlying concepts about what makes an efficient programming language. The two languages are so similar that a programmer proficient at one can easily learn the other. Like C, Pascal is a compiled language. For whatever reasons, Pascal is not used in professional programming circles as much as C is. Many excellent courses are taught using the Pascal language, and several good books are available to guide you through it. Pascal gets an *Intermediate* rating for ease of learning. The following listing shows a sample of Pascal programming.

```
program sample;
var x,a,b: integer;

begin
    for x:=1 to 10 do writeln(x);

    writeln('Hello, world!');

    a:=46;
    b:=72;
    c:=a+b;
    writeln(c);
end.
```

12

As you can see, the Pascal program is very similar to the C program. The left and right braces have been replaced by the words "begin" and "end," respectively, and "printf" has become "writeln." Additionally, the equal sign = has become the := symbol. Aside from these minor syntactical differences, you should be able to recognize the program right away.

FORTRAN Programming

FORTRAN is a very old (in computer years) programming language, used in the 1950s with some of the first electronic digital computers. Because they were used exclusively by engineers and scientists, FORTRAN was designed strictly for mathematical uses, and the name is a contraction for Formula Translator. FORTRAN programs are still very much with us, although new programs generally are written in some other language, except perhaps in mathematical circles.

FORTRAN is a compiled language, and FORTRAN compilers are available for most personal computers. Even for the mathematically inclined, however, FORTRAN is not an easy language to learn, so it gets an *Intermediate* rating.

The following listing shows us yet another variation on the program shown in the previous two listings.

```
      integer *2 x,a,b,c
      do 100 x=1,10
      write(*,10)x
10    format(i3)
100   continue

      write(*,20)
20    format("Hello, world!")

      a=46
      b=72
      c=a+b
      write(*,30)c
30,   format(i4)

      end
```

In this FORTRAN program, you can see that some of the lines are numbered, and some aren't. Also, those that are numbered are not in any particular order. The program begins by declaring four integer variables, *x, a, b,* and *c.* The same variable names have been used throughout all the program listings for clarity. The next line, starting with "do..." is very much like the "for" instruction in the C program. It starts the variable *x* at 1, and tells the computer to repeat everything up to Line 100 until *x* equals 10. The "write" instruction displays the value of *x,* and Line 10 specifies how the displayed value will be "formatted."

Next, another "write" instruction prints the "Hello, world!" message. After that, values are assigned to the variables *a* and *b,* they are added together, and the answer is assigned to *c.* The value of *c* is displayed using another pair of "write" and "format" instructions. Finally, the program ends with an "end" instruction.

Assembly Programming

Assembly language is not really a programming language at all. Programming in assembly language is just one step away from programming at the binary machine code level. Unlike other programming languages, an assembly language source instruction will not translate into several machine code instructions. Instead, each assembly language instruction represents exactly one machine code instruction. The translators for assembly language source files are not called compilers or interpreters either. Rather, they are known as *assemblers.*

NEW WORD: An assembler is like a compiler or interpreter, but not so complex. Assemblers must only translate from assembly language to binary code, which is much closer to your computer's native language.

12

Many programmers write their programs in assembly language when they need complete control over the computer. Others avoid assembly language programming entirely, viewing it as excessively complex or as a waste of time. Because each assembly language instruction exactly matches with the underlying machine instructions, an assembly programmer can control every instruction for maximum performance, while the programmer who uses a compiler must be content with the instructions the compiler generates. Programs written in assembly language tend to be smaller and run faster than programs written using a higher level language.

Unlike other languages, assembly language requires that the programmer know a great deal about the computer on which the program is going to run. At the very least, the programmer must know the exact type of microprocessor used, because each microprocessor chip has a different instruction set. When programs are written in a high-level language (like BASIC, Pascal, or C), the compiler converts each source instruction into machine code. The assembly programmer has to do this manually.

This last listing shows how our sample program would look written in assembly language for an IBM-style PC.

```
      XOR   AX,AX
@01:ADD   AX,1
      CALL  @02
      CMP   AX,10
      JL    @001

      LEA   SI,msg
      CALL  @03

      MOV   AX,46
      ADD   AX,72
      CALL  @02
      RET
msg DB    'Hello, world',0

@02  PROC NEAR
      PUSH AX
      PUSH DX
      MOV   DX,378
      ADD   AX,30
      OUT   DX,AL
      POP   DX
      POP   AX
      RET
@02  ENDP
```

```
@03  PROC  NEAR
     PUSH  AX
     PUSH  DX
     MOV   DX,378
@04  LODSB
     OR    AL,AL
     JZ    @05
     OUT   DX,AL
     JMP   @04
@05  POP   DX
     POP   AX
     RET
@03  ENDP
```

This assembly language listing is extremely involved, so we will look at it briefly. First of all, each line represents a single machine code instruction that the microprocessor in an IBM-style PC can execute. Most of the lines are not numbered, with the exception of a few which must be referenced by other instructions. The names "AX," "DX," and "SI" represent registers within the microprocessor. For our purposes, these are the same as the variables used in the other program listings.

Assembly language programming is very complex and requires a thorough understanding of the microprocessor and computer hardware with which you're working. For these reasons, and others, assembly language programming gets an *Advanced* rating.

Other Languages

There are many other programming languages used today, some more popular than others. Some can be tailored for a particular application; others have a peculiar vocabulary or syntax that appeals only to a small percentage of programmers. The following are some of the other, less popular languages that you might find for your personal computer.

12

COBOL

Until the late 1970s, the most popular programming language for business applications was COBOL. COBOL is an acronym for Computer Business-Oriented Language. Before Pascal became popular, COBOL was the language taught at many high schools, colleges, and universities. Since that time its use has fallen off, although there are still many

COBOL programs in use today. Typically, new programmers learn Pascal, C, or BASIC instead. It gets an *Intermediate* rating.

C++

C++ is an "improved" version of the popular C language. It has all of the same features of C, but with some enhancements that can make your programs more reliable and easier for other programmers to understand. Just as with C, C++ makes a good choice for beginning programmers, but still earns an *Intermediate* rating.

Prolog

Programming is more than just a lesson in logic; there is a measure of artistry and elegance in a well-constructed program.

Prolog is a language used primarily for artificial intelligence (AI) work. AI is a category of computer programming that attempts to mimic the workings of the human brain. Because of its structure, Prolog is well-suited for handling large databases and for producing rules-based expert systems applications. Prolog is an *Advanced* language.

LISP

LISP is another language used extensively in artificial intelligence applications. Its name is a contraction of List Processor. This language lends itself to searching, handling, and sorting long strings of lists of human language text, so it has often been used to implement computerized translators. LISP is used primarily on larger computers, but some very capable LISP compilers are also available for personal computers. Treat it as an *Advanced* language.

Modula-2

Modula-2 is a language created by computer science master Niklaus Wirth, who is also credited with much of the work of developing Pascal. Modula-2 is a strongly structured language, meaning that it is somewhat easier for the compiler to find your programming errors than it is with other languages. Structured programming also promotes well planned-out programs, which generally lead to more efficient and trouble-free software. Like Pascal, Modula-2 is an *Intermediate* language.

Forth

Forth is an acquired taste. It is genuinely unlike most other programming languages and is an extremely bad choice for beginning programmers. It does have some unique features that make it interesting and it tends to run very swiftly. For example, all math is calculated backwards, and the Print command is simply a dot (.). Forth programmers tend to be somewhat evangelical about their chosen language, and will defend its idiosyncrasies to the end.

APL

APL is a language for mathematicians. Even more than FORTRAN, APL (A Programming Language) is designed for mathematical work. Calculus students like to use APL for problem solving. It is extraordinarily complex and has almost no commercial application. It even requires a special keyboard and terminal because its instructions are comprised entirely of special geometric shapes and symbols.

A serious programmer will often have a favorite language, but may learn more than one, as some are better suited to a particular task.

Ada

Ada is a relatively new language, developed by the U.S. Department of Defense. Since 1984, all software projects for the Defense Department are supposed to be written in Ada. For that reason alone there has been a surge in the number of Ada programmers and companies providing Ada compilers. The Ada compilers for large computers are expensive because they have to be tested for compliance with government standards, a process that costs several thousand dollars. Many low-cost Ada compilers for personal computers are also available. Ada was named after Augusta Ada Byron, daughter of Lord Byron, and the Countess of Lovelace. She is generally regarded as the first computer programmer.

Programmable Applications

12

In recent years, a new kind of programming language has been developed that is available to computer users who might normally never consider writing programs. Many database management applications have a sort of programming language of their own to allow database users to customize the database software for their own needs. With this feature, you can generate customized reports, automate repetitive procedures, carry out complex searches with a single command, and perform many other specialized tasks.

Although these are not considered actual "languages" by programming purists, they offer all of the features of a programming language, and serve the same purpose. If you have one of these applications, you should make use of its programmable features. You may find that the application does even more than you expected. You may also find that you enjoy programming and want to learn a more traditional programming language.

Bibliography

More information about programming languages can be found in the following books, all published by Osborne/McGraw-Hill in Berkeley, California.

Albrecht, Bob. *Teach Yourself GW-BASIC*. 1990

Schildt, Herbert. *Turbo C++ for Windows Inside & Out*. 1992

Feibel, Werner. *Turbo Pascal 7 Handbook*. 1993

Hahn, Harley. *Assembler Inside & Out*. 1992

Ribar, John. *C Disk Tutor*. 1992

Schildt, Herbert. *Teach Yourself C*. 1990

CHAPTER

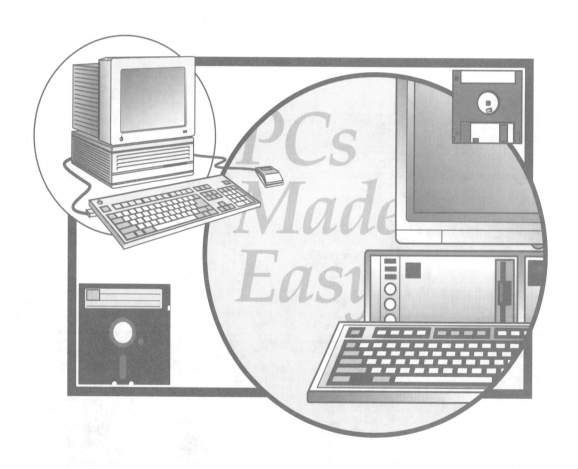

PCs Made Easy

13

HOW DOES IT ALL WORK?

In this chapter we'll follow a program from start to finish as it makes its way through your computer system. Along the way, we'll visit the disk drives, keyboard, display, and memory sections of your personal computer. This chapter shows you a little more about how each part works and, more importantly, how they all work together.

There's nothing in this chapter that you absolutely need to know in order to be a happy, successful PC user. This little tour is intended to satisfy any remaining questions you may have about how your computer gets from here to there. Without getting too technical, this chapter will show you how it goes. The simplified block diagram in Figure 13-1 may help you along the way. It shows all of the major parts of your PC and how they connect to one another. Follow it along as you take a guided tour through your personal computer.

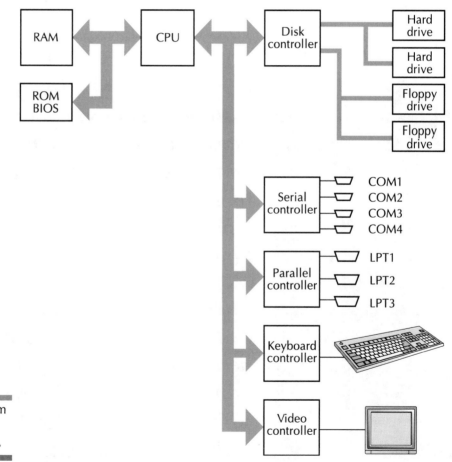

Block diagram
of your PC
Figure 13-1.

Bootstrap

The first thing that happens after you turn your computer on is that it goes through its bootstrap procedure (as described in Chapter 7). This is where it learns how to be a computer all over again. Once the power is turned on, the microprocessor in your PC starts looking around for some instructions to run.

REMEMBER: The microprocessor, or CPU, chip in your computer is the main "brains" of the whole system. Different kinds of CPU chips have different model numbers, like 486 or 68030.

The first place the microprocessor looks is in its read-only memory chips, or ROMs. (You can find these near the upper-left corner of the block diagram.) The ROM chips in your PC hold a program called the BIOS (Basic Input and Output System). Part of the BIOS has the instructions for bootstrapping your computer. Normally, this includes dumb stuff like looking around the system for controllers, plus things like a memory test and a keyboard test. Your PC might run a memory test whenever you turn it on. You may also have noticed that the lights on your keyboard usually blink when your PC is turned on. That's all part of the bootstrap procedure, called the *Power-On Self Test,* or *POST.*

After the POST completes, the BIOS program tells the CPU in your PC to look for the real operating system because BIOS can't do very much by itself. First, the PC will check one or both floppy disk drives to see if there's a diskette in there. If there is, it will try to read what's on the diskette. If not, the CPU will check the hard disk. That's what normally happens.

NOTE: If you put a floppy disk in the drive and close the door, most PCs will try to boot the operating system from it. If the diskette doesn't really have the operating system software on it, your PC may not boot. Just remove the disk and try again.

13

The very first file stored on your hard disk holds the rest of the bootstrap loader. You know it's there because it was put there when your hard disk was formatted. This might have happened at the PC factory before you bought your PC, or you or a friend may have done it. Anyway, it's always the first file on your disk. You can't even see it in a directory listing, because the filename is hidden.

The CPU reads the data from the bootstrap file and writes it into RAM (random-access memory). The procedure is a bit like passing spoons from one hand to the other: read a byte from the disk, write a byte to RAM, read a byte from disk, and so on.

When the whole operating system is copied to RAM, the CPU starts executing it. That's when you see your screen start to display a bunch of messages and you finally see your prompt. For Macintosh users, that's when the "happy Mac" picture goes away and you see your normal Mac desktop.

Keyboard

After your PC has booted the operating system, it waits patiently for you to press a key on the keyboard or move your mouse. At this point it will sit and wait forever. Your computer is incredibly fast, and human fingers are incredibly slow. Underneath each and every key on your keyboard is a little switch, like a miniature light switch. When you press a key, any key, the switch turns on. When you let go of the key and it pops back up, the switch turns off again.

Most of the keyboard keys are the same as those on a typewriter.

Every time one of these switches turns on or off, it "wakes up" a microprocessor inside your keyboard. This isn't the main CPU inside your PC, it's yet another microprocessor in your keyboard. Its only task is to watch what keys you press and tell the main CPU about it. The microprocessor inside your keyboard is a much slower version of the one that's in your PC. In fact, it's just a little bit down the CPU pecking order from the CPU in the original IBM PC.

You can tell just by looking that the keys on your keyboard are arranged in rows. They're also lined up into columns, sort of. The columns slant a bit to the left, but they're still in neat columns. When you press a key, the keyboard processor checks to see what row and column the switch is in. If it's in the bottom row, second column from the left, it knows you must have pressed an "X." (This is just an example, your keyboard may not be arranged exactly this way.) The keyboard processor sends the code for an "X" to your main CPU, where it will be written into a *buffer*. When you release the ⊠ key, the keyboard processor will tell the main CPU about that, too.

NEW WORD: A buffer is a place in memory that the operating system software uses to store miscellaneous data that it will need later on. A keyboard buffer may use a dozen or so bytes of RAM. It's called that because the memory works like a buffer between the keyboard and the microprocessor.

If you keep holding the key down, the keyboard processor assumes that you want to type a lot of "X's" and keeps sending "X" codes to the main CPU. That's why your keys repeat when you hold them down. It won't stop sending "X" codes until you finally release the key. On some PCs you get to adjust the amount of time before the repeating starts, and how fast they'll repeat. This is called the *typematic rate*.

The code for each letter depends on the type of PC. Macs use one kind of coding, and IBM-style PCs use another. In the PC world, they're called *scan codes*. There's one scan code for a key when you first press it, and another scan code for when you let up on the key. There are also scan codes for the left and right Shift keys, the function keys, and all the other keys on your keyboard.

When you press the Enter or Return key, your PC is programmed to start paying attention to what you've been typing to see if it's supposed to do something. It checks the key codes stored in the keyboard buffer in RAM, and compares them against the commands it knows about. For example, on a PC, it checks to see if you've typed DIR, or TIME, or one of the other built-in DOS commands. If you haven't typed one of these commands, your PC will start looking for a matching command on disk.

Disk

As you know, your disk keeps a directory of all of the files you have stored on it. You can see the directory for yourself by typing the DIR command. Every time you add a file to the disk, your PC is programmed to update the directory with the new filename and the correct date and time information. Likewise, when you delete a file, the file's name is removed from the directory.

13

Your PC uses the directory itself whenever you type in a command that it doesn't immediately recognize. It is programmed to look on the disk for a program with a matching name. It's assuming that you know the name of a program, and that you want to run it. The main CPU in your computer will send out commands to the disk controller. They tell the controller to place the disk's read/write heads over the part of the disk where the directory is stored. As the disk spins around and around (see Figure 13-2), the disk controller sends a constant stream of data to the microprocessor as different areas of the disk pass under the heads. The CPU is reading sector marks. These are the magnetic "mileposts" that were placed on the disk when it was formatted. When the disk gets to the sector where the directory is stored, the CPU will start copying the directory.

File Not Found

As the disk sectors with the directory stored on them pass under the read/write heads, the CPU reads the data from the disk controller and

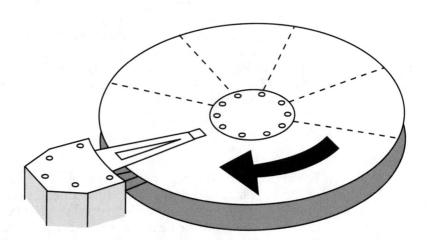

Searching for
the disk
directory
Figure 13-2.

copies it into an unused space in RAM. The whole directory for an average hard disk drive needs two or three sectors' worth of data. Once the directory has been copied into RAM, the CPU will start comparing, letter by letter, what you typed with what is stored in the directory.

If it makes it through the entire directory without finding a match, your PC will print a message:

```
C>foobar
Bad command or file name

C>
```

This says, in essence, "I can't find what you're looking for, sorry." That may just mean that you accidentally made a typing mistake and misspelled the name of the program you want. It may also mean that the program you want is stored someplace where your PC didn't look.

Search Path

Here's a confusing aspect of PCs and the DOS operating system. Even though your PC can tell where every single file on your disk is stored, it won't always check everywhere. It may very well skip over the majority of your disk and only check in a few places. This is supposed to be a benefit, but you'll have to decide that for yourself. DOS has a command called PATH that lets you decide where your PC will look for files and where it won't look. Normally, it won't look in very many places. Unless you use the PATH command, your PC will not search any subdirectories at all looking for your programs. If you have a lot of subdirectories, that can mean that your PC is happily ignoring most of your disk. When you type in a program name and your PC says "Bad command or file name" it may really be saying "I can't find your program, but I didn't look very hard, either." Be sure to read about the PATH command in your DOS manual, and use it if you have created subdirectories on your hard disk.

Check your DOS manual and become familiar with the PATH command; it will save you a lot of time and frustration.

Another reason your PC might say you typed a "bad command," when you know full well the file is right *there,* is because the name you typed might not be the name of a program. There are plenty of files stored on your disk that aren't computer programs. In fact, most of your files probably aren't programs. They don't contain computer instructions;

13

they're data files instead. You can't make your computer run a data file. If your PC searches the directory and finds a data file with a matching name, it will skip over it just as though it didn't exist. You'll get the same message after typing in the name of a data file as for typing in a completely bogus filename.

Program files always have filenames that end with the EXE, COM, or BAT extensions. No matter how hard you try, you can never make your PC run another kind of file. Changing a file's name won't help, either. Don't arbitrarily change the name of a data file to give it a program file's three-letter extension. You'll only cause yourself grief, and the file still won't run.

NOTE: Technically, files with the BAT filename extension are not full-fledged programs, but they run like programs do. These files are called batch files. If you're interested, your DOS manual will tell you how to create batch files of your own.

File Found

Okay, so we know what happens when your PC can't find a matching filename. What happens when it does? First, it looks to see how big the program file is. That information is stored in the directory, so it's easy enough to find out. The CPU checks the size of the file against the amount of RAM it has free at that moment. If the file is bigger than the amount of free memory, you'll get an "Out of memory" message, and the program won't run. Your only option here is to run out to the computer store and buy some more memory.

If the program does fit, the contents of the program file are copied from disk to RAM. When the copy is complete, the CPU in your PC will execute the instructions stored in the program, starting at the beginning. After that, what happens is up to the program.

NOTE: Not all programs take up the same amount of space in memory as they do on disk. Programs with the COM extension are always the same size. Programs with the EXE extension are stored in a special format and can get smaller when they are loaded, but they usually get larger.

Memory

Every byte of program instructions takes up one byte of memory, naturally enough. Most instructions take up three or four bytes. Each byte of storage in your computer's memory is numbered, starting from zero (engineers hate to waste a perfectly good number). The number is called that byte's *address*. Byte locations in memory are like post office boxes in your local post office. Each box is the same size, can hold the same amount of mail (one byte), and has its own unique address, as illustrated in Figure 13-3. The same system works with memory locations.

NEW WORD: A memory address is a number given to a particular byte of memory. Memory addresses are always consecutive and start counting from zero.

Inside the CPU chip in your PC is a memory address *counter*. The counter holds the address of a memory location. When a program starts executing, the CPU reads the very first instruction from memory, runs it, and then reads the next instruction, and so on. After every instruction the CPU adjusts its address counter to the address of the next instruction. If an instruction makes the CPU jump or branch to another part of the program, the address counter gets modified to hold the address of the instruction it's going to jump to.

If you have 1MB of RAM in your PC, the memory locations will have addresses from 0 for the first one to 1,048,575 for the last one.

13

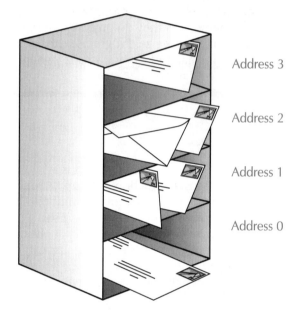

Address 3

Address 2

Address 1

Address 0

Memory is
like a set of
mailboxes
Figure 13-3.

(Remember that 1MB is more than 1 million bytes.) If you have 640K of RAM, the last location will have address 655,359.

Now, for obscure technical reasons, most engineers don't count memory addresses like normal people do. They count with a different numbering system, called *hexadecimal,* or base 16 arithmetic. There's no need for you to learn how to count in hexadecimal, but odds are that you're going to encounter hexadecimal numbers in your DOS manual and in other documentation that came with your PC.

NEW WORD: The hexadecimal numbering system is based on the number 16 instead of the familiar decimal system, which is based on 10. Hexadecimal numbers are frequently used by computer engineers and programmers.

What Are These Numbers with the Letters?

We have 10 fingers and toes, and most of us were taught to count in base 10. For engineers, that means that there are 10 digits, 0 to 9, and when they have counted up to the last digit (9), they "roll it over" and add one to the next digit to the left. That's why 10 follows 9, and 30 follows 29. Easy.

When counting in hexadecimal, the first sixteen numbers are 0 through 15, not 1 through 16.

Now, what if we all had 16 fingers? Would counting still go from 0 to 9? Probably not. Instead, we might have invented 6 extra digits for the numbers 10 through 15, but otherwise use the same counting principles. Computer engineers use the letters "A" through "F" for these extra six digits. Instead of counting "8, 9, 10," they count "8, 9, A, B," and so on. The last digit in hexadecimal arithmetic is F, not 9. And what comes after the number F?

The next number is 10, of course. To most people, the figure 10 means "ten." But to computer engineers who are counting in hexadecimal, 10 means "sixteen" because that's how many they have counted up to after exhausting all of the new digits. They start with 0 and end with F. Adding F plus 1 gives 10.

Decimal	0	1	2	3	4	5	6	7	8	9	10	11	12	13	14	15	16	17	. . .
Hexidecimal	0	1	2	3	4	5	6	7	8	9	A	B	C	D	E	F	10	11	. . .

The only part of this that you need to remember is that you should be wary of numbers printed in computer manuals, especially if you're reading about memory size or addresses. It is customary among engineers for memory to be measured in hexadecimal, and not everybody remembers to convert these to "normal" decimal numbers before putting them in the manual. It's a dead giveaway when the numbers have letters in them.

Remembering Where the Memory Went

Not all of the memory in your PC can be used for storing and running programs. If you've got the full complement of 1MB of RAM, only

13

about 600KB, or just over half of that, is used for your programs. The rest is taken up by other things, as Figure 13-4 shows.

First, DOS itself is a program (your operating system), and it uses up about 60K of space. It starts right at the beginning of memory, at address zero, and fills up the lowest part of your RAM. If you have a lot of add-in expansion boards installed, they may require special device driver programs, and those will take up some more space.

If you use any of the so-called "pop up" programs or memory-resident programs, these will take up a bit of space as well. After these have all been loaded (normally at bootstrap time), then the remaining RAM is free for your programs to use. Or is it?

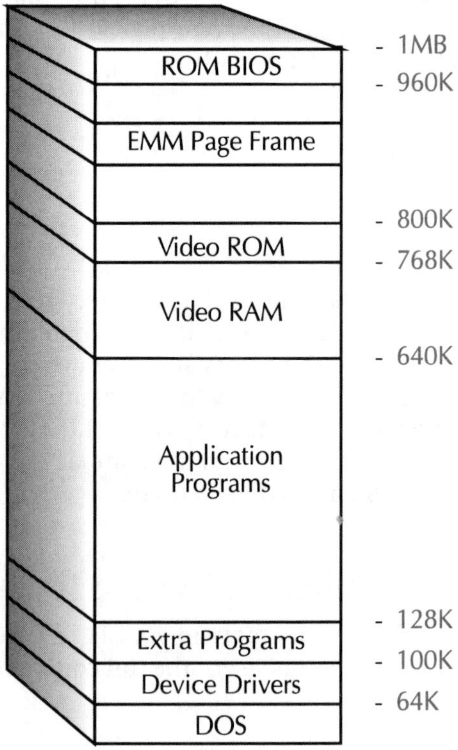

Where your
PC's memory
goes
Figure 13-4.

ROM BIOS	- 1MB
	- 960K
EMM Page Frame	
	- 800K
Video ROM	- 768K
Video RAM	
	- 640K
Application Programs	
Extra Programs	- 128K
	- 100K
Device Drivers	
DOS	- 64K

After the infamous 640K barrier (discussed in Chapter 3), things become crowded again. Starting at that point in memory is where your video display card stores whatever it is displaying on your screen. This may take up 128K of memory or so. Also, most video cards have a ROM chip on them (like the ROM BIOS your PC used to bootstrap itself), and that usually takes another 32K of memory.

After the video card, there is a large unused portion of memory, about 160K. If you have expanded memory and an expanded memory manager (EMM) program, the EMM "page frame" will be somewhere in here. Finally, the last 64K of memory just before the end of the first megabyte will be the BIOS ROMs.

Video Display

Once your program is under way, the CPU must slavishly follow all the instructions it contains. If you're running a word processing application, it will probably clear the screen, display a small menu of options, and wait for you to type something. All of this depends on a working video adapter and monitor.

Although monitors are still available in monochrome, color monitors are a lot more fun.

The video adapter is a plug-in expansion card inside your PC's main system box. It's considered an option card (even though you have to have one) because not everybody wants exactly the same video system. Some people like color, others prefer monochrome (black and white). Some prefer high resolution while others would rather save their money for other things. Your video adapter may be built right into your PC's motherboard. If you have a laptop computer, it certainly is. No matter how they are attached, they all work the same way.

Under program control, the CPU sends data to the video adapter board to make it display the right things. The video adapter has some memory on it, as you saw in the previous section. The principle is simple. The CPU writes the code for an "A" into the video RAM, and an "A" appears on the screen. The exact location in the video RAM (the memory address) determines where the character will appear on the screen. If the CPU writes the code for a "Z" to the same address in the video RAM as the "A," then the "A" disappears, to be replaced by a "Z."

There is special circuitry on your video adapter card to read these codes from the video RAM and send them to your monitor. The card and monitor are connected by a cable. Your monitor works a little bit like a dot

13

matrix printer, in that everything it displays is made up of little dots, called *pixels*. If you look very closely at your monitor, you can see them.

NEW WORD: A pixel is one tiny dot of light on your computer screen. The word is short for "picture element." On a color monitor, each pixel can be a different color. The more pixels on your screen, the sharper the picture will be.

To display something on your screen, the monitor starts at the upper-left corner of the screen and starts drawing dots, or pixels, from left to right. This is called one *scan line*. When it gets to the end of a scan line, it moves down by one pixel and starts a new scan line. The number of pixels in a scan line, and the number of scan lines down the screen, is the monitor's resolution, and it changes from monitor to monitor. A VGA monitor might have 640 by 400 pixels. Generally speaking, the more pixels the better.

If your program calls for displaying graphics instead of text, then the CPU writes individual bits into the video display RAM, instead of character codes for letters and symbols. Each bit controls one pixel, if you have a black-and-white display. If you have a color display, it takes more than one bit per pixel.

With a black-and-white display, the CPU only has to indicate whether a pixel is supposed to be on (light) or off (dark), and that only takes one bit. With a color display, it also has to indicate what color the pixel is supposed to be, and that takes more bits per pixel. With two bits, the CPU would choose between four different colors by alternating the bit patterns (00, 01, 10, 11). With three bits per pixel, you could display eight colors, and so on.

A good-quality display uses 8 bits per pixel, giving you a choice of 65,536 colors. For a truly professional photographic-quality display, you can buy an adapter card with 24 bits per pixel and a monitor that will likely cost more than your entire computer system.

Mouse

To use your application more effectively, you may have a mouse. By moving the mouse around on your table or desktop, you can move a pointer on the screen. With the movable pointer, you can point to things on the screen that you want to move, or delete, or highlight. You can also point to commands if they're displayed on the screen. If you are running Windows, you already know how this works.

To make your mouse work, your computer must normally load a mouse driver. This is a device driver program that gets loaded from disk and runs every time you turn your PC on. Your mouse driver controls how fast your mouse moves and sometimes what the buttons do.

Printer

Now that you've started your application and done the work you wanted to do, it's time to print out the results. Depending on the application, you may press a few keys, select a command from a menu, or even run a different program to get your printed results. No matter what the method, there are a lot of events that have to take place before the first word ever meets the paper.

A printer is not always a necessary accessory for your PC.

First, the CPU in your PC will send commands to the printer controller. That may be either a serial port controller or a parallel port controller, depending on your printer and where you have it attached. (See Chapter 9 for a detailed discussion of the printer.) The commands will get the printer ready to start printing. Each printer has different commands to feed a new sheet of paper, select the proper type style and size (the font), and prepare to print text or graphics. That's why almost all applications need to know what brand and model of printer you have, and what PC port it's connected to.

After sending the appropriate setup commands, your PC will start sending data to the printer. For text printing (like letters and reports) your PC will usually send the ASCII codes for each individual letter to be printed. Then it is the job of the printer to make the shape of that letter on paper. If you have a dot matrix printer, it will make up the shape of each letter with a row of dots, from left to right. As the print head moves from left to right, each pin in the print head will make an impression, until the whole letter is formed. Different dot matrix printers use different patterns to make their letters, so not all printed reports will look the same.

13

Apart from normal characters, your printer must also handle special control characters. These are the other ASCII codes besides the standard letters, numbers, and punctuation marks that you read about in Chapter 9. They are used to control a device, like a printer. Control codes make the printer move over one tab stop, advance a page, underline text, and so forth. When your printer receives a control code, it will carry out some special function.

After your printing ends successfully, you're finished with your work. Now you can use the mouse or keyboard to shut down the application program. At this point, your application program will terminate, or exit, and control will again be turned over to the operating system. The memory that the application took up will be free for the next program. We have now come full circle, from operating system to application program and back to the operating system.

CHAPTER

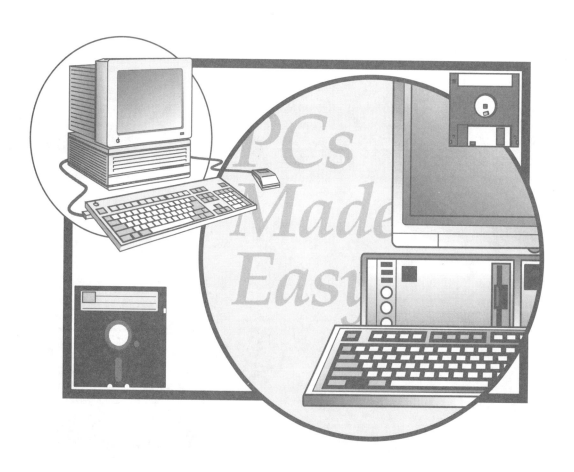

14

DO'S AND DON'TS

This chapter covers computer habits, good ones and bad ones. You'll see some common mistakes that many PC users make, some good rules to learn, and some good habits to cultivate. The tips here generally apply to any personal computer, regardless of type or brand. You might also want to consult your owner's manual for more hints specific to your computer.

Give Yourself Time to Learn

Don't make the mistake of assuming that once your PC is plugged in and turned on, all of your problems will be solved. Unfortunately, this is not the case. Like any new skill, learning to use a new computer takes time. Even though using your PC or learning a new application program is not particularly difficult, it's going to take some time to learn. This is especially true if you bought the computer to replace old manual business techniques. Old habits can be hard to break.

Allow yourself (and others) plenty of time to become accustomed to using the computer. Some people will take to it immediately; others seem to loathe anything invented after their birthday. Don't expect to do anything useful with it for at least a month. Go ahead and do your work using traditional methods while you come up to speed on the computer.

If you're using the PC in your work, the best, and most prudent, policy is to do your work in tandem. That means using both manual and computerized methods for a few months to be sure that everything goes smoothly. Then, you can slowly become less dependent on your old ways and rely more on just the computer.

Practice, Experiment, and Explore

The best way to learn how to use your computer or a new program is to use it! Once you are familiar with the basics, set aside some time several days a week to experiment with your system and the software. Thumb through your software manuals and try out features that you're not currently using. Use an operating system command that you normally have no use for. Make a backup copy of a work file and experiment on it, trying out various features of your application that you don't usually use. You can't break your computer just by using it, and you don't have to worry about losing data if you're working on a backup copy of a file.

Look for New Sources of Information

There's a lot to learn with a new computer and many skills and concepts to acquire. It's always helpful to know where to turn for more information if you get stuck. When in doubt, read the manual. The owner's manual will have a lot of information specific to your

particular machine that you can't get anywhere else. When you have a question, go to your PC manual first.

Sometimes the manual can be too technical or too specific for what you need. Other good sources of information about your new computer or new software are computer books, like this one. There are many titles to choose from, for PC beginners to "power users." The chances are good that there are several books about your particular computer.

Another good resource is someone else who has a PC and a little more expertise than you. If there's a "computer expert" in your office, great. If not, cultivate a relationship with your computer dealer or service center. Many computer dealers offer training courses. There are also several independent training institutes that hold classes on a regular basis in most major metropolitan areas. Your local community college or university also may have beginning computer classes.

 ## Insert Disks Carefully

Even though floppy disks are square and *could* fit into your floppy disk drive in almost any orientation, there is only one *right* way to put them in. If you put a floppy disk in the wrong way, it might get stuck and not come out again. If that happens, you have to find a way to remove it carefully without damaging your disk drive. If you try to use the disk while it's loaded incorrectly, you run the risk of damaging your disk drive as well.

Each 5 1/4-inch floppy disk has an oblong hole near one edge, exposing the recording disk inside. The hole is cut from both sides of the disk, opposite the place where you put the disk label. The front side of a 5 1/4-inch floppy should be smooth, with no rough edges or seams. The back side should have a seam around three sides.

Always insert a 5 1/4-inch floppy disk with the oblong hole going in first and the label last. This usually means that the writing on the label will be upside-down from your point of view.

The smaller 3 1/2-inch floppy disks don't have the same exposed holes that the 5 1/4-inch disks have. Instead, they have a hard plastic shell and a shiny aluminum shutter. The shutter slides open when you insert the disk into the disk drive and pops shut when you remove it again. The front side of the disk has a big space to stick an adhesive label.

The back side of the disk reveals the sliding write-protect tab and also the spindle mounting hub. Always insert 3 1/2-inch disks shutter-end first, with the label going in last. The label side should be facing up, assuming that your disk drive is right-side up in your PC. If your disk drive is laying on its side, you have to figure out which side it's on. Generally, the light and the eject pushbutton on the front of the floppy disk drive are at the "bottom," so insert the disk with the hub aimed that way.

Save Your Work Regularly

A great worry for most PC users is losing data. That can be a very real danger, but only if you haven't taken the proper precautions. A power outage, an unforeseen mechanical failure, or an electronic *glitch* can make your computer stop suddenly. If your work hasn't already been saved, you can only start over again.

NEW WORD: A glitch is a made-up word to describe an electrical failure. To an engineer, it has a very specific meaning, but many people use it to mean anything that's unusual.

No power failure or equipment malfunction can take away work that you've already stored on diskette. The worst that can happen then is that you will lose new data that is still in the computer's memory. Once you've copied that data from memory to floppy disks, it becomes immune to nearly any kind of computer catastrophe.

To protect your investment in your work, you should save your files often as you use the computer. A good rule of thumb is, when saving your work, never wait longer than you are willing to spend to do it over. That may be anywhere from ten minutes to four hours, depending on your personal feelings. Pick a frequency that suits your style best, but definitely get into the habit of saving your work.

Store Your Disks in a Safe Place

Your floppy disks hold your computer-readable information the same way that a file cabinet holds paper records. When a paper document is lost or damaged, that information is gone. The same is true for information stored on a floppy disk, except that the hazards to a floppy disk are not quite as obvious. You should protect and store your floppy disks with at least the same care that you give your paper files. If a diskette holds particularly important information, you should store it in a safe, or some other secure, fireproof place. Keep your disks clean and dust-free and away from heat and magnets. Never bend them. Some additional hints for proper diskette care are given later in this chapter.

14

Make Backup Copies of Your Floppy Disks

Accidents do happen. As careful as you are with your diskettes or other important files, there's always the possibility that something may happen to them. The best protection against accidental loss or damage is to keep multiple copies of important disk files. Buy an extra box of diskettes and make three copies of any disk that you feel you absolutely can't do without. Make copies and, if possible, store them in widely spaced locations. Store one at work, another at home, and if your business is large, send one away to a different office or field location. (Diskette mailing instructions are given later in this chapter.) That way if a disk is damaged, or lost in a fire, you'll always have identical copies of your important data.

REMEMBER: Keeping backup copies of your important files is the single most important thing you can do. Keep your work and your programs safe and make new backup copies regularly.

Don't Fill in Labels on the Disk

Sticking an adhesive label onto your diskettes is an excellent way to keep track of what each disk holds. Usually a box of new blank diskettes will come with labels, one for each disk. It's not important what you write on the label, as long as you write something that will help you remember what the disk is for.

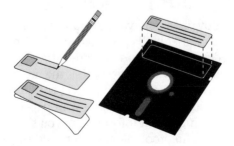

The rule to remember is to fill out the labels *before* affixing them to your disks. Once the label is on the disk, you should not write on it anymore. If you absolutely have to, use a felt-tip pen and a delicate touch. Avoid pencils and ball-point pens. If you press too hard while you write, you'll crease the diskette and possibly ruin the entire disk.

Write-Protect Your Floppy Disks

All floppy disks have a way to write-protect them. A disk that has been write-protected cannot be used for storing new information, nor can information already on it be erased. You can undo the write protection any time. For 5 1/4-inch diskettes, you write-protect the disk by placing a small *opaque* sticker across the notch along the edge of the diskette sleeve. For 3 1/2-inch floppies, you slide the small tab on the back of the disk towards the top edge.

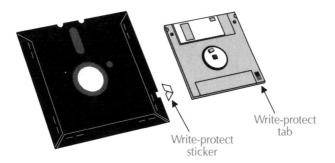

Write-protect
tab

Write-protect
sticker

Obviously, you don't want to write-protect all of your floppy disks, or you'd never be able to use them. You should only write-protect the disks you've used to hold backup copies or other information you don't want to erase accidentally. Write-protecting a diskette won't protect it from damage, but it will prevent accidental erasure in case someone puts the wrong floppy disk in the disk drive.

REMEMBER: Don't try to use transparent cellophane tape for a write-protect sticker. The sticker has to be opaque, because your PC uses a beam of light to detect it. Clear stickers won't show up.

Separate Formatted Disks

All diskettes must be formatted before your computer can store data on them. Disks bought from the store are normally "raw" or unformatted. Formatting a new disk only takes a few moments, but it can be a nuisance when you're ready to store something and you don't want to wait. Formatting all of your new diskettes right after you buy them is a good habit to form. Then there's never a question of whether a disk is ready for use or not.

Another good habit is to keep your formatted disks and your new, unformatted disks in two different piles. Keep the formatted disks clearly marked, so that you don't waste time looking for them.

Don't Store Disks Near Heat or Sunlight

Like records, floppy disks can be damaged by heat or direct sunlight. They are just as susceptible to damage from warping but not as easily replaced. Keep your floppy disks away from direct sunlight around windows. You should also protect them from sources of heat, like heating registers, radiators, ducts, and the top of your computer.

Keep Disks Away from Magnets

Some floppy disk hazards are not as easy to spot as others. An often overlooked peril is a magnetic field, the natural enemy of floppy disks. Floppy disks store information in much the same way that audio or video tapes do, and, like tapes, they can be erased by stray magnetic fields. But since magnetic fields are invisible, how can you avoid them?

Learn to be alert to the kinds of devices that create magnetic fields, and keep your disks a safe distance away. Magnetic fields are generated by electric motors, video screens, and buzzers or speakers. Around the home, this means that you must keep your floppy disks away from televisions and stereo speakers. A distance of about three feet is usually safe. At the office you must not store your diskettes near photocopiers, speakers, air conditioners, or fluorescent lights. Again, a few feet of distance is ample.

Don't let disk get too hot or cold 10°C-60°C 50°F-140°F

 Do not bend

 Do not put near magnetic field

 Do not touch media

Unfortunately, the two biggest culprits that generate magnetic fields can also be the toughest to avoid. Don't set a floppy disk beside a telephone or on top of a computer display monitor. Telephone ringers and all video display screens are terrific sources of magnetism. And, of course, never use a magnet to hold a floppy disk to a bulletin board.

Do Not Fold, Spindle, or Mutilate

Be careful that you don't accidentally crease or crumple a diskette when inserting it into a floppy disk drive. Handle disks gently when removing them, inserting them, or placing them in a storage box. The 5 1/4-inch floppy disks are easily damaged by improper handling. If you want to mail a floppy disk, there are some guidelines for shipping that you should observe.

Sending Diskettes Through the Mail

It's easy to send a diskette through the mail to transport a large collection of data. The only alternatives are sending data with a modem or printing it and shipping the printout. Mailing diskettes is safe and reliable, provided you protect your disks well.

Most office supply and stationery stores sell diskette mailers. These are flat pocket-like envelopes made of very stiff cardboard. They are large enough to hold one or two 5 1/4-inch diskettes. Smaller envelopes will hold a few 3 1/2-inch diskettes. Place your disk in the mailer and then drop the mailer into a larger envelope and address it. Some mailers can be mailed directly and have adequate space for addresses and postage.

Usually floppy disk mailers have special markings with statements like "Do Not Fold" and "Avoid Exposure to All Magnetic Fields" printed on them. When inserting 5 1/4-inch diskettes into a mailer, it is a good idea to put the disk in its protective paper sleeve first and then insert the disk and sleeve into the mailer sideways. That way your addressee can remove the disk from the mailer without removing it from its sleeve.

Back Up Your Hard Disk Regularly

For most PC users, a hard disk drive is a necessity. Nothing comes close to it for speed, ease of access, and storage capacity. The one drawback that hard disk drives have is that they cannot be removed from the system for safekeeping. That means anything disastrous that might befall your computer will also ruin your hard disk drive—and all of the information it stores.

If you have a PC with a hard disk, it is vitally important that you make regular backup copies of all of the files it contains. At least back up your data files; the programs should still be on the diskettes they came on. This is probably the single most important piece of PC maintenance that you can carry out, and it is one of the most commonly ignored. If you have a 50MB hard disk drive in your system, it probably can store more than a year's worth of work. How would you feel if all that work were swept away by an accident? It can happen to you if your computer is dropped, stolen, or has a serious failure. All of your data will be trapped in an unusable hard disk drive.

REMEMBER: Keep plenty of floppy disks handy to make regular backup copies. If you use a tape drive to make backups, keep a stock of tapes on hand. Just don't forget to make those backups.

Most PC users use their floppy disks to make backup copies of the files on their hard disks. Naturally, it's going to take several floppy disks to hold what you have stored on one hard disk. Exactly how many floppies you'll need will depend on the capacity of your hard disk drive, how full it is, and the capacity of each floppy disk. A reasonable estimate is that a few dozen floppy disks should store the data from a medium-sized hard disk, as long as it is not yet completely full.

Backing up a hard disk can be a tedious chore because you constantly have to insert floppy disks in your floppy drive and remove them again until the entire hard disk has been copied. Plan on spending at least half an hour at this task. You should also plan on making a complete backup of your hard disk at least once a month. After you make a full backup, store the floppy disks in a safe place. Your backup floppies should not be used for anything else. Consider the price of a box or two of floppy disks as insurance against hard disk damage.

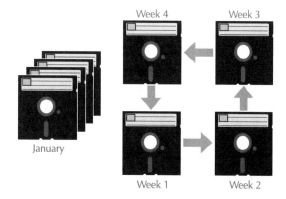

A good habit is to make a full and complete backup copy of a hard disk once a month. Then every week back up just those files that have changed

14

since the last complete backup. This is known as an *incremental backup*. An incremental backup takes much less time than a full backup and uses fewer disks, too, so you're not so likely to skip doing it.

NEW WORD: Making an incremental backup means backing up (copying) only those files that haven't changed since the time you made the last backup. An incremental backup allows you to copy the very minimum number of files and still remain secure.

You might also look at some of the many special-purpose backup programs available that can automate this task for you. Store each incremental backup near the full backup. When four weekly incremental backups have been made, it's time to make another monthly backup. Then you can reuse the incremental backup disks for the next incremental backup, and so forth.

If you're a PC user with a big hard disk (150MB or more), it becomes almost absurd to back up the hard disk to floppies. Instead, you might consider a tape drive. Tape drives are add-in devices like floppy disk drives that are used exclusively for making backups. They're trouble-free, easy to operate, and available for most any personal computer. Tapes make a good backup medium because they are compact, rugged, and hold a tremendous amount of data. Just as with floppies, though, tapes won't do you any good if you don't make regular backup copies and store them in a safe place.

Don't Drop or Jar Your Hard Disk

Hard disks can store 100 to 1000 times more information than a floppy disk, and access it ten times faster. To perform these amazing feats, hard disk drives are manufactured to exacting standards with many parts machined to critical tolerances. All in all, given its complexity, a hard disk drive is a remarkably durable device. But there are limits to what even a good hard disk drive can endure.

The single biggest hazard for a hard disk is a harsh bump or jolt. Like a fine watch, a sudden shock can damage or dislodge some of the critical workings of your hard disk drive. What usually happens is the delicate read/write heads literally crash into the surface of the disk, destroying any data in their path. A *head crash* can also render some or all of the disk's recording surface unusable, so even if the crashed information is restored, you will still lose some portion of the disk's storage capacity. This assumes, of course, that the disk or the heads are not completely beyond repair.

NEW WORD: A head crash is a disastrous, usually unrepairable, failure in a hard disk drive. It is caused by rough handling and happens when the delicate read/write heads skid across the surface of the disk while it is spinning.

Jostling a hard disk is much more likely to cause damage when the disk drive is running than when it is turned off. Keep in mind, the hard disk is always running whenever your PC is turned on. You don't actually have to be using the disk. Even an inactive hard disk drive can be damaged by dropping or jarring. That is why most hard disk drives can park their read/write heads when not in use.

The magnitude of the shock required to scuttle a hard disk drive varies greatly, depending on who made it and what it was doing at the time it was shocked. As a rule, dropping a hard disk drive ruins it, but smaller movements like bumping your system with an elbow or nudging the desk it sits on are fairly safe.

Park the Hard Disk Heads

Nowadays, most hard disk drives automatically *park* the read/write heads every time you turn them off. If you have an older PC (with, presumably, an older hard disk) yours might not park itself automatically. If so, you need to give it special attention. The exact method depends on your particular PC. You might have an application program (perhaps called PARK or SHIPDISK), or you might need to press a particular combination of keys on the keyboard. Either way, if you are planning to move your PC any great distance, you should always park the heads before you turn off the power. After the heads have been parked, you can turn your computer off. Parking the heads should be the very last thing you do. Otherwise, your PC may access the disk for some reason, and un-park the heads again.

14

Clean and Dust Your System

Personal computers don't require much maintenance, but one thing you should do at regular intervals is dust off the computer and keyboard. Keyboards can accumulate an amazing amount of dust and particles, which can lead to irregular or erratic operation. Also pay attention to your computer's cooling vents and keep them free of accumulated dust or other obstructions. If your PC rests on the floor, it will pick up carpet fibers after just a few weeks. A quick wipe with a soft cloth is usually sufficient. Avoid solvents, cleaners, or any fluids. They can mar the finish of your computer's cabinet or cause erratic electrical problems because of static electricity.

Don't Block Air Vents

Take a moment to find out where and how your PC "breathes." Look for the air vents and the fan, usually in the back of the computer. These will come into play when you arrange your PC and peripherals on your desk. The vents are there for a reason, and each one should have about four inches of clearance to allow adequate airflow. Give the fan vent a good six inches of unobstructed room so the computer will not overheat.

Turn Down Your Monitor's Brightness

Like a TV screen, your computer's monitor has a brightness control. Some people like their screens brighter than others, and working conditions sometimes necessitate turning it way up. When you're not using your PC for an extended period, it is a good idea to turn the brightness down, or to turn the monitor off completely. It's okay to turn off the monitor but leave the rest of your PC running.

If you turn down the brightness when no one is using it, you can greatly prolong the life of your monitor. Here's a simple test. Turn your monitor off for a few minutes and look away from it. Then, look back at the blank screen. If you can see a pattern in the glass, your monitor's phosphor coating has already begun to "burn in." It may be time to think about replacing the monitor.

Use a Screen Saver

To protect your computer monitor from "burn-in," you can turn the brightness down (or off) when you're not using it. You can also extend the monitor life just by changing the picture on the screen regularly. Monitors burn in the most when they display the same picture on the screen all the time.

To help prevent monitor burn-in, and to add a little revenue to the coffers, many software companies now sell screen saver programs. These are fun little programs that you can load on your computer that make sure you'll never display the same picture for more then a few minutes. If you leave your computer running, but aren't using it, screen savers will blank out the screen until you come back and press a key. Some of the more inventive screen savers draw cartoons or moving shapes instead of merely blanking the screen.

Don't Switch Power On and Off

Don't make a habit of turning your computer on and off rapidly like a light switch. This is especially important if your PC has a hard disk drive. Switching the power off and on too quickly can make your computer's power supply overheat, and it can damage your hard disk drive. It takes your hard disk a few seconds to wind down to a stop after it's been turned off, and another 10 to 20 seconds to start back up again. After you turn your computer off, always wait 1 or 2 minutes before you turn it back on. Some PCs even have a special lockout, so that the computer won't start again until it's been off for at least a minute.

Unplugging Your System

It should go without saying that you should never unplug your computer without turning it off first. This goes for any peripheral devices that you might have, like a printer, modem, or tape drive, as well. It is never a good idea to unplug any electrical device without turning it off first—that's why they *have* on/off switches—but it's especially true of computer systems.

14

Also, try not to plug your computer into an outlet that is controlled by a wall switch. Turning off the switch has the same effect as yanking out the cord.

Remove Disks Before Switching Off

When you put a floppy disk in the disk drive and close the drive door, it clamps the read/write heads onto the surface of the disk. Floppy disk drive heads don't "fly" the way hard disk drive heads do.

After you turn your computer off, the electricity takes a few fractions of a second to drain out of all the parts. During that time, some parts may still be working while others aren't. It's possible that the disk drives will keep on working without any guidance from the rest of your computer. If this happens, you'll get random data written onto random parts of your floppies.

To avoid this problem, it is always a good idea to remove your floppy disks from drives before you turn off the computer. At the very least, you should open the disk drive door or turn the lever so that the heads won't be in contact with the disk.

Don't Eat or Drink Near Your System

The best way to keep your computer clean and running well is to keep it from getting gummed up in the first place. Avoid the urge to set a cup of coffee on top of the monitor or to eat a sandwich while leaning over the keyboard. Crumbs accumulate and eventually can cause keyboard malfunctions. Liquids, on the other hand, tend to cause more immediately apparent failures.

Keep Cables Out of Walkways

If you have a lot of peripheral equipment attached to your computer, you'll probably have several cables running to and fro connecting them, as well as several power cords. As a safety measure, you should always keep these cables away from walkways and other foot traffic. You may even want to run them through the ceiling if your building uses acoustic tiles. An alternative is to route them along the base of a wall or around door frames. As a last resort, connecting cables may be placed under a rubber cover strip if local fire codes allow this.

CHAPTER

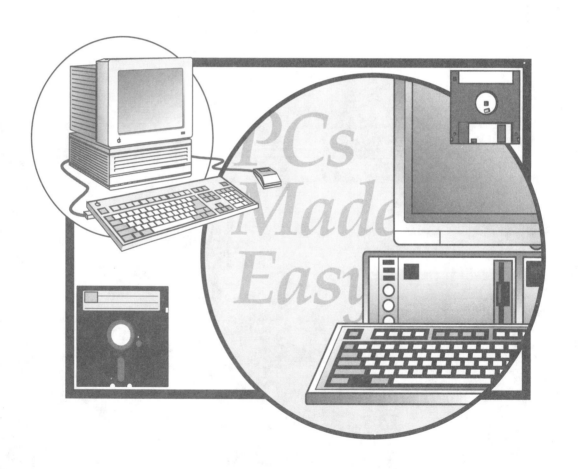

15 BUYING A COMPUTER

Buying a personal computer can be a bewildering experience. There are hundreds of different models to choose from, with a wide assortment of features, styles, options, and prices. Shopping for a computer is not unlike shopping for a new car, except that most new car buyers are at least somewhat familiar with the terminology. (There's an old joke in the computer industry: What's the difference between a used-car salesman and a computer salesman? The car salesman knows when he's lying.)

This chapter covers some of the most important aspects of shopping for and comparing personal computers. You'll find out what some of the most important features are and what the advertising literature might be saying. Then, when the time comes to compare brands, models, and prices, you'll be able to make a "wish list" of features you want, and you'll know which items to steer clear of.

Eight or Nine Easy Pieces

Before going too much further into the hows and whys of buying a new PC, let's take a quick look at what it is you're going to be buying. This won't be an anatomy lesson, just a refresher on how all the pieces go together and what they're called.

In Figure 15-1 you see an exploded view of a typical IBM-compatible PC. This is what it looks like if you open the main computer box and peek inside. The computer consists of a collection of green printed circuit boards (PCBs) with electronic components soldered onto them. They'll just be called "boards" throughout the rest of this chapter.

The biggest board, lying on the bottom of the main PC box, is the motherboard. The motherboard holds all of the most important non-optional components. It holds the microprocessor chip, or CPU—the heart and brains of your entire PC system. The motherboard

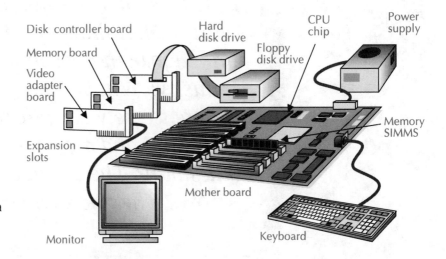

The innards of a computer
Figure 15-1.

probably also holds some or all of your computer's memory (RAM) chips. Your keyboard plugs into a connector near the back of the motherboard, and a big silver box—the power supply—converts the electricity from the wall outlet into something your PC can use.

NEW WORD: The motherboard is the largest circuit board in your computer, holding all of the most important components. Optional expansion boards (called daughterboards) plug into the expansion slots on the motherboard.

Along the rear of the motherboard, arranged in rows, are your expansion slots. These are female connectors that you can plug optional expansion boards into. Pictured in Figure 15-1 are three expansion boards—a disk controller board, a memory board, and a video adapter board. Your system may or may not have these boards, or others. Adding an expansion board is simply a matter of plugging it in and maybe changing a few switches. There are no special tools or skills required.

If you buy a complete system (as opposed to purchasing each part separately and assembling it yourself), it should come with all of the necessary expansion boards already installed.

The Three Most Important Features

Even though there are a lot of bewildering options to consider, you can simplify your choices by paying attention to the three basic pieces of your system. If you concentrate on these three, the others will fall into place. The three most important parts of your new computer are

✦   The microprocessor (CPU)

✦   The disk drives

✦   The video display

They rank in importance in that order. The microprocessor, or CPU, of your new computer is the single most important thing, followed by the disks and the video display adapter and monitor. Decide what you want and how much you're willing to pay for these items. If you're not happy with these choices, the rest of your system won't matter much. These items also have the greatest effect on the cost of a new PC.

Microprocessor

Your choice of microprocessor will determine what software you can use, how fast the computer will be, and how far you can expand its capabilities in the future. Some microprocessors are much faster than others, sometimes by as much as 20 to 1. Naturally, you'll pay more for a computer with a faster microprocessor.

Just as the engine determines the performance of a car, your choice of microprocessor will determine the speed of your PC.

In most PCs, the microprocessor is also the *only* thing that you can't upgrade after you buy the computer. You can change your floppy disks, you can replace your hard disk, you can buy a new monitor, you can even swap out your power supply, but you usually can't upgrade your microprocessor.

Some PCs come with a "vacant" socket to plug in a second microprocessor chip, but adding the second one shuts the first one off. This allows you to move up to a faster CPU without buying a whole new PC.

Microprocessors are extremely complex silicon chips. They are only manufactured by a handful of companies; the biggest ones being Intel Corporation, Advanced Micro Devices (AMD), and Motorola, all based in the United States. These companies then sell their microprocessor chips to the world's PC makers. They don't make the whole PC themselves. That means that many different brands of PCs all use the same microprocessor.

Bit Wise

All microprocessor chips can be divided into three broad classes, based on the amount of data they can handle. At the low end are the 8-bit microprocessors. After that come the 16-bit microprocessors, and leading the pack are the 32-bit microprocessors. A 32-bit CPU can gobble up 32 bits (or 4 bytes) of data at a gulp, or twice as much as a 16-bit microprocessor. That doesn't mean that your computer will run exactly two times faster; that would be too easy. But the difference is

15

very marked. In fact, 8-bit and 16-bit computers are just about impossible to find today, so you'll be getting the cream of the crop no matter what you pick.

Each different kind of CPU has a name or a number, like the model number on a German sports car. You need to study these numbers and remember them, because they identify the CPU in your computer, and that's the most important thing to remember. Look at the following table to see a lineup of all the microprocessors used in all the different generations of Macintosh and IBM-compatible computers.

Microprocessor	Bits	Megahertz
8088	8	4, 6, 8
8086	16	5, 10, 12, 16
68000	16	8, 10, 12, 16
68010	16	8, 10, 12, 16
80286	16	8, 10, 12, 16
68020	32	16, 20, 25
68030	32	16, 20, 25, 33
68040	32	20, 25, 33
80386	32	16, 20, 25, 33, 50
80486	32	25, 33, 40, 50, 66
Pentium	64	50, 60, 66

As you can see, most CPU chips have a five-digit number (which is copyrighted, unbelievably enough), but people usually abbreviate them to the last three digits. You'll hear people shorten "80386" to just "386," and a 68040 becomes an "oh-forty." After the 80286, 80386, and 80486, people naturally expected the next generation CPU to be called the 80586, but Intel threw a curve and called their newest chip Pentium. Odds are, most people will call it "586" anyway. One wonders what the next one will be named.

Speed Demons

Each individual CPU chip is also rated to run at a particular speed—the faster the better. A microprocessor's speed is measured in *megahertz,* and (as you saw in the table) the megahertz ratings range from 4 (snail's pace) to well over 50 (lightning fast). The speed of the CPU in your computer is fixed; it doesn't change speed while it runs.

NEW WORD: A microprocessor's speed is measured in megahertz, abbreviated MHz, and pronounced "*may*-guh-hurts." One megahertz is equal to one million hertz (or cycles per second). It is named after the nineteenth century physicist Heinrich Hertz. The higher this number is the faster your computer will run.

Unfortunately, there's no hard and fast rule to help you decide which CPU is the fastest, or even fast enough for your purposes. A less-capable CPU (say, a 286) running at a fast speed may very well be speedier than a "better" CPU (like a 386SX) running at a slower speed. The chart in Figure 15-2 gives you some idea of how CPU performance overlaps.

CPU	MHZ	← SLOWER	FASTER →
286	16		
	20		
	25		
386 SX	16		
	25		
	40		
386 DX	25		
	33		
	40		
486 SX	25		
	33		
486 DX	25		
	33		
	50		
486 DX2	50		
	66		

Comparing speeds of processors
Figure 15-2.

15

Don't treat this as the final word, though. The design of the computer, the speed of the memory, the presence of a cache, and other factors all affect a computer's overall performance. See the section, "What Are Benchmarks?" later in this chapter for a more thorough explanation of how to measure PC performance.

The CPU and Your Software

Buying the newest, fastest CPU you can afford will delay the day when your PC is obsolete.

Perhaps more important than the raw speed of the CPU is how it will complement your software. The choice of CPU in your new computer might affect what software you can and can't run. Not all CPU chips can run every program.

Each new CPU chip adds features and performance over the older chips, but keeps all the old features, too. Sometimes new software will take advantage of the new features, sometimes not. Any program that runs on an old PC (with, say, an 8086) will run on a new PC, but programs designed for a newer PC may not run on an old one. These programs may need some of the features that only a newer CPU chip can offer.

This should influence your choice of computer and CPU. There are many programs now that need an 80386 chip or better to run. "Better" means a CPU from the 386 family, on up to the 486 and Pentium. If you want to have access to all of these newer programs, you need to pick a computer with at least a 386-family processor. It doesn't matter if it's a 386SX, 386DX, or one of the other 386 variations. All 386 microprocessors can run the same programs.

REMEMBER: Not all personal computers can run all programs. You should try to pick a PC that uses one of the newest CPU chips to give yourself the most freedom and flexibility. Start with at least a 386 microprocessor or better.

The following table ranks the different microprocessors you can get for an IBM-compatible PC. They are listed from the highest performance and most capable CPU at the top, to the oldest, weakest CPU at the bottom.

Microprocessor	Performance
Pentium	Best
80486DX2	Great
80486DX	Very good
80486SX	Better
80386DX	Good
80386SX	Fair
80286	Poor
8086	Bad
8088	Forget it

There are other variations, like the 386SLC or the 486DLC. None of the "letter suffix" variations are really earth-shattering new devices. Most offer small changes on the existing chips, like using a little less electricity than another version, or costing a little bit less.

The different versions of a single type of CPU can have slightly different features.

The best cut-off point for a new PC today is between the 80286 and 80386 microprocessors. Don't spend too much time looking for a 286-based PC. First of all, they're getting harder to find every day, as people move to the 386, 486, and up. Also, there is a growing list of programs like Windows and Windows applications that need a 386 CPU or better to run. These programs won't work on a 286 at all. Finally, as leading-edge PCs gain speed and performance by leaps and bounds, you'll soon find yourself disappointed in the capabilities of your "new" 286-based computer.

Macintoshes don't rely so much on the individual microprocessor as IBM-compatible PCs do. First of all, Macs use a completely different family of microprocessors than the IBM-compatible systems, and you have learned by now that these two computers cannot run each others' software. While there are certainly differences among the Mac CPU chips, they are all pretty much the same when it comes to running Mac programs. Some are faster than others, but what runs on one Mac will run on any Mac.

The table below lists the different CPU chips that you can find in a new or used Macintosh.

15

Microprocessor	Performance
68040	Best
68030	Better
68020	Good
68010	Fair
68000	Poor

Except for the original Macintosh, you won't find any computers with the 68000 CPU chip. Performance really starts to pick up with the 68030 because it adds a cache (see the discussion of caches in the "Memory" section, later). The 68040 is currently the top-of-the-line Mac microprocessor.

Disk Drives

Your disk drives are your computer's long-term storage, and you will depend on them day after day to store and retrieve your vital program and data files. When you look for a computer there are many aspects of disk drives to consider: how many disk drives you need, what size disks you will be using, what format your software comes in, how your disk storage can be expanded, and other considerations.

Floppy Disk Drives

Every PC comes with at least one floppy disk drive. You will want to use your new computer's floppy disk drive for storing programs and data files and for loading new software. Unless you have a tape drive, your floppy disks will probably also be your means to back up your hard disk drive. With floppy disk drives, there are really only two things to consider:

✦ How many?

✦ What size?

PCs Made Easy, Second Edition

Choosing a New Computer

When deciding on a new computer system, the three most important things to look for are the CPU, the disk drives, and the video display. These affect the performance, the capabilities, and the price of a new PC more than any other factors.

The computer's CPU is the most important feature. It controls how fast your computer runs, but also what programs you can and can't use. If you get a PC with an older CPU you might not be able to use many of the newest programs.

The 8088 and 8086 are the oldest CPU chips. Avoid these, because they cannot run many of today's PC programs. There are no new PCs being built with these microprocessors.

The 80286 is the first CPU chip that could use expanded memory, but otherwise it is very old. There are no new computers being built with the 80286, but used 286-based PCs are available as people upgrade their old computers. They are very slow compared to a newer computer and may provide disappointing performance.

The 80386 CPU offers many firsts. A 386-based PC can use extended as well as expanded memory, has a 32-bit data path, multitasking capability, and it can run Windows in enhanced mode. The 386 makes a good start into the PC world; consider it the minimum requirement for a new computer.

Computers with the 80486 processor offer better performance, a built-in cache, and improved floating-point (mathematical) calculation capabilities. These are the basis for most high-performance PCs today.

The newest Pentium, or 586, processor holds the title for best overall performance. It has many features that make it faster, more capable, and more flexible than any CPU that has come before it.

Sure, floppy disk drives come in high density and low density, as you saw in Chapter 4, but you don't even want to consider putting low-density floppy drives into a new PC. Low-density floppies are already becoming scarce, and they'll be completely extinct before long.

Besides, a high-density floppy drive can read and write low-density diskettes, so you're not giving up anything.

How Many Floppies?

Ideally, you would have four floppy disk drives; two of each size. That would let you copy both 5 1/4-inch diskettes and 3 1/2-inch diskettes, all without swapping disks. However, most PCs are set up to handle only two floppy disk drives, so two is a more practical limit.

One floppy drive is the bare minimum for any decent personal computer. Without it, how would you get software onto or off of your PC? Often a bare-bones advertised price leader will have only a single floppy disk drive included. Having only one floppy disk drive can be frustrating. It makes it more complicated (though not impossible) to copy diskettes.

What Kind of Floppies?

If you plan on sending your floppies through the mail, the 3 1/2-inch disks are a little sturdier.

Choosing between 5 1/4-inch and 3 1/2-inch floppy disk drives is mostly a matter of personal taste. They work equally well, although a 3 1/2-inch floppy disk can store slightly more than its bigger brother. If you're going to have two floppy drives in your PC, the best answer is to get one of each. That way you can always use a disk that someone has given you, or make a disk to give to someone else.

With one drive of each size, you give up the capability to make easy disk duplications, but that's a small price to pay. Many programs today come complete with two copies of the software; one on 5 1/4-inch disks and another copy on 3 1/2-inch disks. It doesn't look as though either size will become obsolete in the near future. Despite the slight advantages of the smaller disk size, there are too many 5 1/4-inch floppy disks already in circulation for them to disappear any time soon.

Hard Disk Drives

Hard disk drives, or Winchester disks, used to be a novelty in the personal computer world because they were so expensive. Now they're nearly universal. It's a rare PC today that doesn't have a hard disk drive in it.

Hard disk drives are more expensive than floppy disk drives, and they're not as easy to upgrade. That means that you'll want to give more serious consideration to what kind of hard disk to put in your PC because you'll be living with it for a long time. When selecting a hard disk drive, there are three things to consider:

✦ Capacity

✦ Access time

✦ Interface

When it comes to hard disk capacity, more is, frankly, more.

Hard disk drives come in different physical sizes, just as floppy disk drives do. In fact, they come in the *same* sizes, namely 5 1/4-inch and 3 1/2-inch. Hard disks also come in different heights, within the confines of those sizes. Some hard disks are taller than others and some are short, "half-height" disks. The physical size of the hard disk drive has absolutely nothing to do with how it works for you. Don't pay any attention to the size of the disk at all. It doesn't have to match your floppy drive size, for example, or anything else. The only time it might possibly be a consideration is if the disk is physically too big to fit in your PC.

Hard Disk Capacity

Unlike floppy disk drives, the physical size of a hard disk drive is completely irrelevant.

The storage capacity of a hard disk drive is fixed and can't be changed. Unlike a floppy disk drive, you can't just remove the disk and insert a new one. An average hard disk drive in a personal computer might store about 80MB or so. A big hard disk drive might hold more than 200MB. If you think you'd be hard pressed to accumulate 200MB of data, you might be surprised. Like garages, hard disks have a way of filling up.

As computers get faster and faster, and hard disk drives get cheaper and cheaper, programs grow larger and larger. It used to be that a 128K program was a monster, and only the best-equipped PCs could ever hope to run it. Nowadays even normal word processing programs take up 15MB of disk space and more. If you plan on using Windows, that will take up another 10 to 20MB of disk space, easily. It is fair to assume that programs won't be getting any smaller in the future.

15

Naturally, the greater the capacity of your hard disk drive, the more it's going to cost. You will have to weigh the relative merits of the various disks for yourself. A rough rule of thumb says that hard disk storage costs about $2 per megabyte, so a 150MB disk might be somewhere around $300.

Access Time

The second important feature of a hard disk drive is its speed. Apart from the obvious fact that you don't have to hunt around for the disk and insert it in the drive first, any hard disk drive can load information several times faster than a floppy disk drive. The amount of time it takes to retrieve information from a hard disk is known as the *access time,* or seek time. Access time is measured in milliseconds (ms), or thousandths of a second. Access times from 30 to 40 ms are average, the low 20s are pretty good, and under 20 ms is very fast. Even though the difference between the access time of two hard disks might be only a few thousandths of a second, that time adds up over the months and years. Fast access time is definitely a plus, and you may have to pay more for it.

Choosing a Hard Disk Drive

After the microprocessor, the most important aspect of your PC is the size and type of its hard disk. Hard disk drives are difficult to replace, so choose one that will last several years.

The most important characteristic of a hard disk drive is its storage capacity, since this can never be increased. Estimate how much data you plan to store, plus the size of your operating system and application programs. Then double or triple your estimate.

Second in importance after the hard disk's capacity is its speed. All hard disk drives are fast compared to floppy disk drives, but among hard disk drives, some are as much as twice as fast as others. When a disk is used for several hours per day, year after year, the time you save with a faster disk adds up quickly. Faster disks cost more, and so does increased capacity.

Hard Disk Interface

Somehow your hard disk drive has to connect to your PC's motherboard. There are different methods for doing this, and each has pluses and minuses. The technical term for the connection between the hard disk and the motherboard is the *interface*. There are three basic interfaces that you should be familiar with:

✦ ST 506 interface

✦ IDE interface

✦ SCSI interface

The three interfaces are listed here in order of popularity. There are no big differences in how each one works, at least from the point of view of a PC user. The differences are mostly technical, but they can influence how you add a new hard disk drive or other peripheral device to your computer.

The ST 506 interface (named after the Seagate Technology model 506 disk drive) is the most common. Using this method, two flat "ribbon" cables connect the disk drive to a disk controller card, as shown in Figure 15-3. The controller card then plugs into one of your PC's

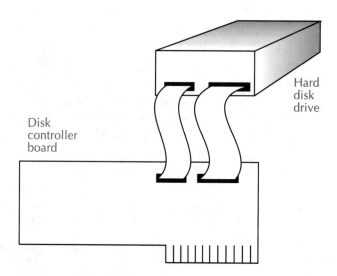

Connecting a disk drive to a controller
Figure 15-3.

15

expansion slots. That's it. The disk controller card may be able to control one, two, or four disk drives this way. It depends on the particular card—something you should look into when choosing your PC.

The IDE (Integrated Drive Electronics) interface eliminates the disk controller card by plugging directly into your PC's motherboard. The electronics that used to be on the disk controller card are miniaturized and placed on the disk drive directly. This method saves you the expense of buying a disk controller card, and it frees up an expansion slot in your PC.

The SCSI interface is the most complicated, but offers the most options for expansion. An SCSI disk drive plugs into a disk controller with a flat ribbon cable. The disk controller then plugs into an expansion slot in your PC's motherboard, much like an ST 506 hard disk and controller. Some SCSI controllers have their own microprocessor on them and run special software that speeds up your computer's disk accesses. A SCSI controller can control up to seven disk drives or other devices. Besides just hard disk drives, you can connect tape drives and CD-ROM drives to your SCSI controller.

NEW WORD: The SCSI interface is used to connect hard disks, floppy disks, tape drives, and CD-ROM drives to personal computers. SCSI stands for Small Computer System Interface and should be pronounced (when necessary) as "scuzzy."

Although each different disk controller method has things to recommend it, you should probably stay with one of the first two kinds. For a start, there are more ST 506 and IDE hard drives available than SCSI disks. SCSI disks also cost more. Unless you know that you're going to want a CD-ROM or other SCSI device, you can save the cost of the SCSI controller, which is many times more than a standard disk controller.

Video Display

You'll be spending a lot of time in front of your new computer's display monitor, so pay special attention to getting one that's right for you. You will have different choices for the monitor itself, and for the video board that controls the monitor. These two work as a matched pair, so don't rush out and buy one without considering the other. Best of all, pick them out as a pair from the same computer dealer. The three criteria to consider in a display system are

✦ Resolution

✦ Screen size

✦ Dot pitch

A good monitor can be a big investment. Some can cost more than the rest of your entire system. But you'll be looking at it for a long time, so this is not a place to cut corners.

The Display Adapter Board

In the IBM-compatible PC world, there are many different video formats to choose from. As PCs got better and faster, the standard video system delivered with them changed. IBM's early PCs came with one kind of display, and the later ones came with another. Fortunately, all of the various display systems are compatible with one another. When a new one came out, it offered all of the features of the previous ones, plus more. That means that software that runs on an old screen will run on a newer one, but not necessarily vice versa.

Pick the monitor that looks best to you and that will give you the most enjoyment.

The IBM people dreamed up three-letter acronyms for each generation of video display system, and you need to be familiar with these terms because they are used everywhere. The table below lists each one, from oldest to newest.

Abbreviation	Description	Resolution	Colors
MDA	Monochrome Display Adapter	Text Only	2
CGA	Color Graphics Adapter	320 x 200	4
EGA	Enhanced Graphics Adapter	640 x 200	16
VGA	Video Graphics Array	640 x 400 320 x 200	16 256
S-VGA	Super VGA	800 x 600 1024 x 768	256 256

The Monochrome Display Adapter is the dinosaur of the PC world. It can only display text (letters and numbers), no graphics. It's also only good for two colors, black and white (or green). You'd have difficulty finding one of these anymore, and it's not worth trying very hard.

The CGA display was the first one to display any graphics. (The first one from IBM, that is. Apple computers had been showing off graphics for years.) The graphics were, by today's standards, very poor and only used four colors. They were about the quality of a child's painting.

The EGA display can display some passable graphics without sacrificing the quality of the text. It can also use 16 colors, making the displays a bit more interesting. This is good enough for pie charts, word processing, and most games.

Color monitors are especially appreciated on games. The software is so advanced, you won't want to waste it on a monochrome monitor.

The VGA display combines the quality of the graphics and text so that both are quite good. This is the one you want to consider most seriously when you pick a new display. It is usually the minimum offered with new PCs. A VGA display can emulate (copy) the CGA and EGA displays as well, so programs written for PCs with those video boards will work just fine if you have a VGA board. The VGA standard is also the only one to offer 256 colors. This has a dramatic effect on the clarity of your picture. Even though the resolution of a standard VGA is no better than an EGA display, the additional colors have a striking effect on the realism of the picture.

Beyond VGA is the Super VGA, with all of the same features but even better resolution. A 1024-x-768, 256-color picture must be seen to be believed. It is almost as good as looking at a color photograph. Again, the wide choice of colors makes an amazing difference. Super VGA boards can, of course, emulate all the earlier display standards as well. This is the one to choose for top-quality video.

Your video display board normally plugs into one of your PC's expansion slots on the motherboard. As an alternative, some motherboards offer the video display adapter built right in. This will save you an expansion slot and can save you money as well. What you give up is flexibility for the future. If your video display adapter is built into the motherboard, you can't change it later.

Some of these built-in adapters use what is called a *local bus* interface. This is a method for speeding up your video. Instead of connecting the video electronics as though they were part of an expansion board, they

Making Resolutions

The quality of the picture on your screen depends on three things: the resolution of the display, the number of colors, and the clarity of the monitor.

Resolution measures the number of dots, or pixels, that make up the picture. There are a certain number of pixels across the screen, called the horizontal resolution, and a different number of pixels counting up and down, called the vertical resolution. The higher the overall resolution (the greater the number of pixels), the better your display will look.

More colors can also make a display more interesting. If you are displaying images and pictures, more colors can make the display much more realistic. The additional colors can be used to add subtle shading and highlights.

The size of the pixel dots on the screen is called the dot pitch. The smaller the dot pitch, the better, because smaller pixels are less noticeable and blend together better.

are connected to the CPU like memory. This can make some graphics applications run faster. Again, with local bus video, you give up expandability for the future.

NOTE: Local bus video adapters are included as part of the motherboard, instead of as an extra board that plugs into an expansion slot. The local bus adapter offers faster graphics execution at the expense of future expandability.

Yet another new wave in the video graphics world is the move to accelerated video adapter boards. An accelerated video board has its own microprocessor on it, like a smaller version of the one that runs your whole PC. The video CPU is programmed to do one thing: draw graphics on your screen. With another CPU working for you, your graphics can run much faster. These work particularly well if you are

15

using Windows. The drawback is, in order to take advantage of the accelerated video functions, your application programs have to "know" that the board is there and make use of its advanced features. Currently, not many programs can do that, with Windows the major exception. Most other programs ignore the extra CPU and treat the accelerated video board like a standard VGA board, wasting the extra money you paid.

The Monitor

Your monitor and video board work together as a pair. If you pick out a high-quality video board with lots of resolution and colors, you'll need a top-of-the-line monitor to show them off. Your monitor must be able to do all the same things that the video board can do, or else you won't be able to enjoy all of the features.

Your video board and monitor don't necessarily have to match, but you'll only enjoy the features of the "weakest link."

Like video boards, monitors have different resolutions. Some can display more pixels than others, or more colors. It's normally okay to mismatch the monitor and the video display board; what you get will be the "lowest common denominator" between the two. For example, if your video board can generate 1024 x 768 resolution (Super VGA) but you have an EGA monitor, you'll get an EGA-quality display. You won't damage your monitor, and perhaps sometime in the future you can upgrade it and keep the video board.

Some monitors use *interlaced* scanning and others are *non-interlaced*. These terms describe how the monitor draws the screen, and they're not terribly important. A non-interlaced monitor (often abbreviated as NI) will display a somewhat sharper picture than an interlaced one.

NEW WORD: An interlaced monitor alternates drawing every other row of pixels on the screen. A non-interlaced monitor draws every row of pixels, from top to bottom. Interlaced monitors cost a little bit less, but non-interlaced monitors provide a somewhat clearer picture.

You can choose how big your monitor will be, the same as choosing a television. This is entirely a matter of personal taste. A bigger or smaller screen won't affect the quality of your display at all. Most people have screens in the 12-inch to 14-inch range, measured diagonally. Beyond about 14 inches, the price of the monitor jumps dramatically. A 21-inch monitor can cost three times as much as a monitor with a 14-inch screen. If you are doing professional desktop publishing or page layout work, this may be well worth the price.

The final feature to consider when selecting a monitor is the dot pitch. Dot pitch is the distance from one pixel to the next. The smaller the dot pitch, the better your display will look. Big, fat pixels tend to make the display look grainy, like sitting too close to the TV.

NOTE: You can't skimp and use your television set in place of a monitor, at least not if you want to be able to read the screen. Not since the days of the earliest home computers have PCs been able to use TV sets. The quality of the TV display just isn't good enough.

Dot pitch is measured in thousandths of an inch, or mils. A dot pitch of 0.23 is quite good, while a monitor with 0.40 dot pitch would give a much blurrier picture. On the other hand, monitors with coarser dot pitch also cost less.

Other Important Features

After the "big three" there are other features to consider when buying a PC. They don't rank quite as high because they are easier to upgrade later on, and because they're less expensive (so you won't feel so bad about settling for your second choice). The second group includes:

✦ Memory (RAM)

✦ Option expansion capabilities

The memory in your PC is certainly very important (it wouldn't run without it), but you can always add more. In fact, adding memory is probably the most common upgrade that people perform. That brings us to the second point, expansion capability. How your PC supports this, and how many options you have, may sway your decision for one PC over another.

Memory

Your computer's RAM is where program instructions are stored while a program is running, and where your computer keeps its work before you save it to disk. The amount of memory you have determines what kinds of programs you'll be able to use. Bigger, more complex application programs require more memory than simple programs. Some operating systems, too, require more RAM than others. The basic DOS operating system on most PCs can run with hardly any memory, but Windows requires at least 2MB to be useful; 5MB or more is recommended.

The good news is, there's really nothing to know about memory when you're buying a PC. It doesn't come in sizes or brands or colors. You only need to concern yourself with how much you're getting. If you're upgrading an existing computer, one other feature you might be concerned with is access time.

NOTE: The access time of a memory chip measures how fast it can "remember" data when the CPU calls on it. The access time is measured in nanoseconds, abbreviated ns. A nanosecond is the amount of time it takes light to travel about six inches.

How much memory you get in your new PC will affect its price, of course. If you're getting a 286 computer, 1MB of RAM is probably enough, at least for a start. With a 386 PC, plan on at least 2MB; more if you're going to run Windows or any large, complicated applications. The same goes for a 486 machine; start with at least 2MB.

Most application programs will say on the box how much RAM they need to run. If you're curious, read the box to see what it says, and then double that estimate. (Software companies tend to underestimate the minimum hardware requirements.) As a very rough rule of thumb, the more an application program costs, the more RAM it's going to need.

If you're upgrading a PC by adding memory, pay special attention to the access time of the memory chips you buy. Each PC uses memory chips with a particular speed. When you add new chips, or a SIMM module with RAM chips already on it, make sure that they are at least as fast as the ones already in your PC. Average access times hang right around 70 to 100 nanoseconds. It's perfectly all right to buy memory chips that are faster (lower ns number) than necessary, but you should never use ones that are too slow. When in doubt, check your PC's owner's manual or take your computer into the dealer's shop for the upgrade.

Wait States

When you are browsing the PC advertisements, you may see something called a *wait state*. A wait state is an extremely technical concept, and it's not going to be defined in detail here. Suffice it to say, wait states are slightly bad things, to be avoided whenever convenient. A wait state occurs when the CPU chip in your computer is faster than the RAM chips, and the CPU must wait for the memory to catch up.

Wait states slow your computer down; cache memory speeds it up.

Most PCs are designed to avoid these wait states, but some computers may incur one or two if they are using slow RAM chips. All other things being equal, a computer with one wait state will be a wee bit slower than another one without wait states.

Cache Memory

Some of the newer and more powerful PCs use a special kind of memory called a *cache*. A cache is used in addition to the main RAM in your computer. It is very small, usually about 64K to 256K. It can greatly speed up the operation of your computer for many kinds of work, without increasing the cost by too much.

Caches don't make sense for all computers. Slow computers never have caches, and very fast computers nearly always have them. If a particular computer doesn't come with a cache, you won't be able to add one later on. You may be able to expand an existing cache, however. If your computer comes with 64K of cache memory, you might be able to expand that to 128K or 256K in the future. Expanding the cache isn't like adding normal RAM; you have to take your PC into the dealer and have it upgraded in the shop.

The faster your computer is, the more important a cache becomes. Caches don't make sense for 286 computers, for example. A 386 PC may or may not have a cache, and a 486 computer or better should certainly have one. If you're comparing 386-based systems, you'll see that a cache adds to the cost of the computer, compared to those without one.

Expansion Bus

15

It is an old cliche that work expands to fill the time allowed. It seems just as true that programs expand to fill the available memory. Data seems to expand to fill the available hard disk space. Graphics programs overwhelm your video display adapter or monitor. After a few months or years, you may find yourself wishing for a whole new computer.

One of the great benefits of the PC is its expandability. You can add nearly anything to your computer system through the easy-to-use, plug-in expansion slots on your PC's motherboard. You can change the video adapter board, expand the memory, add a new tape controller, plug in a stereo audio board, and add a cable television tuner.

Until just a few years ago, all IBM-compatible PCs used the same kind of expansion slots. They didn't have an official name, they were just called expansion slots. Then a collection of PC makers got together and came up with a newer, better kind of expansion slot, and they called it *EISA*. About the same time, IBM decided to change the expansion slots too, and they called theirs *Micro Channel*. Now the world has three different ways to expand PCs.

NEW WORD: There are three different and competing expansion slot standards for IBM-compatible PCs. The original ISA (Industry Standard Architecture) slots are still the most common. The EISA (Extended Industry Standard Architecture) adds features while maintaining compatibility with ISA boards. The Micro Channel slots are used primarily by IBM computers.

By far the most common kind is still the original kind of expansion slot, now called *ISA*. Most PCs have ISA expansion slots and use ISA-style boards. (These are also called *AT bus cards,* after the IBM PC/AT.) There are some EISA-compatible PCs that use EISA expansion boards, but they are not nearly so common. One of the nice features of EISA computers is that they can use ISA expansion boards along with EISA expansion boards, so you have a choice. Finally, the computers with Micro Channel expansion slots (like the IBM PS/2 line) will only accept Micro Channel plug-in boards, and these are not yet in widespread use.

For most people, a computer with ISA-style expansion slots is the way to go. It will give you far greater freedom and flexibility when you want to expand your PC. There are literally thousands and thousands of different ISA-compatible expansion boards to choose from. In the Macintosh world, all Macs use an expansion standard called *NuBus*. The NuBus has never changed, and all Macs use the same expansion boards.

Smoke and Mirrors

There are other, less important, features that many new PCs have. A lot of these are pretty useless, added by PC makers to differentiate their PCs from the competition's. You should be able to recognize these and evaluate them for what they are.

Turbo Switch

An item you'll see on most new PCs is the "turbo switch." This supposedly lets you run your PC in a super-fast "turbocharged" mode—offering the ultimate in high-end computing technology (or so they would like you to believe). In actual fact, the turbo switch *slows your computer down,* making it run like a much older computer.

Here's the big idea. There are still a lot of valuable programs around that used to run on the original IBM PC or the PC/AT (the first 286-based PC). By today's standards, those machines are pathetically slow. If you run one of these old programs on a new 66 MHz 486-based computer, it will run far quicker than it was ever intended to. Normally, that's good, but some programs don't work if they run *too* fast. Enter the turbo switch. When you press the switch, the CPU in your computer is deliberately slowed down to about one-fifth of its normal speed. You'll notice the difference right away if your PC is drawing something on the screen. Some older programs that would have crashed, run just fine when the "turbo" is turned off.

Turbo Lights

To go along with the aforementioned snail mode (oops, turbo mode) switch, many PCs offer some interesting lights on the front panel of the computer's main box. Some have just a simple red or green light, while others have more elaborate displays with two- and three-digit numbers.

When you press the turbo switch, the lights light up. For example, it may be green when the switch is off and red when the turbo is engaged. The more ornate ones show one number (say, "16") when the switch is off and another, much bigger number (like "125") when you press the button. Rest assured, no matter which kind it is, it has nothing to do with what your computer is doing. The numbers do not measure the speed of the processor, the amount of work it is doing, the relative humidity, or anything else meaningful. They are simply lights. They are designed to change when you press the turbo switch. That's all.

Coprocessor Socket

Until the advent of the 486 microprocessor, most PCs were not very good at calculating complex mathematical equations. That may come as a surprise to many, because we think of computers as calculating machines. Sure, they were good enough to balance a checkbook or figure inventory levels, but really complicated calculations in physics, chemistry, or trigonometry were beyond most PCs. To remedy this, microprocessor makers offered a *coprocessor* chip especially designed for math functions. The coprocessor works alongside the main processor, taking over the math problems and leaving the rest alone. Those people who needed one could add a math coprocessor to their systems.

NEW WORD: A coprocessor (also called an FPU) is a special-purpose microprocessor dedicated to mathematical functions. You can add a coprocessor to most PCs. They speed up specific application programs that perform complex calculations.

There are different coprocessor chips for each microprocessor. They have model numbers just like the CPU chips do. There's the 8087, which works with the 8086, the 287 for the 286, and the 387 for use with a 386 CPU. The 80486 DX has no coprocessor, because the math functions were finally added into the CPU itself. The coprocessor chip (or FPU, for floating-point unit) fits into a socket on the motherboard. Most PCs have such a socket near the main CPU. Hardly any of them come with the coprocessor already installed. You can buy the coprocessor chip by itself at many computer stores, or you can take your PC to a dealer and have one installed.

The coprocessor only speeds up a very specific set of mathematical calculations, and then only with the proper software. It won't speed up normal application programs at all. If you have applications that might benefit from a coprocessor, they will usually spell out that fact in large print. Those applications that need a coprocessor usually need it badly.

Key Lock

Some PCs offer a lock on the front of the case and a matching key. When you turn the key in the lock, the PC will continue to run, but it won't pay attention to the keyboard or the mouse. This is only useful if you want to start running an application program and then walk away from the computer, secure in the knowledge that nobody can molest the computer while you're away.

Some locks go one step further and prohibit access to the inside of the system. When the lock is turned, the lid of the main system case is locked down so that nobody can open it, even with a screwdriver. For the security-minded, this can be used to safeguard precious expansion boards or hard disk drives.

Bundled Software

The whole point of having a personal computer is to run software, of course. The choice of application programs is up to you, and you will select these according to your tastes, needs, and budget. But every PC has to have an operating system, and for that you don't have very many choices. For an IBM-compatible PC, you will want to have DOS, and for a Macintosh, you need the Macintosh System.

Apple Computer loads each and every Mac with the Macintosh System software before you buy it, so you don't have to worry about this little item at all. Every Mac is ready to go, right out of the box. Just plug it in and turn it on, and it works. In the PC world things are not so simple.

Your PC may come with DOS already loaded on it ("installed," in the parlance), but it's more likely you will have to buy a copy of DOS and load it yourself. This isn't really any more difficult than loading a new application program for the first time, and the DOS manual comes with instructions on how to do it. If you want Windows, you will have to buy and install that software as well.

Many PC retailers offer their computers with DOS and/or Windows already loaded and running. This service may cost a little bit extra, above and beyond the price of the software itself, but is well worth it for many people. If the operating system is already installed, you know that you will be able to start work right away, instead of spending your first few hours just setting up.

What Are Benchmarks?

Shopping for a new computer, like shopping for a sports car, is filled with competing claims about performance, options, and speed. Every PC is faster and less expensive than the last one, with more and better features. If speed is what you're after, you'll certainly get it from the newest PCs that are available. But how do you measure the speed of a computer?

This is actually an older and more complicated question than many people imagine. Ever since there were two computers people have tried to measure which one was fastest. The fast fact is, there's really no easy way to tell. Computers do so many different things that it's difficult to come up with one overall performance rating for the whole system. You have to measure one thing at a time.

To measure a computer's speed you have to run a *benchmark*. A benchmark is a program, usually small, that can be run on a lot of different computers. The benchmark program does one particular task, over and over, and then reports how long it took to complete. The quicker the program ran, the faster the computer is—at that particular task. Different benchmarks measure different things, like mathematical calculations, or disk access, or general processing, or graphics.

NEW WORD: A benchmark is a program that does no useful work, but can time itself to see how long it took to run. Benchmarks are used to compare the relative speed of two or more different computers.

A benchmark you'll hear a lot about is the Norton System Information program. This benchmark produces a System Index, or *SI*, rating number. The higher the SI rating, the faster the computer is supposed to be at general-purpose computing tasks. The SI ratings are "normalized" for the original IBM Personal Computer. That is, an original IBM PC will produce an SI rating of 1.0. All other numbers are then considered relative to this baseline. A good 386-based PC with a cache might score 25.0 or better—that's 25 *times* faster than an original IBM PC!

Another valuable benchmark is the Landmark speed rating. The Landmark also compares computers to the original IBM PC and provides a relative performance index. Other benchmarks include the Whetstone, which evaluates complex mathematical calculation speed, and the Dhrystone (yes, it's a pun), which is more general purpose in nature.

You'll find benchmark numbers quoted in ads and brochures. Their numbers are like MPG; your actual performance may vary.

A new benchmark that is growing in popularity is called the SPECmark. The SPECmark is actually a collection of benchmark programs. Recognizing that one program cannot accurately measure the overall performance of a system, a collection of computer makers calling themselves the Standard Performance Evaluation Corporation (SPEC) developed the SPECmark suite of benchmarks. Each individual program measures different aspects of the system, and the results are combined to produce an overall SPECmark rating. This is a much better indicator of overall system performance than many of the more specialized benchmarks.

Finally, there is the MIPS rating. The acronym MIPS stands for Millions of Instructions Per Second. It has been used for years to compare how many machine-language instructions a given computer can execute. These numbers are normalized to the ancient DEC VAX 11/780, a refrigerator-sized computer popular in the 1970s. A VAX produces a rating of 1.0 MIPS, or one million instructions per second. Most PCs can easily surpass this. The MIPS rating is so useless and impractical that it has been called the Meaningless Indicator of Performance for Salesmen.

Laptop Computers

One of the fastest-growing segments of the personal computer market is laptop computers. A *laptop* computer is a portable, battery-operated

15

computer that you can take anywhere and literally set on your lap to use. Laptop computers are complete, full-featured computer systems with keyboard, display screen, disk drives, and everything. A good laptop computer is every bit as capable and powerful as a full-sized desktop machine.

Computer users who travel a great deal, like salespeople, contractors, consultants, or service agents, find that laptop computers are ideal for their way of doing business. A laptop computer can be used on an airplane during a long flight, in a car, in a hotel room, or while waiting in a lobby. In many cases, there is no need to supplement the capabilities of a laptop computer with another desktop computer in the office.

Laptops used to be a second computer. Now they're powerful enough to be your only computer.

Over time, "laptop computer" has come to mean something different than a "portable computer." A portable computer (also called a "luggable" computer) denotes a PC that is small enough to be carried around without help, but still requires an electrical outlet to plug it in, instead of running on batteries. These used to be popular with travelers who had a place to plug them in when they arrived at their destination.

Weight

The major benefits of a laptop computer are its light weight and portability. Having a computer this small means that you can pack it along with other items in your suitcase or briefcase. Most portable computers are roughly 8 x 11 inches—about the size of a notepad—and only a few inches thick. If you really do plan to hold the computer on your lap as you type, you may want to pay attention to the overall weight of the machine. If it weighs much more than a few pounds, you're liable to get sore knees.

Unfortunately, a computer's weight is directly proportional to its capabilities. The more powerful and full-featured it is, the heavier it's going to be. You'll have to balance these two criteria when shopping for a laptop computer. A major portion of a laptop computer's weight is its battery pack. Be sure when reading brochures and listening to the sales pitches that the weight of the battery is included in the total weight. Often, it's not. The battery can account for as much as one-third of the computer's total weight, so don't forget about it.

TIP: Don't forget to include the battery in the weight of your laptop computer. It can make up a large portion of the total weight and it's not always counted in the literature.

Battery Life

Probably the single most appealing feature of any laptop computer is its ability to work anywhere, any time. Whether it's on an airplane or on the beach, your computer will always be ready to go—at least as long as its battery is charged. The bigger and more powerful the computer, the shorter its battery life. Pay close attention to this aspect of the computers you evaluate. If the battery life is shorter than you plan to be using the computer at one stretch, you have three options. You can buy extra batteries and swap from one to the other while you work, you can take a break to let the battery recharge, or you can run the computer while it is plugged into a wall outlet. Nearly any laptop PC will let you work while it's plugged into a wall outlet and recharging.

Make sure you have enough battery power. Imagine running out on an airplane with no place to recharge.

A small laptop computer can run for up to six hours on a fully charged battery, providing that you don't use the disks very often. The motors and mechanical parts of a disk drive draw more power than the rest of the computer's components put together. A powerful 486-based laptop computer with a big hard disk drive might only be able to run for an hour or two before the battery needs a recharge. Batteries don't recharge nearly as quickly as they discharge, unfortunately, so plan on letting your battery charge for four to six hours, or overnight.

The rechargeable nickel-cadmium (Ni-Cad) batteries used in most laptop computers exhibit an odd symptom known as *battery memory*. If you don't drain the battery all the way until it's "dead" before you recharge it, it might not recharge all the way again. Over time, this can permanently shorten the life of your battery, even though you may be recharging it for several hours. If at all possible, drain your computer's battery as completely as possible before you recharge it, and then charge it completely. This will "train" the battery for the longest life.

TIP: Wait until the last possible minute to recharge your laptop computer's batteries. Then charge them up all the way. Constantly topping them up will shorten their life. All the way empty and all the way full is the rule.

Warranties

A personal computer is an expensive purchase, so it's a good idea to check into the warranty provided with any system you are considering. A minimum warranty should cover the entire system for at least 90 days. Many personal computer manufacturers warrant their equipment for one year.

Often, some of the components of the computer system will be warranted separately, such as the monitor. This is because those pieces are usually purchased wholesale by the computer maker, and they pass along the warranty to you. Printers and other peripheral devices will also be covered separately.

Check to see who will perform warranty service in the event of a breakdown. Ideally, you would get on-site service—the repair technician comes to you. Some PC companies offer such on-site service within 24 hours of your phone call. Your local dealer might service your machine directly if you bring it into the shop. If not, check to see if the repair depot is nearby. If depot service is called for, and it's not close by, who will pay for the shipping? Often you are expected to pay freight one way and the PC company will pay the return.

After you get your PC home, be sure to fill out the warranty registration card and send it in. Do this right away. There may be separate warranty cards for various parts of your system, so look carefully to be sure you've found all of them. If your system came bundled with software, each program will have a registration card as well. Now you can plug your system in, turn it on, and enjoy!

Reading PC Advertisements

If you're shopping for a PC through mail order or reading your local newspaper, some of the advertisements can be confusing. Most of the ads seem to be aimed at engineers or, at the very least, at people who already know exactly what they're looking for. Abbreviations are everywhere. It's difficult to advertise something as complicated as a computer system intelligently in just a few inches of column space.

This section will help you decode some of the claims and abbreviations so that you know what you're getting—or at least what you're looking at. You've already seen many of the terms in this chapter or in previous chapters of this book. First look at Figure 15-4, which shows a representative sample from a computer dealer's newspaper advertisement. Let's take a look at this and decode what's there.

The first rule of reading computer advertising is to ignore the picture. The computer pictured in the ad *might* actually represent the computer described in the text, but there's no guarantee. You're better off ignoring the picture and judging the system based solely on the description.

The headline starts off with "486DX/33." This describes the most important thing you need to know, namely the microprocessor. It has a 486DX CPU running at 33 megahertz. A good start, to be sure. Next it says "floor standing system," which describes nothing more than the size and shape of the case the system is in. It's a tower system, meaning it stands on one end.

486DX/33 Floor Standing Computer System

- 33 MHz i486DX • 4MB RAM
- 210 MB HD • Dual FDs • Mouse
- .28 NI SVGA Color Monitor
- Windows 3.1 • MS -DOS 5.0
- 3 1/2" XYZ Diskettes
- 3 1/2" Disk File

2699⁹⁹

Typical
computer ad
Figure 15-4.

15

The next line repeats the fact that the computer has a 486DX running at 33 megahertz. It also says the system includes 4 megabytes of main memory (RAM). It doesn't mention how much you could add to that, but it is safe to assume that you could indeed move beyond the initial 4MB in the future.

Next you can see that this system comes with a "210 MB HD." What's an "HD"? That's the hard disk drive. This one has a 210 megabyte capacity. It also has dual FDs, meaning two floppy disk drives. The ad doesn't say whether these are 5 1/4-inch or 3 1/2-inch floppy drives, or one of each. You would have to see the system for yourself or call the dealer to know for sure. Although it doesn't say so, you can assume that any system with disks includes a disk controller board. Finally, this line also says that the price includes a mouse.

The next line describes the video monitor that comes with the system, but not the video adapter board that controls it. The monitor itself has a 0.28 dot pitch, and it works in non-interlaced (NI) mode. It is Super VGA compatible, and it is a color monitor. (Don't assume that all monitors are color unless it says so.)

For software, this system comes with the operating system (MS-DOS version 5.0) and Windows version 3.1. There are no application programs included. It doesn't say that the software is already loaded and ready to run, so you should assume that it is not. It probably means that you will receive two boxed copies of the software when you buy the computer. If so, be sure that the boxes are sealed and in their original packing.

Now, what's missing from this description? It seems like a very complete system, and one that many people would be very happy with. One large omission is the cache. Does this PC have a cache memory? Any good 486 system should certainly have one; even many 386-based PCs have a cache. Yet the ad makes no mention of a cache, something that usually gets a lot of ink. You should assume the worst (no cache) until you discover otherwise. Some other items left off the list are the keyboard and the serial or parallel I/O ports. These may not be included.

Three other small omissions are the access time of the hard disk drive, the type of video adapter board, and the expansion capabilities. Although the color monitor does offer Super VGA resolution and quality, the video board that controls it might not. The board also might not offer all 256 VGA colors. Many low-cost boards do not. It is even possible that the system doesn't include a video adapter board at all. For the hard disk drive, although the size of the disk (210MB) is fine for most purposes, it may be very slow. The expansion slots are not mentioned, so you have no idea how many there are or what type of boards you can use. When in doubt, assume the standard ISA (AT bus) slots.

The next advertisement, in Figure 15-5, shows a smaller, less expensive system. In this one, the headline declares it is a 386SX computer running at 16 megahertz. The "386SX-16" shorthand is common in these kinds of ads. The next few lines tell you that it comes with 2 megabytes of main memory (RAM), which can be expanded to 14 megabytes (an unusual number) in the future; a 40 megabyte hard disk drive (HDD); and your choice of one 5 1/4-inch or 3 1/2-inch floppy disk drive (FDD). The fact that there is only one floppy disk drive may mean that the computer is physically too small for two, or the system may just be offered that way to keep the price down.

The next line states that the system comes with a built-in VGA card. This means that the video adapter board is built right into the motherboard, instead of using an expansion board. It does not mean that it uses the local bus video interface (if it did, it would say so).

386SX-16*Plus*

- **2MB RAM** exp. to 14MB
- **40MB** HDD
- 5.25" or 3.5" FDD
- Built-in VGA Card
- 101 key keyboard
- 12" Mono VGA monitor
- Optional MS-DOS 5.0 $49
- Optional Windows 3.1 $59
- One-year on-site warranty

$499

A smaller
system's ad
Figure 15-5.

While the built-in VGA controller keeps one expansion slot free, it also denies you the possibility of upgrading it in the future.

A 101-key extended keyboard is included (always important) along with a 12-inch monochrome VGA monitor. It is unfortunate that the monitor isn't color, unless you plan on doing little more than word processing. If you want a color monitor, you'll have to pay to upgrade it. On the plus side, the advertisement states that the system comes with a one-year on-site warranty. Presumably, that is included in the advertised price, and not an extra-cost option.

Now we get to the bare-bones advertisement in Figure 15-6. This one is fairly typical of smaller computer dealers offering cut-rate prices. The ad isn't flashy, and you have to read it carefully to know what you're getting. This one is arranged as a table so you can look up what you want.

The first column on the left lists the CPU type and speed. The first entry, "386SX25" means a 386SX microprocessor running at 25 megahertz. Below that is a 386SX running at 40 megahertz with a 16 kilobyte cache, followed by a 386DX at 40 megahertz with a 64 kilobyte

SYSTEM	MB + CPU	BASIC SYSTEM
386sx25	85	228
386sx40/16C	145	288
386-40/64C	168	308
486sx25	208	348
486-33/64C	278	408
486dx2-50/64C	553	688
486-50/64C	608	758
486dx2-66/64C	688	818
Vesa LB 486-33	468	598
Vesa LB 486-50	588	718
Orchid VL 50	788	908

Buying basics

Figure 15-6.

BASIC SYSTEM CONFIGURATION: MB & CPU, 0MB RAM, IDE 1:1 2HD/2FD CONTROLLER (2S, 1P, 1G), 1.2 MB FD, INTERNAL CLOCK/CALENDAR, MATH COPROCESSOR, SOCKET, MINI TOWER CASE W/POWER SUPPLY & 101-KEY KEYBOARD

cache. The second and third columns list the price for just the motherboard (MB) and CPU, and the price for the "basic system."

The price in the second column is just the motherboard with the CPU chip installed; there is no case, no disks, no keyboard, nothing. Unless you will be building your own PC from parts, this is not what you want. The third column gives the price for their "basic system." What does the basic system include? Read the small print at the bottom to find out.

The PC market is competitive; you get what you pay for. Also, prices are dropping every day. Waiting for the "best deal" may never come.

Below the table it says that the basic system includes the motherboard and the CPU (obvious enough), but no memory to speak of (0MB RAM). That means that even the basic system won't run until you add a few megabytes of memory. It does include a disk controller board for up to two IDE hard disk drives and two floppy disk drives. The disk controller board also includes two serial communication ports, a parallel port, and a joystick, or game port. This is all encoded in the description "IDE 1:1 2HD/2FD controller (2S, 1P, 1G)."

The basic system also includes one high-density 5 1/4-inch floppy disk drive ("1.2 MB FD"), a clock/calendar chip (which is standard equipment on all PCs), a math coprocessor socket (for future expansion), a mini-tower case, a power supply (happily), and a 101-key extended keyboard.

What's missing from this system? Quite a bit. First of all, there's no memory, so you'll need to add as much as you think you need. There's also no hard disk drive, no video adapter board, and no monitor. The basic system, as configured here, won't run. It will get you on your way, but you'll need to add a few hundred dollars' worth of "options" before you can start computing.

Armed with your newfound wisdom and knowledge, now you're ready to go out there and pick out your ideal PC! Don't forget, once you've got it up and running, refer back to the earlier chapters as a guide when you need it. Use this book as a source while you're still learning to get along with your computer. Good luck!

APPENDIX

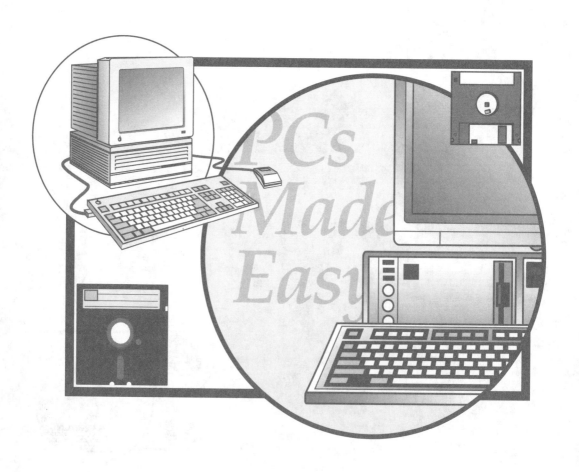

GLOSSARY

This glossary should give you a quick reference to all of the most used — and most unusual — computer words. If you don't find what you need here, you can also look in the index at the back of the book.

Access Time The amount of time it takes a disk or memory chip to fetch data. Disk drive access time measures the time to move the read/write heads to the desired track of the disk. This time is measured in milliseconds. Memory chip access times measure the time to retrieve binary data for the microprocessor. This time is much shorter and is measured in nanoseconds. *See also* Nano-; Milli-; Track.

Active Matrix A type of flat-panel display used for portable laptop and notebook computers. Active-matrix displays are better at displaying fast-moving objects on the screen than standard liquid crystal displays (LCDs).

Adapter An optional PC board that you can plug into the inside of a personal computer. The adapter board adds functions to your PC. *See also* Board.

Address A number that indicates where a byte of data is stored. If a computer's memory were compared to a row of post office boxes, with each box holding one byte, then the address is the P.O. box number.

Alternate Key The Alt key on an IBM-style PC keyboard. The Alt key is used like a Shift key; you press it down at the same time that you press another key to perform some action.

Analog An engineering term used to describe a type of electronics circuitry. The opposite of digital electronics, analog electronics uses varying voltage levels, while digital electronics uses only two. An example of an analog electronic device is a transistor radio. Computers are digital electronic devices.

Append To add to the end of something. If you add an extra paragraph to the end of a document with your word processor, you are appending text.

Application A particular class of software. Examples of application programs are word processors, graphic art programs, spreadsheets, database management programs, and so forth. An application program is distinct from an operating system. The application program is the software that you use to get your work done. *See also* Operating System.

Argument A word or number that you supply to a program when it asks for it. It is an answer to a question or a bit of information. Argument was originally a mathematical term like parameter. *See also* Parameter.

A

ASCII Abbreviation for the American Standard Code for Information Interchange; typically pronounced "askee" (never "askee-too"). This is an internationally recognized convention for representing letters and numbers of the Roman alphabet in the binary notation that all computers use. For example, the ASCII code for the letter "T" is 01010100.

Assembler A program used to help write other programs. If you create a file with assembly language programming instructions in it, the assembler will convert that file into binary instructions, which your computer can then run. Assemblers are used to translate programs written using assembly language; compilers and interpreters are used to translate programs written using other programming languages. *See also* Compiler; Interpreter.

Backlight A feature of some laptop computer display screens. The backlight shines through the LCD (liquid crystal display) making it easier to read in dim light.

Backspace Key A key in the upper-right corner of most computer keyboards. The Backspace key serves the same purpose as it does on a typewriter; it moves the cursor one character to the left. On a computer it deletes the last letter you typed.

Backup A second copy of a file, or group of files, backups are usually kept on floppy diskettes or on tape. You should back up your important files often, and store the backups off-site for greater security.

BASIC One of many programming languages, BASIC stands for Beginner's Allpurpose Symbolic Instruction Code. It is the easiest programming language to learn.

Baud A unit of speed, like miles per hour. The speed of serial data transmissions is measured by baud rate, for example, 2400 baud or 9600 baud. Baud rate is almost, but not quite, the same as bits per second. The term is a corruption of the French name Baudot.

Benchmark A computer program that is designed to measure how fast a computer runs. The benchmark program does no useful work. Instead, it produces a number, or benchmark rating, that can be used to evaluate the relative speeds of different computers.

Binary Having only two different digits, namely 0 and 1. Normal arithmetic uses base ten, or decimal numbers. Digital computers use a base two (binary) system because it is easier to implement with digital electronics. A deeper discussion of the binary number system can be found in Appendix B.

Bit One digit in the binary number system. You could think of a bit as a contraction for binary digit. A bit can be either a 0 or a 1.

Board A printed circuit board. These are the flat, stiff green boards to which electronic components are soldered.

BPS An abbreviation for bits per second. This is a measure of data transmission speed, sort of like miles per hour. BPS is also called baud rate. *See also* Baud.

Bug A mistake in a computer program. Computers execute the instructions given them without checking to see whether those instructions make sense or not. Consequently, a typing mistake or other error in the programmer's source code can cause undesirable effects. These are called programming bugs. This term gave rise to phrases like "still a few bugs in the system."

Bundled Software Software that is given away with the purchase of a computer; a package deal. Buying a computer with bundled software can get a new user up and running quickly, but it may not always be good-quality software, or particularly useful.

Byte A measure of information, or data. Eight bits make a byte. This is like an eight-digit number, except the digits may only be 0 or 1. One byte can represent all the numbers from 0 to 255, or all upper- and lowercase letters and punctuation marks, or a small portion of a picture.

C One of many programming languages. C is a popular language used by many professional programmers.

Cable A collection of wires grouped into a bundle. A telephone cord is an example of a cable with (usually) four wires in it. Cables are used to carry data between computers and peripherals. Cables can be round, like a rope, or wide and flat, like a ribbon. *See also* Peripheral.

Cache A special kind of memory used in some computers. A cache (pronounced like cash) is a small amount of extra, high-speed memory in addition to the slower, more common RAM that is used to hold the data that the microprocessor uses most often.

CAD Acronym for computer-aided design. This is a class of software used by engineering professionals to help them create drawings. Architects use CAD software to design buildings, engineers use it for designing bridges, and so forth. CAD software can handle the tedious work of drawing straight lines, taking dimensions, rotating figures, lettering, and so forth.

Caps Lock Key Used like a shift lock key on a typewriter. Pressing the Caps Lock key allows you to type uppercase letters without holding down the Shift key for every letter. Pressing the Caps Lock key again turns it off. The Caps Lock key generally works for uppercase letters only. For example, pressing Caps Lock and then the 1 key will not produce an exclamation mark.

Card Another word for a printed circuit board. *See also* Board; PCB.

Cartridge Disk A removable hard disk. Usually, the disks are not removable from a hard disk drive. A cartridge disk allows you to remove the disks and take them somewhere else.

CD-ROM Acronym for compact disc read-only memory. It is possible to use a CD as a data storage medium in many personal computers, with the addition of a CD-ROM disk drive.

Central Processing Unit *See* CPU.

Centronics The name of a printer manufacturer. Centronics popularized the parallel printer interface, so their name is often used to describe such an interface.

Character A single letter of the alphabet, a digit, or a punctuation mark.

Checksum A number used to check the validity of data. Checksums are calculated using complex algorithms designed to produce a nearly unique checksum for every combination of data. When the data is transmitted, the checksum is calculated again, and if it matches the transmitted checksum, the data is probably correct. An invalid checksum indicates a storage or transmission error. The last few digits of a credit card number are usually a checksum.

Chip An integrated circuit, so-called because integrated circuits are etched into tiny squares, or chips, of silicon.

Clock Speed The speed at which the internal "heartbeat" of a personal computer runs. This is measured in megahertz, or millions of cycles per second, and the faster the better.

Clone A computer that is designed to be a copy of another, better known computer. For example, Compaq manufactures IBM PC clones.

Close To stop using a file and save it on disk. This is the reverse of opening a file. Closing is meant to suggest physically closing a paper file folder.

Compatible A more acceptable term than "clone" for a computer that is designed to be a copy of another computer.

Compiler A program that is used to create other programs. It fulfills the same purpose as an assembler or an interpreter. A compiler converts a file of programming language instructions into a file of executable binary instructions. *See also* Assembler; Interpreter.

Computer A digital electronic device designed to carry out a limited number of instructions, in an infinite number of patterns.

Computer-Aided Drafting An alternative definition for CAD or computer-aided design. *See also* CAD.

Configuration Program A small utility program that comes with most application programs. The configuration program (or installation program) allows you to customize the application software for your particular computer and your way of doing things.

Context Sensitive A phrase describing software that can modify its behavior depending on what you are doing. For example, many application programs have a Help command; a context-sensitive application would provide you with different kinds of help depending on what you were doing at the time.

Control Characters Special invisible characters that are typed by holding down the Ctrl key while pressing another key. Control characters are used extensively by most personal computers for controlling peripherals and marking the boundaries of files.

Control Key A special key at the lower-left corner of most personal computer keyboards, used for typing control characters. *See also* Control Characters.

Controller An electronic circuit board that controls a particular peripheral. For example, most disk drives are connected to a disk drive controller board, which is, in turn, connected to the computer. The controller converts the computer's instructions into electrical signals used to control the mechanical motion of reading and writing the disk.

CPS Abbreviation for characters per second. This is how the printing speed of many printers is measured. A 20 CPS printer is slow; 100 CPS is quick.

CPU Abbreviation for Central Processing Unit; also known as a microprocessor. This is the main integrated circuit of the entire computer. The CPU chip is equivalent to the engine in a car. CPUs are usually identified by a number, such as 68020 or 80386. *See also* Microprocessor.

Crash This could mean one of two things. A hard disk can experience a head crash, which is a critical failure caused by the read/write heads losing their cushion of air and colliding with the disk's surface at high speed. Crash can also describe a computer which has ceased to function.

CRT Abbreviation for cathode ray tube. This is a technical description of a television or computer monitor's glass picture tube. CRT is also loosely used to describe any monitor or terminal.

Cursor A mark on your display showing where the computer will put the next character it displays. This is a little like the position of the print ball or carriage on a typewriter. Cursor comes from the Latin word for "runner."

Cylinder   A disk's surface is divided into circular tracks, like the grooves on a phonograph record, except that the tracks are all separate and do not spiral. There are tracks on the top of the disk and matching tracks on the bottom. If there is more than one disk in the disk drive, they are all divided into tracks as well. The "stack" of tracks is called a cylinder. *See also* Track.

Daisy Wheel   A plastic or metal disk used by some printers, with letters, numbers, and punctuation marks embossed on fingers around the outside. It is called a daisy wheel because the disk resembles a daisy, with one symbol per "petal."

Database   A collection of related information. A database is a computer's equivalent to an index card file. Information in a database is entered, sorted, searched, and displayed using a database management program.

Database Management Software   Software to manipulate the information in a database, commonly abbreviated DBMS. A DBMS can sort the database, display selected information, search for specific information, and perform many other tasks.

DBMS   Abbreviation for database management software.

Debug   The act of removing bugs from a program so that it runs properly. *See also* Bug.

Decrement   A verb meaning to subtract from a number.

Dedicated Word Processor   A machine very much like a personal computer, but designed for word processing tasks only.

Default   An automatic choice. Computer programs often give you a series of choices to make. If no selection is made, an automatic choice, known as the default choice, will be made for you. Unlike banking, default does not have negative connotations in computing. The default choice is meant to anticipate what most users would have chosen anyway.

Delete   To remove or erase something.

Desktop Publishing   Using a computer to produce very complex documents, with many sizes and styles of text, formatted columns, figures, and artwork.

Destination A term used to describe a disk, file, or computer when a transfer of information is taking place. For example, to copy a file from one disk to another disk, you copy from the source disk to the destination disk.

A

Device Driver A special kind of software concerned with controlling a specific piece of hardware, such as a color monitor, a daisy wheel printer, or a mouse.

Digital An engineering term that describes something with only two states. Digital is the opposite of analog. Digital electronics uses only two voltage levels, typically 0 volts (ground) and +5 volts. Digital is to electronics what binary is to numbers. *See also* Analog.

Directory A list of files stored on a disk. Most computers keep a machine-readable directory directly on each disk. The directory generally includes the names of each file on the disk, along with each file's size, type, and date of creation or last modification.

Disk A round, flat, medium used to store digital information in magnetic form.

Disk Drive A mechanical device used to store and retrieve information on a disk.

Diskette Another name for a floppy disk.

Distribution Disk The floppy disk that new software comes on. You should always make a backup copy of the distribution disk(s) right away, if possible, and then store the originals in a safe place.

DOS Acronym for disk operating system; rhymes with "moss." Almost any personal computer's operating system software is a DOS, but the term is generally used to refer to the Microsoft/IBM disk operating system.

Dot Matrix A type of printer. Dot matrix printers produce letters, numbers, and punctuation marks by making a pattern of small dots on paper. Dot matrix printers are fast and inexpensive.

Down A generic term meaning not working. The period during which a computer is not working is known as downtime.

Download A verb meaning to receive information from another computer.

EBCDIC Acronym for Extended Binary Coded Decimal Interchange Code. EBCDIC is an alternative to ASCII, although not as widely used. EBCDIC is used almost exclusively by large IBM computers. *See also* ASCII.

Edit To alter information. You can use a word processing program to edit a document, a spreadsheet program to edit financial figures, or a database to edit records, for example.

Editor A program that allows you to edit. In particular, a program that allows you to edit a text file; a word processor.

EMS Abbreviation for Expanded Memory Specification. A hardware and software standard that allows 80286-based computers and above to use more than 1MB of RAM.

Enter Key Also called the carriage return key, or just the Return key. You must usually press this key to tell the computer that you are finished typing for the moment. Otherwise, it will wait forever for you to finish your command.

Escape Key A special key, usually at the upper-left or right corner of the computer keyboard, that is used for various things. Depending on your software, the (Esc) key might be used to abort a command, use a menu, or delete a file, to name just a few.

ESDI Acronym for Enhanced Storage Device Interface, an interface used on some hard disk drives. This is an alternative to SASI, SCSI, or ST 506. *See also* SASI; SCSI; ST 506.

Ethernet Ethernet is a type of computer network. Networks are used to tie computers together using a high-speed communications medium, such as Ethernet, which allows them to share files and exchange information.

Execute A verb meaning to carry out, or run, as in "execute a program."

Expansion Port A socket or plug for the addition of optional hardware in order to expand the capabilities of the computer. An expansion port may be located inside the PC (expansion slot), or outside.

Extended Keyboard Any keyboard with more than the minimum number of keys needed to operate the computer. Typically, a keyboard with ten or more special function keys (F-keys) and an extra set of cursor-control (arrow) keys.

File The basic form of long-term storage. A file is a collection of related information that you store on disk. A file might contain names and phone numbers, sales figures, binary instructions for the computer to execute, or anything else.

Firmware A computer program stored in a permanent memory chip, instead of on a disk. The special memory chips that hold programs are called ROMs (read-only memory). Firmware programs are typically very short.

Fixed Disk Another term for a hard disk or Winchester disk. The term is used primarily in IBM manuals. *See also* Hard Disk; Winchester.

Floppy Disk Also called a diskette, a floppy disk is a small, flat recording medium that can be removed from the disk drive. Floppy disks come in two basic sizes, 3 1/2-inch and 5 1/4-inch. Floppy disks may store more than a megabyte.

Folder A term used by the Macintosh line of computers to describe a collection of related files; also called a subdirectory. *See also* Subdirectory.

Format To prepare a completely blank disk to receive information. Formatting a disk creates track and sector marks so that the computer can later find what it has written. Disks only require formatting once. Reformatting a disk will erase all information on it, with little hope of recovery.

FORTRAN The name of a programming language, which is an abbreviation for formula translator. FORTRAN is used primarily for creating scientific and engineering application programs.

FUBAR Fouled Up Beyond All Recognition.

Function Key A special key on the computer keyboard that performs specific functions determined by the software you are running. Normally, different types of programs use the function keys for completely different purposes.

Giga- One billion (approximately) or 1,073,741,824 (exactly). From the Greek for "giant."

Gigabyte 1,073,741,824 bytes.

GIGO Garbage In, Garbage Out. An observation that computers cannot turn invalid information into useful data, or lead into gold. A computer can only manage and organize information it already has. If the information that you input is worthless, the output will also be inaccurate.

Graphics Computer-generated pictures, as opposed to words and numbers. All personal computers can display words and numbers, or text, but not all of them can display graphics. *See also* Text.

Hacker A term used to describe an amateur computer programmer; a dabbler.

Handshake A means to allow two devices to agree on how to transfer information. For example, when a computer is transmitting characters to a printer, the printer must have some way to tell the computer (which is much faster than the printer) to stop transmitting for awhile. Likewise, the computer must have some way to tell the printer that there are no more characters to transmit. This is known as handshaking. Handshaking can be accomplished by transmitting agreed-upon control characters along with the data (software handshake), or by using extra wires in the interface cable (hardware handshake). *See also* Control Characters.

Hard Copy Printed output, as opposed to a display on a screen.

Hard Disk A high-capacity, high-speed recording medium used to store digital computer information. Hard disks cannot be removed from the hard disk drive.

Hardware Electronics. Computer hardware includes the CPU, motherboard, memory, keyboard, monitor, and disk drives. Hardware is the opposite of software. *See also* Software.

Head The part of a disk drive that converts magnetic fields into electrical current, and vice versa. This is the equivalent of a tone arm on a phonograph.

A

Head Crash   A catastrophic failure of a disk drive. Normally, a disk drive's read/write heads skim just above the surface of the disk's recording medium. If the disk drive is jarred, or the air contaminated, the head may crash into the disk, destroying the head and some portion of the disk as well.

Hz   Abbreviation for hertz, or cycles per second. A unit for measuring frequency.

IC   Integrated circuit. *See also* Chip.

Icon   A picture intended to represent an idea or a concept. For example, a red circle with a diagonal slash through it is an international symbol for "don't" or "no." The Macintosh line of computers relies heavily upon icons to convey the meaning of its commands. Users point at icons to carry out commands, rather than typing them in on the keyboard. Windows relies heavily upon icons as well.

Increment   A verb meaning to add to a number.

Incremental Backup   A periodic backup copy of files made to augment a complete system backup. It is more efficient to make complete backups only occasionally, and then back up only new files at regular intervals.

Index Hole   A small hole (about 1/8-inch diameter) just off-center on a floppy disk. The disk drive shines a light through this hole once every revolution to make sure that the floppy disk is spinning at the proper speed.

Ink Jet Printer   A type of printer that works by squirting precisely measured quantities of ink at the paper. Ink jet printers are very quiet, but often require special paper.

Install   A procedure for customizing software to run on your particular computer. Installation usually consists of answering multiple-choice questions about your computer, your printer, your display screen, and so forth. When installation is done, the software can be used.

Interface   Something that allows the connection of two or more dissimilar devices. An interface can describe the connection between a computer and a modem, computer and printer, or computer and disk drive. Common interfaces are serial, parallel, SCSI, and Ethernet.

Interpreter A program used to create other programs. Similar to an assembler or a compiler. An interpreter reads an instruction written using a programming language and converts it to one or more binary instructions that the computer can execute. Interpreters convert each programming instruction as it is encountered. *See also* Assembler; Compiler.

Invalid Illegal, bad, inaccurate, or incorrect.

I/O Port I/O is an abbreviation for input/output, and port is a general term describing a plug, jack, socket, or connection. Therefore, an I/O port is a connector on a computer used for importing and exporting information to or from other devices, such as a printer, mouse, modem, and so on.

K Abbreviation for kilobyte, or 1024 bytes.

Kilo- Greek prefix for "one thousand." In computer jargon, kilo- is usually treated as 1024 instead of 1000, because 1024 is an even power of two.

Kilobyte 1024 bytes.

Kilohertz One thousand cycles per second (hertz). A measure of frequency, often abbreviated KHz.

LAN Acronym for local area network. *See also* Local Area Network.

Landing Zone A portion of a hard disk drive's disk where there is no data stored. The read/write heads are allowed to come to rest on this area of the disk when the disk stops spinning.

Language A system of words and symbols used to program a computer. There are many different programming languages used worldwide, including Pascal, C, BASIC, and FORTRAN.

Laptop A computer that is small enough to be carried around, and runs on batteries as well as electrical power.

Laser Printer A peripheral that prints by using a laser beam to draw letters and figures onto a magnetic drum. The drum is then covered with a fine black powder, which is then transferred onto paper.

LED Light-emitting diode. A kind of high-tech light bulb; usually red, but it can also be green, amber, or orange.

Letter Quality A description of a good-quality printer. A printer that produces documents good enough to send in a formal letter.

LIM Lotus-Intel-Microsoft, the three companies that sponsored the EMS specification. *See also* EMS.

Linker A program that is used to create other programs. Unlike a compiler, interpreter, or assembler, a linker does not translate programming instructions into binary instructions. Instead, a linker joins already-translated programs into one larger program. *See also* Assembler; Compiler; Interpreter.

Local Area Network A network that spans a relatively small area (less than a mile), and connects a moderate number of computers (2 to 100).

LPM Abbreviation for lines per minute. A measure of a printer's speed. *See also* CPS.

Machine Code Also called binary code. Machine code is the only programming "language" that computers understand. It is made up of the binary digits 0 and 1, in various combinations. Each particular sequence of binary digits (bits) is a machine instruction. A sequence of instructions makes up a program.

MB Abbreviation for megabyte, or 1,048,576 bytes.

Mega- Prefix for one million, from the Greek for "great." In computer jargon, mega- is generally treated as 1,048,576 instead of 1,000,000, because 1,048,576 is an even power of two (specifically, 1024 x 1024).

Megabyte 1,048,576 bytes.

Megahertz One million cycles per second (hertz). This is a measure of frequency, often abbreviated MHz.

Memory   Any of a number of electronic or magnetic mechanisms to store a digital electronic bit of information. Memory can be a RAM chip, a disk drive, or a magnetic tape.

Menu   A list of choices displayed on the screen, from which the user is supposed to make a selection. Choosing a command from a menu is often easier than typing one in voluntarily.

Micro-   Prefix meaning one-millionth part, from the Greek for "small."

Micro-controller   Any of a hundred different small microprocessors used for very inexpensive applications, such as controlling appliances, hand-held games, and thermostats.

Micro-processor   The key integrated circuit in any personal computer. The microprocessor is the chip that fetches and executes the binary instructions of a program. Also called a CPU. *See also* CPU.

MIDI   Acronym for Musical Instrument Digital Interface. A common interface between computer systems and electronic musical instruments.

Milli-   Prefix meaning one-thousandth part, from the Latin for "thousand."

MIPS   A measure of a computer's performance. MIPS stands for million instructions per second. A computer's speed might be rated at 5 MIPS, for example. MIPS has also been called "meaningless indicator of performance for salesmen."

Modem   A device which acts as an interface between a computer and a telephone line. A modem allows a computer to transmit information to, and receive information from, another computer system over telephone lines. The term is an abbreviation for modulator/demodulator.

Monitor   The display screen of a computer system, also called a CRT or (inaccurately) a terminal.

Monochrome   From the Greek for "single color." In particular, this refers to a computer display that cannot display more than one color. Black and white, green, or amber monitors are all monochrome monitors.

A

Mouse A small hand-held device for positioning the cursor on the display screen. A mouse (so-called because of its appearance) works by moving it across a desk or pad. The cursor will move a similar amount in the same direction. *See also* Cursor.

Multitasking The ability to run several programs, or tasks, simultaneously. This is a feature that some operating systems have, and some do not. A multitasking operating system makes it easier for the computer user to switch between different jobs or tasks than a non-multitasking operating system.

MUNG Mush Until No Good.

Nano- Prefix meaning one-billionth part, from the Greek for "dwarf."

Network A system of cables and software that allows several computer systems to communicate amongst themselves.

Num Lock Key A key in the upper-right corner of an IBM-style PC keyboard. The [Num Lock] key converts the nearby cursor-control keys into a calculator keypad. Pressing the [Num Lock] key again switches back to cursor-control mode.

Nybble Four bits, or half of a byte.

Object Code File A disk file that contains machine code instructions. This kind of file is normally created by a compiler, interpreter, or other programming language translator.

Offline Not currently transmitting or receiving data. A device which is functioning but not active.

Online Active and connected. Ready to run.

Open To open a file is to begin using it. Open is meant to suggest the opening of a paper file folder. Saving a file is also called closing it.

Operating System A complex class of software that oversees most of the low-level functions of operating a computer, such as reading input from the keyboard and mouse, displaying characters on the monitor, and so forth.

Optical Character Recognition The ability of a scanner to recognize and "read" the printed matter that it is scanning; often abbreviated OCR. *See also* Scanner.

Parallel In computer jargon, a method of transferring more than one bit of information simultaneously. Usually accomplished by using multiple wires, one for each bit.

Parameter Information or options. *See also* Argument.

Parity An extra bit of data used as a check to verify that the rest of the data was stored or received correctly; a checksum.

Park Something you do to a hard disk drive to protect the disk's read/write heads from damage. Not all hard disk drives can be parked, and not all need to be.

Pascal A programming language, similar to C, named after the mathematician Blaise Pascal.

PCB Printed circuit board. The flat boards that are used to create electronic assemblies.

Peripheral An optional piece of computer equipment; an enhancement. Printers, modems, and scanners are popular peripherals.

Pixel Short for picture element. A pixel is one small dot of light on a computer or television screen.

Platter The disk in a hard disk drive. Most hard disk drives have three or more platters.

Plotter A peripheral used primarily by engineers and architects that draws figures using a pen and paper.

PPM Abbreviation for pages per minute. It is one way to measure how fast a printer can print; typically used with laser and LED printers.

Print Screen Key A special key on the right side of an IBM-style PC keyboard used for printing a copy of whatever is currently displayed on the computer's

A

screen. The label on the keycap is often abbreviated PrtSc. [Prt Sc] is usually used with [Shift] to get the desired result.

Printer A peripheral that produces a hard copy of a file on paper.

Processor *See* Microprocessor.

Program A carefully ordered sequence of computer instructions; software. Everything that a computer does is guided by some program.

Programmer One who creates programs.

Prompt Something displayed on a computer screen that is meant to cue the user that some input is expected.

Public Domain A legal term describing a program that may be freely given away, but not sold.

RAM Acronym for random-access memory. The main memory chips of a computer, which come in two kinds: dynamic and static.

Resolution A measure of how sharp and clear a computer screen is. Because of FCC standards, all television screens have the same resolution, or number of pixels. Computer monitors, on the other hand, come with a wide assortment of resolutions. Monitor resolution is measured in pixels, across and down. A typical monitor might have a resolution of 320 x 200 pixels.

ROM Acronym for read-only memory. Two other terms you will see are PROM (programmable-) and EPROM (erasable-). A memory chip that stores a particular program permanently.

RS-232 Identification number given to a specific serial interface used by most personal computers.

Run To execute a program.

SASI Acronym for Shugart Associates' Standard Interface, pronounced "sassy." A disk drive interface, not commonly used anymore. *See also* SCSI; ESDI; ST 506; ST 412.

Scan To take an image of something using a scanner. *See also* Scanner.

Scan Code A system similar to ASCII used by IBM-style PCs. When a key is pressed, its scan code is sent to the computer. Another scan code is sent when the key is released. This allows the computer to identify special keys that have no ASCII code.

Scanner A peripheral that converts an image of a picture or printed page into electronic form. The image can then be edited on the computer. A scanner performs the reverse function of a printer.

Scroll To move the image displayed on a computer screen up, down, or sideways to make room for more information.

Scroll Lock Key A special key at the upper right of an IBM-style PC keyboard. The Scroll Lock key controls how the image on the screen will move when new information is displayed.

SCSI Acronym for Small Computer System Interface, pronounced "scuzzy." A successor to SASI, it is a common interface between computers and disk, tape, or CD-ROM drives.

Sector A portion of a disk. A formatted disk's surface is divided into circular tracks and pie-shaped sectors. A track and a sector define a crescent-shaped area of the disk. *See also* Track.

Seek Time *See* Access time.

Semi-conductor A physics term describing the electrical properties of certain physical elements, such as silicon, germanium, and arsenic. All integrated circuits are composed of various semiconductors.

Serial In computer jargon, a method of transferring one bit of data after another, single-file.

Silicon The most well known semiconducting element, used in the fabrication of integrated circuits. The Santa Clara Valley in California, where many electronics companies are located, is often called Silicon Valley. This is not the same thing as silicone.

Simulation A program that tries to copy the operation of some other machine. Flight simulators make popular game programs.

SMD Surface-mount device. *See also* Surface Mount.

SMT Surface-mount technology. *See also* Surface Mount.

Software See Program.

Source A term used to describe a disk, file, or computer when a transfer of information is taking place. For example, to copy a file from one disk to another disk, you copy from the source disk to the destination disk.

Source Code File A file on disk, created by a computer programmer, that contains programming language instructions. This file can be read and edited with a standard word processing program. The source code file is then translated by a compiler, interpreter, or other programming language translator to produce an object code file. *See also* Object Code File.

Spreadsheet An application program that is used for evaluating financial or statistical information.

ST 412 A popular interface between floppy disk drives and computers. It is named after the particular model number of floppy disk drive that popularized it.

ST 506 A popular interface between hard disk drives and computers. It is named after the particular model number of hard disk drive that popularized it.

Start Bit An extra bit of data added to the beginning of a serial data transmission, which is used to notify the receiving equipment that a byte of data is beginning.

Stop Bit An extra bit of data added to the end of a serial data transmission, which is used to indicate to the receiving equipment that the end of a data byte has been reached.

Streaming Tape A kind of magnetic tape that is used for making backups. *See also* Backup.

Subdirectory A collection of related files on a disk. Many operating systems allow the computer user to partition a disk into subdirectories (or folders) so that related files can be kept together. This can make it easier to find a particular file later on.

Supertwist A particular type of LCD (liquid crystal display), used primarily on laptop computers.

Surface Mount A relatively new technique for making electronic printed circuit boards even smaller, by eliminating the need to drill holes in them to solder in the integrated circuits. Instead, the IC chips are soldered to the surface of the board.

Tape Drive Similar to a disk drive, but for tapes. Magnetic tapes are often used as a convenient medium for backing up disk files.

Terminal A peripheral that includes a video display screen and a keyboard. A terminal communicates with a computer over a serial interface or a network. Most personal computers do not use terminals. Used primarily by medium or large multiuser business computers.

Text Words, numbers, and punctuation marks. Typewriters can print text, and all personal computers can print and display text, too. Not all PCs can produce graphics, though. *See also* Graphics.

Thimble A small device used by some printers, similar to a daisy wheel. A print thimble is shaped like a small cup, with letters, numbers, and punctuation marks embossed around the rim. *See also* Daisy Wheel.

Track One of many concentric rings around which data is stored on a disk. Disk tracks are like grooves in a phonograph record, except that they do not spiral, and they are not physically cut into the disk.

Uninter-ruptible Power Supply A special power supply that continues to work after a power blackout. These can be handy if the computer is being used for especially important work. This is often abbreviated UPS.

Upload To transmit data to another computer. *See also* Download.

User A person who uses a computer.

VDT Abbreviation for video display terminal. *See also* Terminal.

Virus A class of program that is created maliciously, to infiltrate and corrupt computer data and disk files. Viruses are extremely difficult to detect or remove.

Wait State A small period of time when the computer's microprocessor is doing nothing; wasted time. Wait states can occur when the computer is designed with a microprocessor that is faster than the memory used.

Wetware The human brain.

Winchester Another name for a hard disk drive, from the Winchester repeating rifle.

Word Processor An application program used for writing and editing documents, such as letters, memos, or books.

Workstation A computer; generally used to describe machines somewhat larger and more powerful than a personal computer.

Write-Protect Tab A small opaque sticker used to protect a 5 1/4-inch floppy disk from accidental erasure. When a write-protect tab is placed over the write-protect notch on a diskette, the computer will refuse to write new information onto the disk, or to erase information already on it.

WYSIWYG What You See Is What You Get, pronounced "wizzy-wig." A feature of desktop publishing and Windows programs.

APPENDIX

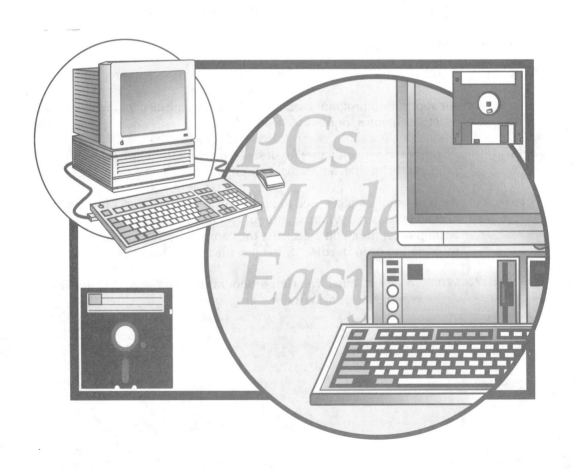

BINARY AND HEXADECIMAL NUMBERING

Computer engineers and programmers work in an arcane world all their own. We live in a time where personal computers are moving from that world into the realm of everyday objects used by people with no technical training. Sometimes, that can be a difficult transition. Engineering terms are still commonly used, and technical jargon is widespread. You can't even take something as simple as numbers and counting for granted. You may come across numbers written in base two (binary) or base sixteen (hexadecimal) from time to time. There is (hopefully) no need for you to become proficient in either one of these mathematical curiosities, but a little guided tour may be of some help.

Binary Numbers

Computers store and manipulate all information in an electrical, on/off method. To the electrical engineer, this is *digital* format. To the programmer or mathematician, it is *binary*. To you, the user, it should be *invisible*.

In your computer's digital electrical system, all things must be either on or off; there is no in between. To your computer's software, everything is either true or false, with no maybe. And when calculating binary numbers, everything is either 0 or 1.

Zero and one? How do you count with just 0 and 1? Everything that your computer stores—numbers, names, pictures—must be represented with just two binary digits. But how do you write a number like 6429 when all you have is 0 and 1 to work with?

People throughout the world count in base ten, or *decimal* notation. Presumably, this is because of our ten fingers and toes. Most modern cultures write out numeric values using the Arabic digits 0 through 9. If you want to represent one object, you write the number 1, or for nine objects you write 9. When you add one to nine, you get ten, but there's no digit for ten. Instead, you must "roll over" the units digit, going back to 0, and increase the figure on the left by one, producing 10.

In binary notation, the system works the same way. The only difference is that there are only two different digits, so the numbers roll over more often. Here's an example.

Zero objects is represented with 0 and one object with 1—no surprises here. If you add one to one, you get two—but there's no digit for two! We're out of digits, so we must "roll over" the units digit to 0 and increase the next digit on the left by one, giving us 10. This is the binary number for two (*not* ten). It sure *looks* like ten, and someone writing numbers in binary notation has to make sure to say so, so there's no confusion. "Rolling over" the digits is like using a car's odometer that only has 1 and 0 digits on it.

To continue with the example, adding one more to two gives three, written as 11. What happens with four? You must roll over the rightmost digit to zero, and increase the digit to its left. But that digit is already 1, so you must roll it over to 0 as well, and start a third figure, so four looks like 100. Table B-1 shows how the first sixteen numbers (from zero to fifteen) look in binary notation.

Note that fifteen is the largest number you can write with just four bits. All four bits are already 1. The number sixteen needs five bits. With five bits you can represent 32 different numbers, from 0 to 31. Six bits let you go to 64 numbers, and so on. In binary, adding one more bit doubles the range of numbers you can represent. In "normal" decimal counting, each new digit increases the number of combinations by ten. See Table B-2.

B

Binary	Value
0000	Zero
0001	One
0010	Two
0011	Three
0100	Four
0101	Five
0110	Six
0111	Seven
1000	Eight
1001	Nine
1010	Ten
1011	Eleven
1100	Twelve
1101	Thirteen
1110	Fourteen
1111	Fifteen

The First
Sixteen Binary
Numbers
Table B-1.

| | Decimal | | Binary | |
Digits	Number of Combinations	Largest Number	Number of Combinations	Largest Number
1	10	9	2	1
2	100	99	4	11
3	1000	999	8	111
4	10,000	9999	16	1111
5	100,000	99,999	32	11111

Comparing Decimal and Binary Counting Table B-2.

Your PC doesn't bother with less than eight bits at once, called a byte. With eight bits there are 256 possible combinations, so you could write all the numbers from 0 to 255 with eight bits. (If you want to kill half an hour, you can try this yourself.)

If you want to convert numbers between binary notation and "normal" decimal notation, you can use a simple chart like the one in Figure B-1. It assigns a decimal "value" to each binary digit, or bit. If that particular bit is a 1, look up its decimal value and add it to your total. If a bit is 0, skip it. When you're done, add up the values for all eight bits and you have the decimal equivalent of a binary number. In the example, the binary number 10001101 is equal to 141 (128 + 8 + 4 + 1). This system also works in reverse, converting decimal numbers to binary, although it is more tedious. You will find that there is exactly one way to represent every decimal number in binary.

If you want to expand the chart to work with decimal numbers greater than 255, simply add more binary bits to the left. Make each new bit worth double its predecessor. For instance, a ninth bit would be worth 256. Therefore, 6429 requires thirteen bits and would be represented as 1100100011101.

Hexadecimal Numbers

If you understood binary (base two) counting, you shouldn't have any trouble with hexadecimal (base sixteen). On the other hand, if binary arithmetic was a problem, then hexadecimal, well...

B

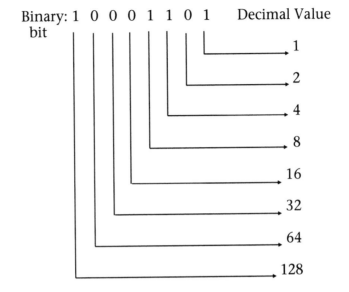

An example of converting binary notation to decimal notation

Figure B-1.

Suppose that instead of just two digits, or ten digits, you had sixteen to use. Instead of stopping at 1 (as in binary), or at 9 (for decimal), you could count all the way up to fifteen. The hexadecimal system uses the letters "A" through "F" for the extra six digits after 9. The last digit in hexadecimal arithmetic is F. The next number after F is 10. Although it looks like ten, in hexadecimal math it means sixteen.

With an imaginary one-digit odometer, you can count up to 9 in decimal, or up to F (15) in hexadecimal. A two-digit odometer runs up to FF (255). Each added digit increases the possible total by—you guessed it—sixteen.

A P P E N D I X

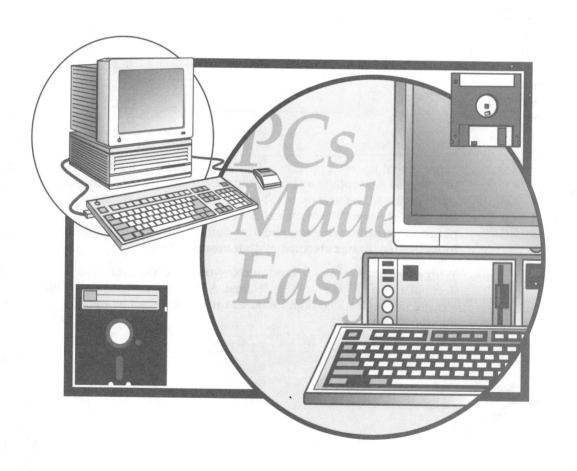

ASCII CODE

The binary numbering system may work fine for numbers, but how does your computer store letters of the alphabet using just 1 and 0? Surprisingly, it still uses binary numbers, borrowing a technique that's more than 100 years old.

The concept of representing characters with numbers is hardly new. The Morse code, first used by telegraph operators, has been around since the late 1800s. With Morse code, different letters and punctuation marks are represented by different long and short taps on the telegrapher's key. The long and short pulses (dashes and dots) are akin to the 1 and 0 of binary numbers.

Each *character* (letter, punctuation mark, or symbol) is stored as a number. A special number has been assigned to each letter of the alphabet and to most of the punctuation marks you're likely to use. The set of numbers for these characters is known as the ASCII code. ASCII stands for American Standard Code for Information Interchange, pronounced "askee" (not "askee-too"). You could say that the ASCII code is a direct descendant of Morse code. Morse code uses no more than six dashes and dots for any one character, while the ASCII code uses seven bits. That's mostly because the ASCII code has more symbols than Morse code, and because ASCII makes a distinction between upper- and lowercase letters. While Morse code and ASCII code do not use the same binary patterns, the parallels are striking.

Despite its nationalistic name, the ASCII code is used worldwide; the only major countries not using it are Japan and some Middle Eastern countries, because their alphabets contain too many symbols for the ASCII code to work. The ASCII code defines characters for the first 128 binary numbers. An ASCII code chart follows in Table C-1.

Notice that the ASCII chart distinguishes between upper- and lowercase letters of the alphabet. This allows your computer to recognize the difference when you're typing, and to store the correct form. Otherwise all of your word processing documents would be in all capitals (or all lowercase).

Another interesting feature of the ASCII code is that the values 48 through 57 represent the digits 0 through 9, respectively. This is something of a paradox. Is the number 0 stored as the binary number 00000000, or 00110000 (the binary form of 48), as the ASCII chart would suggest? The answer is: it depends.

Your computer makes a distinction between numbers used for calculating and numbers that you print. That is, a number like 42 is stored differently depending on whether you want to actually use it as a number (add and subtract with it, for example), or whether you want to print it in a sentence. Confusing, to be sure, but true. It might seem less confusing to use the values 0 through 9 to represent the figures 0 through 9, but that's the way ASCII is.

The values 1 through 26 in ASCII are the control characters. These are the invisible characters you get when you hold down the [Ctrl] key on your keyboard and press another key. There are 26 control characters, corresponding to the 26 letters of the alphabet. When you use the [Ctrl] key, your computer doesn't distinguish between upper- and lowercase letters. There is no such thing as Control-Capital-M.

0	Null	32	(Space)	64	@	96	`
1	Ctrl-A	33	!	65	A	97	a
2	Ctrl-B	34	"	66	B	98	b
3	Ctrl-C	35	#	67	C	99	c
4	Ctrl-D	36	$	68	D	100	d
5	Ctrl-E	37	%	69	E	101	e
6	Ctrl-F	38	&	70	F	102	f
7	Ctrl-G	39	'	71	G	103	g
8	Ctrl-H	40	(	72	H	104	h
9	Ctrl-I	41	)	73	I	105	i
10	Ctrl-J	42	*	74	J	106	j
11	Ctrl-K	43	+	75	K	107	k
12	Ctrl-L	44	,	76	L	108	l
13	Ctrl-M	45	–	77	M	109	m
14	Ctrl-N	46	.	78	N	110	n
15	Ctrl-O	47	/	79	O	111	o
16	Ctrl-P	48	0	80	P	112	p
17	Ctrl-Q	49	1	81	Q	113	q
18	Ctrl-R	50	2	82	R	114	r
19	Ctrl-S	51	3	83	S	115	s
20	Ctrl-T	52	4	84	T	116	t
21	Ctrl-U	53	5	85	U	117	u
22	Ctrl-V	54	6	86	V	118	v
23	Ctrl-W	55	7	87	W	119	w
24	Ctrl-X	56	8	88	X	120	x
25	Ctrl-Y	57	9	89	Y	121	y
26	Ctrl-Z	58	:	90	Z	122	z
27	Esc	59	;	91	[	123	{
28	FS	60	<	92	\	124		
29	GS	61	=	93	]	125	}
30	RS	62	>	94	^	126	~
31	US	63	?	95	_	127	(Del)

The ASCII
Code
Table C-1.

A P P E N D I X

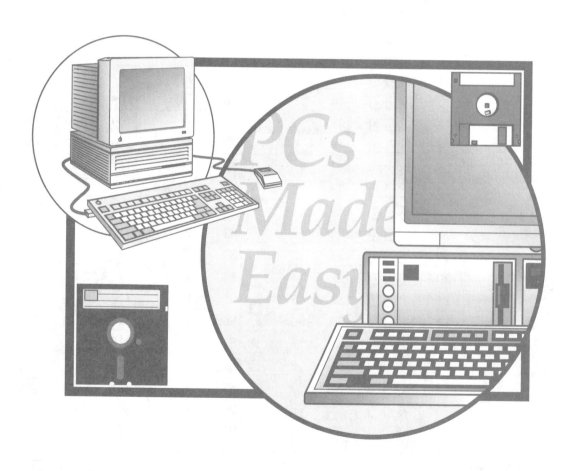

GRAPHICS FORMATS

After seeing how a computer represents and stores numbers and characters, it might seem that storing pictures in a digital format might be the most difficult one of all. Actually, representing pictures (also called graphics) is quite easy and straightforward.

Images on your computer screen are created in basically the same way as pictures on a television. Each picture is made up of thousands of tiny dots on the screen. If you look at your TV or computer monitor closely enough, you'll see each individual dot.

As you learned in Chapter 13, each of these points of light is called a pixel, short for "picture element."

Displayed on Screen

On a monochrome (one-color) computer screen, each pixel can be either on (bright) or off (dark). This corresponds very nicely to the binary numbering system in your computer. To store a picture on disk or display it on the monitor, your computer simply assigns one bit to each pixel in the picture. If a certain pixel is dark, your computer stores a 0; if a pixel is turned on, your PC stores a 1. A typical monochrome PC display might have 320 pixels across the screen horizontally and 200 pixels vertically, for a total of 64,000 pixels on the screen. That means that it takes 64,000 bits, or 8000 bytes, to store a single black-and-white picture.

Color displays are a wee bit more complex, because each pixel can be a different color. The more colors your computer can display, the more complicated the process is. Different colors are made by mixing red, green, and blue, the three primary colors of computer graphics. Instead of storing each pixel with one bit of data, each pixel needs multiple bits; some for the red portion, some for the green, and some for the blue. Now each pixel can light up with various amounts of red, green, and blue light all mixed together, depending on the red, green, and blue values in the data. For a simple 16-color CGA display, the same 320-x-200 image takes three times as much memory, or 24K, to store in color.

Among the three colors of red, green, and blue, it is possible to create any color at all. Color television sets all work on exactly the same principle. The reason some video adapter boards can display more color than others is because they devote more bits to the red, green, and blue portions of each pixel. With more bits, there are more combinations with which to vary the color values.

Stored on Disk

When it comes time to take the picture from your screen and store it on disk, things get even more complicated. There are literally dozens of different ways to store the same picture in a disk file. Different application programs use different formats, and different computers

(PC and Mac) use different formats, too. It seems there are as many graphics file formats as there are computers.

All of these different and incompatible graphics file formats were invented for good reasons. Some preserve the colors in a picture better than others. Some take up less space on your disk. Some are easier to convert from color to black and white, and some are just plain inexplicable. Each one has pluses and minuses, and different application programs usually each have a "favorite" format that they work with. Table D-1 gives you just a small sample of some popular PC file formats. The moral of all this is, if you want to exchange graphics with someone else with a PC or a Mac, the two of you will have to make sure that your applications are using the same file format.

If you want to use an incompatible format, it may be possible to convert the graphics file from one format to another. There are special application programs available to do this. Your application may also be able to "import" graphics files from other applications that use a different format.

D

File Type	Application
.DXF	AutoCAD CAD Drawing
.GIF	CompuServe Color Graphics
.CUT	DRHalo Paint Program
.IMG	GEM Image File
.PIX	Inset Systems Picture
.PCT	Macintosh PICT Format
.MSP	Microsoft Paint
.PCX	ZSoft PC Paintbrush
.TIF	TIFF (Tagged Image File Format)
.BMP	Windows Wallpaper
.WPG	WordPerfect Graphics

Sample Graphics File Formats
Table D-1.

INDEX

433

Index